THE FEMININE ECONOMY
AND ECONOMIC MAN

THE FEMININE ECONOMY
AND ECONOMIC MAN

Reviving the Role of Family
in the Post-Industrial Age

Updated Edition

Shirley P. Burggraf, Ph.D.

PERSEUS BOOKS

Reading, Massachusetts

ISBN 0-7382-0036-0

Library of Congress Catalog Card Number: 98-88746

Perseus Books is a member of the Perseus Books Group

Cover design by Jean Seal
Text design by Octal Publishing, Inc.
Set in 11 point Transitional521 BT by Octal Publishing, Inc.

1 2 3 4 5 6 7 8 9—0302010099
First paperback printing, December 1998

Find us on the World Wide Web at
http://www.aw.com/gb/

To Ray and Elizabeth

CONTENTS

PREFACE

There is much wishful thinking in our public discourse with respect to the family. Many traditionalists seem to think that by chanting "family values" and by coming down hard enough on women the family can reclaim its central place in our culture. Many nontraditionalists hope that with enough parental leave and enough child care everyone can have careers and families and no one will have to make any hard choices. Both sides of the debate seem to be underestimating the strength of shifting economic forces operating on family life, and neither side is getting much help from economists.

Between policy proposals that assume women should stay home whether they want to or not, and those that conversely assume women should get out of the house, are various European-styled programs for socializing some of the costs of childrearing with things like subsidized day care and/or child allowances. Whatever the merits of such proposals, they would operate only at the margins of the costs that most families incur. The argument pursued in this book is that the family is not a marginal institution in our economy, either in terms of the resources it absorbs or in terms of the wealth it produces in the form of "human capital." *The family is actually the primary engine of economic growth, and yet it has never been recognized as such.*

The economic value of family investment in caretaking and the opportunity costs of women's time in the home have been virtually invisible in the market economy. Because the work of nurturing has been largely unpaid and, not coincidentally, largely done by women, it has seemed unimportant compared to such imposing economic variables as the unemployment rate or the national debt. We have, however, reached a point at which family functions can no longer be taken for granted. Many of the most challenging problems with which our society is attempting to cope— productivity and economic growth, Social Security insolvency, failing schools, welfare reform—are tied together through the family more directly and substantively than is generally recognized and will surely prove intractable unless we first attend to the institution that is the primary producer of our social capital.

The lengthening period of child dependency on parents and schooling, coupled with the growing importance of parental guidance in today's complex society, makes parental investment of time and money an increasingly valuable economic resource. At the same time, increasing opportunities outside the home, especially for women, have drastically raised the opportunity costs of parental time. Traditional returns to parents in the form of labor on the farm, in the family shop, or in financial insurance for old age have evaporated. In the context of a service-oriented, information economy in which intellectual capital is the critical resource, we are confronted with the striking anomaly that parents who are conscientiously and effectively rearing children are, literally, the major wealth producers in our economy while the family continues to be viewed as economically dependent on the market economy.

I argue that the modern family is coming unglued, not because family functions are no longer valuable to society, nor because of some profound deterioration of moral fiber or because of a basic change in human nature, but because the economic ties that have traditionally bound families together, male to female and the generations to each other, have frayed to the breaking point. I also argue that what has happened to the family is best understood in the context of our whole social structure of supporting and caretaking roles, a structure which, given its history, it seems appropriate to call "the feminine economy." Getting "women's work" done when women are no longer volunteering their unpaid or underpaid labor is what much of the public discussion of family values is really about.

Talking honestly and realistically about the economic dimensions of family is a necessary step toward demystifying and depolarizing some of our most divisive social issues. Such a discussion in no way implies that economics is all there is to the family. As the family has many of the characteristics of an economic institution, however, I will argue that the best way to deal with the social problems associated with family breakdown is to understand that the family is, among other things, an economic system in transition. Although it is inevitably somewhat distasteful to talk about family issues in the language of economists and accountants, some practical discussion of dollars and cents is required if we are ever to resolve the unfinished family business left over from the cultural revolution of the sixties.

It is worth noting that the life-insurance industry had a similar problem of perception to overcome when it began in the mid-nineteenth century. Prominent ministers such as Henry Ward Beecher initially condemned the concept of putting a price on human life as sinful and sacrilegious. As the urbanization of our economy progressed, however, and as the breadwinner's earning ability replaced land as the major form of wealth, a breadwinner's death increasingly left widows and orphans to be burdens on society. The same ministers eventually came to see buying life insurance as a responsible thing to do. Today, although life insurance is still banned in some parts of the world (Syria, Libya), no one in a modern Western society would confuse the value of a person's life-insurance policy with the value of a person as an individual. Life insurance is simply a way of using a market mechanism to take care of an important dimension of family business, a dimension made necessary by changing economic conditions.

The family's economic conditions have changed rather drastically in recent decades. In times past, our whole social system effectively assigned gender roles at birth. There was a social agreement that provided substantial reinforcement for people to marry, for women to bear and rear children, for men to support their families, and for the generations to take care of each other within the family. The modern family has, however, lost most of that social infrastructure as the balance between family costs and benefits has progressively deteriorated. As a result, industrial countries in the twenty-first century are, in effect, going to have to write a new social contract for the family if the family is to continue to perform its essential social functions.

Because the family is the primary producer of our workforce and of our citizenry, stress on the family constitutes what is arguably the single greatest imminent threat to the American standard of living. For the family to once again do its job of effectively producing wealth in the form of human capital, we are going to have to socialize more of the costs and/or privatize more of the return on family investment. Most family-assistance proposals have focused on collectivizing family costs, but it seems reasonable to ask whether privatizing more of the social wealth produced by families may be a more viable alternative than trying to replace family functions with government programs and mandates.

Whichever direction public policy takes with respect to the family, we are going to have to take the feminine/caretaking/family economy as seriously as we take the competitive/market/business economy of economic man. The caretaking economy and the competitive economy are two sides of the same economic reality, neither of which can function without the other.

ACKNOWLEDGMENTS

The family web has many threads. It is impossible to talk realistically about the economics of family without reference to other disciplines such as political theory, psychology, sociology, philosophy and ethics, history, biology, and anthropology. While this is primarily an economic argument about issues of family business, I am indebted to many scholars in other fields to an extent that may not always be clear throughout the discussion. This analysis attempts to recognize that family issues have biological, psychological, sociological, political, and ethical dimensions and to reference with deep respect some of the major sources of knowledge, insight, and debate in other fields. At many points, however, the discussion is forced to skim the surface of a subject in order not to lose the thread of the main argument. More background is provided in the footnotes, but the referenced sources are in most cases just a sample of intellectual contributions on the topics mentioned.

In addition to the academic and government sources cited here, I have also drawn extensively on the insights and perceptions of journalists who have been reporting from the front lines of our culture wars and on various columnists and commentators who have defined important issues. Those sources have managed to identify and articulate many problems and social concerns in our post-'60s culture that formal academic models have yet to assimilate. Writers such as Joan Beck, Erma Bombeck, Ellen Goodman, Ann Landers, Anna Quindlen, and William Raspberry are, in their own ways, serious students of modern family life and have contributed enormously to general understanding of what is happening in our culture. Their stories often are relegated to footnotes in this discussion for the same reason that academic stories are, and their contributions to the argument similarly exceed their visibility on the page. Likewise, the contributions of various artists.

I am indebted to artists, novelists, screenwriters, and actors who contribute to understanding what is happening in our human relationships in their unique ways—they create names and faces and specific situations for abstract questions. One scene or one character from a book or a movie can sometimes express more about the essence of a social problem than all the journalists, academic analysts, and government statisticians combined. I have used clips from various forms of popular culture that say something better than mere words can express about what is happening to family relationships.

At a personal level, there are many institutions, colleagues, friends, and family who have contributed to making this project possible. An especially large debt is owed to the Bunting Institute of Radcliffe College for supporting my research at a critical time. The Bunting Institute, its amazing director Florence Ladd, and the Bunting staff provided a uniquely stimulating and supportive environment in which women scholars, writers, and artists could learn and grow and develop their own voices.

The forty 1994-95 Bunting Fellows were a special group who often disagreed in our seminars with parts of the concept developed here but whose challenges and criticisms contributed enormously to shaping the argument. I am grateful to all of them and must especially thank the Social Science Workshop participants (Leslie Brody, Kate Cloud, Kate Elgin, Ruth-Arlene Howe, Martha May, Helena Meyer-Knapp, Susan Pedersen, Dorothy Quincy Thomas, and Karen Wyche) for their contributions to my thinking processes. The voice I was trying to develop at the Bunting was the voice of an economist who is also a parent and a feminist. Economists, parents, and feminists don't generally have very much to say to each other per se; but the lines of communication rather desperately need to be opened if we are to understand what is happening both to the family and to the economy.

Another institution to which I am indebted is Florida A & M University, especially to its students and their families who have taught me many lessons over the past 25 years. Any professor who teaches college students for 25 years has to be awed by the love, faith, hope, determination, sacrifice, and sheer parental heroism that families invest in getting their children through childhood and adolescence and into young adulthood.

Special thanks go to my editor, William Patrick, whose editorial pen has contributed much to this project.

Finally, the extent to which I have had to be absent from family and friends in order to write about the value of family life has been both painful and somewhat ironic; but it also illustrates the point argued here about the everyday trade-offs associated with families. Fortunately, my family and my friends have done many things to make the personal trade-offs of this project bearable, for which I owe them a tremendous debt.

1 INTRODUCTION

WANTED

Parents willing to bear, rear, and educate children for the next generation of Social Security taxpayers and to carry on the modern culture of learning and progress. Quality parenting preferred. Large commitments of time and money required. At least one parent must be willing to work a double shift and/or sacrifice tenure and upward mobility in the labor market. Salary: 0. Pension benefits: 0. Profits and dividends: 0.

THE PROBLEM

Will anyone be answering this ad in the twenty-first century? While there is an obvious social need and considerable personal motivation for families to produce healthy, disciplined, and productive children, from a purely economic standpoint it is an increasingly heroic thing for individuals to try to do. Particularly when costs of parental time and college tuition are computed, childrearing is a daunting financial task for poor and middle-class families that often constitutes a path into poverty.

Although the family is the system within which half the human race (the female half) has predominantly labored throughout history and which the other half (the male half) has supported economically, it has generally been taken for granted by society as just something people do, and ignored by economic analysts concentrating on the market economy. What is becoming increasingly

1

clear, however, is that the family is an economic institution that we take for granted at our peril.

One way to look at what is happening to the family is from an economist's customary perspective; that is, as a resource-allocation problem. There are many indications that the family is receiving a declining share of the economy's resources. Labor-force statistics indicate that women are allocating their time out of the home and into the market labor force on a massive scale while the numbers of illegitimate births, female-headed households, and delinquent child-support payments suggest that men are deserting their parental roles at a similar rate. Traditional family roles are being sacrificed by both men and women who are investing their time and resources elsewhere.

Disinvestment in our most basic social institution is rapidly bringing our culture to a critical point in social evolution and creating unprecedented problems for social and economic policy. There is considerable pressure to find alternative means of distributing the costs of family functions that individuals are no longer able and/or willing to bear. The critical decision to be made is what kind of allocation system can best direct resources where our society wants them to go.

The 1980s were a decade in which many social issues came to the fore. Americans began asking why our schools don't work; why so many students appear to be unprepared, undisciplined, and unmotivated; why there are so many divorces and single-parent families; why there are so many abortions, illegitimate births, crack babies, and latchkey kids; why there is so much teenage violence and so many unskilled workers resulting in declining productivity.

In response to growing public concern, the 1988 presidential campaign was declared "the year of the family" by both Republicans and Democrats. The political debate since then has revolved around whether women should have fewer choices in the marketplace (the right-wing agenda of reduced enforcement of discrimination laws, elimination of affirmative-action policies, restriction of abortion); or, if women are going to have more choices in the marketplace, how government should assign responsibility for maintaining family functions in the home (the left-wing agenda of subsidized day-care programs and mandated parental leaves from employers).

After a decade of exposure to this numbing exchange, the question has to be asked: Are there any options beyond either trying to put women back behind the veil by denying them choices in the marketplace or setting up a bureaucracy that in effect makes the family redundant? At a lecture on the University of California at Berkeley campus in 1969 at the height of the '60s protest movement against "the system," the late economist Abba Lerner explained to the student radicals of Berkeley that the list of system choices for the human species is very limited. Basically, it consists of:

- Traditional caste systems in which roles are assigned at birth and enforced by social sanctions.
- Bureaucratic systems in which resource-allocation decisions are made by centralized planning using the tax and enforcement powers of the state.
- Market systems that allow individuals to pursue their own interests within a system of property rights, contracts, and market prices.

Most public-policy debates concerning health care, trade protection, farm subsidies, environmental regulation, and so on focus on the role of government intervention versus the role of the marketplace. What is unique about the family values debate is that it is being argued only in terms of government intervention versus a traditional, sentimentalized view of the family with no consideration of the role of markets and private incentives. Our search for answers to the family's problems has been limited because we have framed the problem very narrowly.

CONSIDER THE CHOICES

CASTE SYSTEMS

The lost social order bemoaned by conservatives was essentially a gender caste system in which roles were determined at birth. Our grandparents' generation could assume that people would marry, that women would bear and rear children, and that men would support their families. Few professions were open to women, and men had few alternatives to obtaining the services of a wife. Divorce, desertion, and illegitimacy were considered almost unmentionable scandals. Spinsterhood, bachelorhood, and childlessness were calamities to be pitied.

Why have things changed so much? For many reasons, but the focus here is on the economic factors involved in commitment to family. The traditional family appears to have lost much of its economic base and thus much of its attraction for men and women in the modern, postindustrial economy. Women have discovered that they can in fact compete successfully in the marketplace and can take care of themselves economically *if* they aren't trying to take care of others as well. They have choices about what to do with their time and talents that their grandmothers didn't have, and they are becoming increasingly aware of the economic costs and risks of remaining in the home.

At the same time that women's economic choices outside the home have broadened, the economic incentives for men to support homes and families have decreased substantially. Many of the goods and services that the family once provided (everything from sex to food preparation to old-age insurance) are now available on the open market or in social programs. The most conspicuous example of the latter is the Social Security system, which provides substantial economic support in old age to people who in previous generations would have depended on their children. Each worker is now required to contribute 15.3 percent of income to pay for Social Security pensions and Medicare, but parents have no claim on their children's earnings by virtue of being parents.

Can we turn back the clock and revive the system of predetermined roles? Two centuries after the Declaration of Independence spelled out the principles of personal liberty on which this country was founded, it seems hardly necessary to defend the moral right and human need of all individuals, women and men, to participate fully and freely in the social contract and in the process of personal choice. Trying to force people into unwanted roles violates the most basic tenet of Western culture. The amount of coercion it would take to keep today's men and women in traditional roles against their will is beyond the practical or justifiable power of the state.

If the traditional family system in which people automatically assumed their roles is, short of a highly totalitarian state, no longer viable, what options does society have for getting the functions performed that are still socially indispensable? If individuals are more frequently choosing to invest less time and money in family, and if it is beyond the power of the state to command otherwise, where does that leave the mechanism of cultural stability and continuity that the family has traditionally provided? What will happen to our culture if fewer and fewer people make the necessary commitments to family and children? Who will support us in our old age if there aren't enough productive workers to maintain the Social Security system? How can we get more nurturing and caring work performed in the economy of the next century?

BUREAUCRACIES

The answer proposed by many family advocates is to ask government to support the family with agencies and programs. On the theory that if individuals aren't doing it the government must, there has been considerable pressure to use the powers of government to shift some of the costs of parenting onto taxpayers and employers. Not surprisingly, such proposals often meet considerable resistance from those on whom the burden would fall.

A basic question has to be asked: how suited is the welfare state to undertake the tasks of nurturing and caretaking that have been proposed for it? Can universal day-care programs provide the specific love, motivation, and discipline that a particular child needs? Should families who disagree with the concept be forced to pay taxes to hire workers to care for someone else's children? How far can programs such as legally mandated parental leaves go toward meeting the individual needs of employers and families? While some employers (perhaps many) will find family policies to be in their best interest, others will be bankrupt before employees return from their parental leaves; and even the most generous employers will lose employees because a few months of leave are not enough for many families. Will employers who are forced to share the costs of family caretaking against their will create as many jobs or hire as many people with family obligations?

In an era when our economy has to compete for business around the world, can we reasonably expect employers across the board to be able to add on the operating costs of generous family policies and remain competitive? Will the families whose parents lose their jobs be helped? There may well be things that governments can efficiently and appropriately do to help families; but there is no government program that can perform the one-on-one, hands-on tasks of parenting, teaching values, enforcing discipline, turning off the TV for homework, wiping tears, or setting examples.

There is also the very real possibility that some governmental attempts to help families, most notably our welfare system, have actually made the problems worse. When the prospect of losing government subsidies makes work and marriage too expensive for the most economically vulnerable, how can we construct means-tested programs without creating such perverse incentives that people become trapped in unemployment and illegitimacy?

If returning to a traditional family system in which people are forced by social custom to assume particular roles is not a viable or acceptable option and if it is exceedingly difficult for the government to transfer family functions to either employers or taxpayers, perhaps it is time to consider the last option on Professor Lerner's list.

MARKET SYSTEMS

Market systems allow individuals to make their own decisions within a system of contracts and property rights. Market remedies for family stresses haven't been considered until now because there is no functioning market for what parents do. The family currently lacks a legal infrastructure for operating in the market economy. Individuals have no economic rights as parents and no claim to the fruits of their parental investment. People who never have children; parents who neglect, abuse, or abandon children; deadbeat parents who don't pay child support, all have as much claim (in many cases more) on the earnings of the next generation through the Social Security system as do the most dutiful parents.

The essence of the family values problem is that our society says one thing about the value of investment in children publicly while the economic system conveys something very different privately to individual parents and caretakers. However valuable children may be to society, they are still a very expensive proposition for their parents. Can our economic system be made to tell a more truthful story about the value of parental investment to the individuals making the investment decisions? Can a market be created in any reasonable way that will send the right signals to parents about the social value of investing in children?

RETHINKING THE FAMILY CONTRACT

Caste systems, bureaucracies, markets—it's not very romantic or enticing to think of the family as being part of any economic system. It's not something any society has had to think about when family roles could be taken for granted. The family has to be part of some kind of economic system (consciously or unconsciously), however, in order to have access to an economy's resources. As one commentator has said, "The underlying problem for the twentieth century is how to create a system that allows all parents to invest in their children, both emotionally and financially."

In his classic book on property and contracts written at the turn of the century, a noted economist, Richard T. Ely, distinguished between conscious and unconscious processes of acquiring wealth. As an example of unconscious wealth Ely cited an obedient, diligent, and faithful son. Ely went on to say that "with development of civilization, particularly on the economic side, social self-consciousness continually wins new fields and gains on the unconsciously operating social forces."

Ely's words seem especially definitive and prophetic at this stage of development in our civilization. As individuals become increasingly conscious of the real costs of producing obedient, diligent, and faithful children and as society realizes that such children don't just pop up like mushrooms, and that starting a family involves as much effort, investment, and risk as starting a business, we are going to have to think about the family in some unaccustomed ways. It is time, it seems, to bring the investment aspects of family decision making into our economic and political consciousness.

When we become conscious of the family as the socially productive institution that it is, one that has for centuries absorbed much of the human race's energies and resources in order to perform essential social and economic functions, and when we confront the fact that the family can no longer be taken for granted just because it operates outside the marketplace and thus off of the economic radar screen, the question of how to reverse the current disinvestment in family appears critical. The traditional family is breaking down because individuals are investing their time and money elsewhere, but the social need for many of the family's traditional services remains. How can individual decisions and society's needs be reconciled?

The first step is to understand the necessity and scope of the choice that has to be made. The countries of Eastern Europe understand that they are in a process of transition between two major economic systems and are devoting considerable attention, debate, and analysis to the process of *perestroika*. They are consciously trying to redesign a new system for providing many of the necessities of life. Fortunately, the system they are trying to design is new only to them—they can follow well-developed capitalist models capable of producing the goods and services of a market economy.

In a now-famous speech to the Commonwealth Club of San Francisco shortly after the Los Angeles riots, former Vice President Dan Quayle ascribed "lawless social anarchy" to a "'Murphy Brown' morality," referring to a TV character's embrace of out-of-wedlock motherhood. Many observers would probably agree about the crucial role of families (although not necessarily traditional patriarchal families) in transmitting social values, but it is going to take more than lectures on morality to motivate people to make the necessary commitments to family. If we collectively want more resources spent on family functions than individuals are choosing to invest, we have to design a system that provides the necessary incentives— a system that enables the family to compete with the marketplace for the resources that it needs to do its job.

2 THE FEMININE ECONOMY

THE INVISIBLE HAND OF CAPITALISM

When Adam Smith wrote *The Wealth of Nations* late in the eighteenth century to explain the elementary principles of market economics, he coined a famous phrase—*the invisible hand*—that has come to symbolize the essence of capitalist theory. In Smith's words:

> As every individual endeavours as much as he can both to employ his capital in the support of domestic industry, and so to direct that industry that its produce may be of the greatest value; every individual necessarily labours to render the annual revenue of the society as great as he can. He generally, indeed, neither intends to promote the public interest, nor knows how much he is promoting it. . . . he intends only his own security; and by directing that industry in such a manner as its produce may be of the greatest value, he intends only his own gain, and he is in this, as in many other cases, led by an invisible hand to promote an end which was no part of his intention.

The concept of a free market's capacity to harness private self-interest in service of the public welfare and to reconcile the profit-maximizing behavior of individuals with the public good without any centralized plan or control is surely one of the most provocative ideas ever conceived. Until very recent times, however, the invisible hand concept has applied almost exclusively to men because women's unpaid labor was never factored into the economic equation. The feminine economy has operated mostly outside the system of explicit prices and contracts that characterize the market economy. Women's work has never even been seriously measured or counted as an important part of economic output. As far as economic statistics are concerned, our grandmothers who bore numerous children and labored from dawn to dark caring for their families did nothing valuable with their time.

THE TRULY INVISIBLE HANDS

The term feminine economy sounds like a contradiction of terms. Whereas feminine is usually associated with such qualities as soft, nurturing, intuitive, and caring, economy denotes production, efficiency, competition, and rationality, which have a more masculine connotation. What is feminine is not generally considered economic and the economy is not usually thought of as feminine in nature. To what, then, might the term feminine economy refer? As used here, it refers to the unique functions that mostly women have traditionally performed: mothering, teaching, nursing, supporting, volunteering; in essence, the caring roles as opposed to the competitive ones—the hands that have rocked the cradle, set the dinner table, tended the sick, guided the children, and generally provided support, comfort, and nurturing.

The feminine economy might also be called the caring economy, the support economy, or the family economy—the place or the set of relationships within which people have traditionally cared for each other and supported each other rather than competed. It is the system that has served the human race throughout history (and in most of the world still does) as an organizer of the female labor force. It is the system that has been the primary producer of human capital (i.e., productive human beings), the system that has been the major provider in the dependency phases of the human life cycle (youth, illness, and old age), and a system that has provided the human infrastructure for male workers in competitive roles.

It is simply and grossly incorrect to say that women went to work in the 1970s and 1980s. It certainly would have been news to our grandmothers to say they didn't work because they didn't get paid a wage and were therefore invisible to statisticians. What women have done in the past 30 years is change jobs—from the household sector to the market sector and out of female occupations into more competitive roles.

The magnitude of this massive reallocation of effort is only dimly reflected in economic statistics and only dimly perceived by social scientists and policymakers because only half of the transaction has been recorded. An addition to the market labor force is counted when a housewife takes a paid job; and the dollar value of measured production goes up when an educated woman who in an earlier generation would have been a teacher, nurse, secretary, or full-time housewife becomes a doctor, lawyer, or manager instead. The accompanying reduction of output in the support economy, however, is never subtracted from any of the major economic indicators.

Single-entry bookkeeping that records women's entry into the market labor force or promotion within the labor force as all gain and little or no loss has caused economic statistics to miss what Daniel J. Levinson, professor of psychology at Yale, described as the early stages of a major step in social evolution. Nevertheless, everywhere in our culture there is a commonsense perception that something valuable is missing for which no one can account. Even if the gross domestic product is going up, we feel that our standard of living and our true state of well-being have declined.

Since it seems illogical to assume that for centuries half the adult population did nothing very valuable with its time, a major question needs to be asked: If women were already doing something economically valuable and/or socially useful in the feminine economy, how has our society adjusted to the loss of that output as women transferred the major portion of their labor to the marketplace? In many areas of our culture, the answer has been: by trying to ignore it. The situation is in some ways comparable to the response of many former slave owners to emancipation at the close of the Civil War. Some plantation families tried desperately to maintain their traditional lifestyle by pretending they still had slaves.

According to historians of the period, some plantation mistresses who unaccustomedly had to wash their own clothes contrived to hang the clothes in their attics rather than let anyone see them doing "slaves' work." Some families even had their daughters blacken their faces and serve dinner to company in order to keep up appearances of the plantation lifestyle. Like former slave owners who went to ludicrous lengths to avoid facing a new reality, modern society has yet to deal realistically with the fact that women are no longer doing many of the things they once did. Like those postwar plantation masters, we are still pretending there is a servant in the house when in reality no one is home.

THE CASE OF THE MISSING HANDS

WORKER PRODUCTIVITY

The statistical blind spot concerning what women have traditionally done pervades our culture, analytical work, and public policy in many ways. Young professionals still expect to earn the same salaries and promotions their predecessors had, even though their predecessors were typically married men with someone backing them up at home. Surely it is an irrational expectation to believe that one person can do two jobs as well as one or that it is possible to put in the same number of hours at the office and be as productive as your predecessors were when, unlike them, you also have to deal extensively with the domestic side of life as well.

Economists still measure labor productivity as they always have—the ratio of output to number of workers employed—*without adjustment for the fact that there used to be millions of invisible employees.* Employers who once got two (an employee with a backup spouse at home) are now most often getting just one. Managers who used to get overqualified secretaries and assistants are now more likely to be getting what they pay for as the talented and ambitious woman goes for an MBA instead, yet the manager's productivity ratio is still measured the same way by statisticians; and economists wonder why it is declining!

THE SOCIAL SECURITY SYSTEM

In the public policy arena, the whole Social Security system is based on the implicit assumption that families will continue to produce human capital in the form of productive children at something close to their historical rate. The "present value" of the implicit debt of the Social Security system to people currently in the system (workers and retirees) on the basis of current contribution records and benefit formulas is more than $21 trillion, an amount that is roughly comparable to the total tangible wealth in the U.S. economy. Medicare promises tranfers of a similar magnitude! What asset backs up these enormous promises to pay? Only the future earnings of our children, many of whom are not yet born—let alone reared and educated. *Who*, exactly, is designated in these economic assumptions to do the bearing, rearing, and educating? *Who* is assumed to be investing the necessary resources to develop the human capital to yield a $21-plus trillion return to keep Social Security afloat?

Children are produced by families—borne by women, traditionally reared primarily by mothers, and supported economically by fathers. But, it is mothers who are now "going to work" at better-paying jobs, and it is fathers who are divorcing (or never marrying) mothers and abandoning children altogether, and it is stable middle-class couples whose fertility rate has fallen below replacement. Are large numbers of well-socialized and competent children with the characteristics necessary to support the Social Security system so easy to produce that it doesn't matter whether anyone takes care of them?

THE SCHOOLS

The family per se is not the only venue in which the migration of female labor has left no one minding the store. Many of our mothers and grandmothers with college educations went into teaching almost as a matter of course; but few of our bright, ambitious daughters think of teaching as their inevitable occupation. The public schools were once an institution that combined a captive labor force with a captive audience—now they have only the captive audience. Talented and dedicated people still go into teaching and some even stay, but the woman who graduates at the top of her class is now much more likely to be heading into law or medicine or an MBA program than was her counterpart in our grandmothers' generation.

Decline in the traditional numbers of talented women going into teaching is, of course, not the only factor putting pressure on our schools. Considerable stress is also coming from the fact that children are bringing so many more problems to school because of upheavals in the home environment. Schools, it is said, have to do more for children because families are doing less; but the same trend that is taking mothers out of the home is also taking many of the best teachers out of the schools. Traditional caretakers are no longer to be found either at home *or* at school. Resulting decline in school performance is a surprise only because women's work has been taken for granted for so long and because its contributions have been so grossly undervalued.

The fact that women's contributions in their traditional roles are sorely missed in no way casts blame on women for making intelligent choices. Why should women value their traditional roles as important when society assigns them little value? Why, when lawyers make $100,000 and teachers are paid $30,000, shouldn't a woman make the economically rational decision?

THE CHURCH

This is a painful time in our culture as many observers are noting in diverse contexts. In an article about the schisms occurring in major religious denominations over issues of human sexuality such as homosexual marriage, abortion, and ordination of women, one reporter claims that the media are missing the real story. "The real story is that patriarchy is dying. It is not our [the media's] fault that we have missed this story, for not many in the church are saying it out loud yet. It's too scary. And so rather than focus on the real change that is happening, everyone from theologians to bishops to priests to laypeople to the media focuses on the symptoms of that change . . . Nearly all mainline Christian churches have evolved along a patriarchal model in patriarchal societies. So when people come along suggesting that perhaps there is another model, another angle from which to view Christianity, all hellfire breaks loose."

THE NEED FOR AN ALTERNATIVE MODEL

It is truly scary to see the major institutions on which our civilization has been built—family, church, school—so threatened and so uncertain of their roles, with their foundations crumbling beneath them. As the reporter just quoted noted, however, there are alternatives to the patriarchal model. The model the reporter sees emerging for the church is one based on "the wholeness of women as well as men." Human wholeness is a concept that obviously has many important dimensions—spiritual, psychological, biological, sociological. It also has an economic dimension.

An economic system that says someone is worth $200 an hour as a lawyer but worth nothing as a parent and worth relatively little in other caretaking occupations such as teaching and nursing is not a whole economic [healthy] system. An economy that treats speculation in the stock market as socially productive but investment in children as worthless is hardly a balanced system. In a world in which people are free to choose between caring and competitive roles, an economic system that disproportionately rewards the competitors and beggars the caretakers will eventually lose its ability to compete because resources are increasingly diverted away from society's basic function of providing a civilized context for human life.

[What is an economy for?]

Wholeness between work and family, between "men's work" and "women's work," between competitive roles and caring roles, is going to require an economic system that can somehow manage to balance the masculine/feminine, competitive/caring, work/family equation. Such a system will have to take the feminine economy at least as seriously as it takes the market economy.

3 HOMO ECONOMICUS AND FEMINA ECONOMICA (ECONOMIC MAN AND ECONOMIC WOMAN)

> If any human society—large or small, simple or complex, based on the most rudimentary hunting and fishing, or on the whole elaborate interchange of manufactured products—is to survive, it must have a pattern of social life that comes to terms with the differences between the sexes.
>
> —Margaret Mead, in *Male and Female: A Study of the Sexes around the World*

> Circumstances change and societies need to adapt to those changes. A pattern that worked well when fertility and infant mortality were high and the economy was agricultural or industrial may not work as well for a postindustrial society.
>
> —Victor Fuchs, in *Women's Quest for Equality*

GENDER DIVISION OF LABOR: THE DOUBLE COINCIDENCE MODEL

Men and women are different. How different and with what consequences is a subject of unending debate in many areas of life. In the economic arena, the major manifestation of gender difference has been the extensive specialization and division of labor by sex that has characterized most cultures throughout history. As important and conspicuous as the division of labor between the sexes has been, however, economic theory has had little to say on the subject of gender, tending instead to view the customary division of labor as a sociological and/or a biological constant. Economic analysis has been able to focus on the market economy by taking the nonmarket economy as a given, assuming that its work (i.e., women's work) has little economic value and/or that the work will continue to get done as it always has.

Division of labor by gender has been a characteristic of virtually all known economic systems. For what would appear to some extent (the extent is hotly debated) to be compelling biological reasons, the family economy has been based on a set of gender characteristics and complementarities related to the reproductive roles of male and female. Men have specialized in jobs requiring strength, mobility, and aggression while women have specialized in jobs perceived as compatible with maternity. With the possible exception of slavery in the American South, no socially enforced labor system in modern times has approached the scale, significance, or pervasiveness of traditional masculine and feminine roles.

In hunting and gathering societies, men hunted and women gathered while tending hearth and children. In agricultural societies, men tilled the land while women tended home and children. In industrial societies, men worked in the market labor force for competitive wages while women who could afford to stay out of the factories cared for home and children or worked in low-wage jobs or noncompetitive jobs such as teaching and nursing that were extensions of their caretaking roles. It has also been the role of men to serve as society's warriors in the tribal, feudal, and industrial stages of economic development.

Specialization and division of labor generally enables people to do many more things together than they are able to do separately. As Adam Smith memorably stated in the opening lines of *The Wealth of Nations,*

> The greatest improvement in the productive powers of labor, and the greater part of the skill, dexterity, and judgment with which it is anywhere directed, or applied, seem to have been the effects of the division of labor.

The family's success as a social institution throughout history has undoubtedly been due in large part to its unique ability to harness the diverse talents and capacities of its members into an efficient production unit based on the specialization and division of labor.

When our economy was predominantly rural, both men and women worked at home and shared the fruits of their labors in a form of barter exchange. It was only when industrialization created jobs away from home that monetary exchange and the devaluation of women's unpaid labor became so problematic. Barter was too awkward for transactions outside the family, requiring as it does a *double coincidence* of wants—a man who produces nails and wants to buy a car has to find someone with a car who would rather have nails—whereas monetary exchange requires only a *single coincidence* of wants—a want to buy nails and a want to sell a car—for the transactions to occur. The essence of sexual relationships and sexual roles from an economic standpoint could be said to be the extensive double coincidence of wants that exists between males and females, a degree of coincidence that has made specialization and division of labor within the family possible without monetary exchange.

Marriage between male and female has been both a biological and an economic partnership and has served to satisfy many mutual needs ranging from sexual desire to reproduction to economic survival. From the standpoint of economic efficiency, there would appear to be many advantages to a system of gender specialization so natural and so complementary that no monetary transactions are required. An accepted natural order of sexual roles that assigns lifetime jobs at birth enables a culture to reap more of the benefits of specialization by starting role training at an early age with a minimum of conflict about who is going to do what, thereby minimizing the transactions costs of specialization. Human civilization has operated on a two-sphere, double-coincidence model of gender roles centered in the family throughout history; and in most of the world it still does. Why, then, should the system be changing now in a few countries?

UNISEX TECHNOLOGY AND THE MODERN ECONOMY

There is no shortage of after-the-fact explanations of the changing role of women in modern economies. Some analysts emphasize rising productivity and rising wages in the market economy that have made work outside the home increasingly profitable. Others point to commercial substitution of products and appliances within the home that have made the services of a housewife less necessary and less valuable. Reliable birth control, feminist awareness, sex discrimination laws, and, perhaps most importantly, a postindustrial economy that values brains more than brawn have given women many more opportunities for competing in the marketplace.

Such a powerful combination of forces—the pull of higher wages and more diverse opportunities outside the home, the push of displacement by appliances and commercial products within the home, and the press of women for economic equality—makes it seem unlikely that any gender system of labor that categorically assigns women to "women's work" within the home or in home-related occupations will continue to survive very far into the twenty-first century. The technological base that has made the traditional gender division of labor within the family so productive for so long is rapidly disappearing. There is simply no need for young girls to learn how to spin, weave, sew, bake bread, make soap, can pickles, or other domestic arts taught at home any more than boys need to learn how to hunt game or hitch a horse to a plow. In the computer age, it is more profitable for both boys and girls to be in school learning the technology of our culture, which has few if any gender specifications.

Two hundred years is just a blink in evolutionary time; but within two centuries, we have developed from a frontier economy in which women were dependent on men for economic and physical survival (hunting, tilling the land, fighting) to an industrial economy with caretaking, clerical, retail, and processing jobs at which women could support themselves at a low level but were still dependent on men for earning better wages and for fighting wars, to a postindustrial economy based on knowledge, information, and service skills at which women seem to be as naturally adept as men.

Although many institutional rigidities and social prejudices concerning women's abilities may still exist, in a technological sense the economic playing field has been virtually leveled between the sexes. Since men no longer need women for many household services and since women are no longer at a biological disadvantage for most jobs, the double-coincidence model is losing most of its relevance. With the exception of a few employers such as the National Football League, there aren't many jobs for which men have any natural advantages over women who choose to forgo commitment to marriage and family; and there are few household goods and services that cannot be acquired in the marketplace.

MASCULINITY, FEMININITY, AND THE ATTITUDES OF ECONOMIC MAN

Sexual roles, however, have never been just a matter of dividing up the physical work—who bakes the bread and who plows the field, who changes diapers and who works for IBM, or even the physical acts of reproduction. The social dimensions go much deeper and involve a psychological division of labor as well. The essence of the feminine versus masculine roles has been a matter of attitude as well as of specific duties—the basic posture of caring or competing, nurturing or achieving, working for internal rewards or for external recognition and compensation. Although the technology of household and/or market production may change drastically, as it has in a relatively short time in industrial countries, the human need for the yin and yang of life, the caring and competing, the feelings and the calculations, the id and the ego—what society has traditionally considered to be the feminine and masculine perspectives on life—is hardly obsolete.

Saying that society needs both the masculine and feminine perspectives is not to say that males are incapable of feminine feelings such as caring, or that females cannot be as competitive as males. It is simply to assert that society needs both the caring and competitive roles and attitudes, however they may be divided between men and women. Our current crisis stems from the fact that, while many of the efficiencies of gender specialization that once formed the base of the family economy have lost their economic value, degenderization of economic production roles has put stress on the caring functions of the family *for which there are no technological substitutes*. Not only is there a reallocation of time in a degendered workforce, there is almost inevitably a change of attitude when people take on more competitive jobs. It takes a specific set of attitudes and behaviors to compete in the marketplace, a personality configuration defined by social scientists as "economic man."

The concept of economic man—essentially a definition of economic rationality—plays a central role in market theory. *Homo economicus* is said to be the driving force, the *sine qua non*, of capitalism. His definitive characteristics are individualism, selfishness, competitiveness, and above all rationality. The role of economic man is to optimize; that is, to maximize the satisfaction of his personal needs, preferences, and wants to the fullest extent possible given the quantity of resources to which he has access. Markets are assumed to consist of the interactions of economic men, each of whom is pursuing his own interest but who collectively form a market system in which everything of value can be bought and sold.

Economic man produces things as cheaply as possible, sells things for as much as possible, and acquires as much wealth as possible. Everything economic man has is for sale to the highest bidder, and everything he does is for the purpose of acquiring wealth at the expense of his competitors. Leisure and altruism may be considered needs or preferences to be balanced with other needs and preferences, but every minute is subject to the calculations of the optimization process. Economic man can never rest and can never be satisfied. He is a selfish, competitive fighter who is totally calculating about how he allocates his time and resources. What Professor McCloskey has called "a cross between Rambo and an investment banker" is the totally competitive individual, the gladiator, the driving force of capitalism.

Since models that assume economic rationality (i.e., that individuals behave like economic man) are the basis of most economic analysis, and since such models frequently yield good predictive results about the market economy, it appears that economic man is an accurate description of much economic behavior. Clearly, however, economic man doesn't describe all human behavior, nor does it even describe economic behavior in all its dimensions. The concept of economic man provides no clues as to how the human race survives the dependency phases of the human life cycle when the individual is unable to compete; and yet those phases have always claimed a substantial share of the economy's resources, the major resource being the efforts and labor of women. As our dependency phases in both youth and old age get longer, the missing components of economic man will be an increasingly serious problem in explaining how our economy operates.

THE TRADITIONAL ECONOMIC WOMAN

Prior to the large-scale entry of women into the market labor force and into more competitive jobs, it was the role of economic woman to support economic man in his competitive activities—not to compete with him. Nurse, teacher, secretary, wife, and mother were the roles of economic woman. It is these supporting roles in our economy that are at risk now that economic woman is acting more like economic man by competing for traditionally male jobs while there is a much smaller crossover of men into traditionally female roles. As a result, our culture is profoundly threatened by the loss of what we have taken for granted for so long—the assumption that the necessary caretakers would always be there. The resulting sense of social threat is surely a major part of the feminist backlash and a contributor to the intense feelings that surround the abortion issue.

The essence of femininity surely isn't about cooking or cleaning or even the physical act of giving birth. By filling the caring roles, women have provided the safe harbors; the places of respite, nurture, and recovery; the escape from the nonstop stress of the competitive arena in which economic man engages. The womb is the ultimate safe haven and the ultimate symbol of care and nurture. If a helpless baby can't be safe in its mother's womb, where can the human race be safe?

The womb is also, however, the ultimate symbol of the economic trap that can condemn a woman to a lifetime of economic dependence and/or poverty. Women have become painfully aware of how much the womb's functions can cost them in terms of lifetime earnings and options. The cost is essentially an "opportunity cost"—what a woman is otherwise capable of doing and capable of earning and capable of achieving as long as she has no caretaking responsibilities.

Anyone born before 1950 can remember the prevalence of myth and prejudice (in Betty Friedan's words, a "feminine mystique") about the relative competence of women in competitive roles. As Sandra Day O'Connor and Ruth Bader Ginsberg discovered after graduating from top law schools and then being offered jobs only as legal secretaries, any woman who tried to enter a predominantly male profession encountered a wall of resistance. It has been a most remarkable and undeniable achievement of the women's movement in the post-1950s era to disprove society's general assumption that women can't do it. Courageous individuals such as Justices O'Connor and Ginsberg have demonstrated resoundingly that women can in fact function at the highest levels of their professions.

One important and inevitable consequence of such demonstrations of the potential of women in competitive, high-paying jobs is to raise substantially and to make much more explicit the opportunity cost of staying home or remaining in a traditional caretaking role. Since partners in prestigious law firms can make upwards of $1,000,000 a year, $1,000,000 a year is literally what full-time motherhood can cost the bright, ambitious woman who chooses to stay home to care for her family. Even in law firms that provide "mommy tracks" as an alternative to partnership tracks (35 to 40 hours a week instead of 60-plus), the opportunity cost can still be extremely high. If mommies get $100,000 a year while partners get $1,000,000, the opportunity cost of being even a part-time mother is $900,000 a year.

Since there is no particular reason to believe that women in the 1990s are any more genetically endowed with talent or drive than our grandmothers were, the opportunity costs of women's work have always been there; but the costs were hidden because no money changed hands and there were no explicit prices. Women who had the ability to be Supreme Court judges were worth just as much to society then as now. The perception that women have worked at home for free or worked in women's jobs at relatively little cost has always been a form of social illusion because the value of their potential output in the market economy has always been an opportunity cost of the resources invested by women in home, family, church, school, charity, and so on. There isn't and never has been any "free lunch" in the feminine economy—only the appearance of one.

The principle of opportunity cost was recognized by Congress when it eliminated the draft in favor of the volunteer army. A military draft can force people to work for less than the market value of their services, but the value of those services in the marketplace is lost whether or not Uncle Sam pays in full. In terms of lost production, the draftee costs the economy at least as much as the volunteer and probably more because the volunteer is likely to be someone with fewer opportunities in the marketplace (i.e., with a lower opportunity cost) than the draftee.

The same principle applies to anyone who is denied the opportunity to compete freely in the marketplace and to be paid the full value of his or her services. Categorically assigning women who could be $200,000 doctors to be $35,000 teachers costs society $200,000 in alternative output even though the school board only writes a check for $35,000. Society may in fact get $200,000 worth of services and social benefits from the teacher, but no one should imagine that the social cost is limited to the amount on the paycheck.

When people talk about the importance of family values, it's not clear they understand that there is and always has been a very large cost associated with the caring roles, nor is it clear exactly who they think should pay the cost. Costs have been hidden from view because women's work has been paid relatively little, but the cost has been there every time a talented woman has remained in a caretaking role rather than achieving her potential in a competitive job. Caring has never been free, but it has been mostly women (and the men who supported them) who have borne the cost. Now that the costs are less hidden, women are naturally starting to think and to act more like economic man.

There is an emerging economic actor the world has never seen: a rational, independent, and informed female who understands the concept of opportunity cost and who can act accordingly. There is an economic woman, *femina economica*, who calculates the value of her time and talents in alternative roles and occupations and increasingly goes where the returns are greatest, a female who follows the same market signals that men follow. According to the basic theory of capitalism and Adam Smith's invisible hand, market prices serve to guide resources where society wants them most. Given what the market says about the relative value of doctors, lawyers, managers, engineers, plumbers, and mechanics versus housewives, teachers, and social workers, it is a safe prediction that as women increasingly exercise their choices with the same kind of economic rationality that many men do less and less time and talent will be invested in society's caretaking functions.

Why should women invest their lives and resources in low-paying occupations and accept lower status and smaller returns when they have more profitable choices? Why should men support wives and female family members in low-paying jobs when there are more profitable alternatives? Obviously, both men and women have to care enough about family, children, and community to pay the opportunity cost of letting a family member engage in activities that pay less than their comparable worth in more competitive occupations; but no matter how much they care, they also have to be able to afford it.

What is happening to family values is that they are becoming increasingly and prohibitively expensive for the individuals involved.

WHAT SOCIETY STANDS TO LOSE: THE SEXUAL LINCHPIN

One prominent social critic who has given considerable thought to changes in gender roles blames women and women's liberation (i.e., women's participation in the process of rational economic choice) for destroying our culture. The following quotes from George Gilder's *Sexual Suicide* give the essence of his arguments:

> Marriage and procreation are a countercultural assertion.

> Against a fetish of individualism and a spurious equality, against an erotic hedonism that sees sex as a mere sensuality, against such ideological abstractions and glandular pulsations, our social fabric seems invisible. Like the Pentagon, our social science often reduces all phenomena to dollars and body counts. Sexuality, family units, kinship, masculine solidarity, maternity, motivation, nurturing, all the rituals of personal identity and development, all the bonds of community, seem "sexist," "superstitious," "mystical," "inefficient," "discriminatory." And of course they are—and they are also indispensable to civilized society.

> So the way is opened for the feminists. The movement barges into all the private ceremonies, sexual mystiques, and religious devotions of society as if they were optional indulgences rather than definitive processes of our lives.

> The principal flaw of most of the literature of women's liberation is its incomprehension of the real power of women. . . .The feminist program thus usually consists of taking jobs and money away from men, while granting in return such uncoveted benefits as the right to cry.

> If women become equal in terms of money and achievement, there is only one way equality between the sexes can be maintained in a modern society. Women must be reduced to sexual parity. They must relinquish their sexual superiority, psychologically disconnect their wombs, and adopt the short-circuited copulatory sexuality of males. Women must renounce all the larger procreative dimensions of their sexual impulses.

> Women control not the economy of the marketplace but the economy of eros: the life force in our society and in our lives.

Gilder makes an eloquent case for the social value of women's traditional roles and the trade-offs involved in achieving economic parity between the sexes. He argues quite strongly that the survival of civilization depends on the socialization of men's short-term sexual impulses into women's long-term capacity for procreation and nurture of human development. Gilder claims that if women abandon their procreative roles for competition with men they are responsible for the "sexual suicide" of our culture.

The questions Gilder raises are very serious, but the only remedy he has to suggest for what he perceives as the progressive breakdown of civilization is simply to argue that women should understand the superior social value of their traditional roles and give up trying to compete with men in the marketplace. Gilder puts all of the responsibility on women for accepting and subsidizing what he admits is a "sexist, superstitious, mystical, inefficient, and discriminatory" system of gender roles.

Gilder's eloquence on the biological, social, and psychological importance of traditional gender roles is, unfortunately, not accompanied by any analysis of the economic forces that necessarily influence the decisions of both men and women in committing to family roles. He neglects to notice that no matter how socially vital and necessary women's traditional roles may be intrinsically the marketplace says they are worth very little and that something more than exhortation and scolding may be appropriate, just, and necessary to achieve a better balance between the caring and competitive functions.

Why should women see their traditional roles as valuable when our major social system for determining the relative values of things—the market system—says that women's traditional work isn't worth very much? Why should anyone think that people aren't getting the economy's message loud and clear that time invested in family or in the traditionally feminine occupations is worth very little compared to the alternatives for bright, ambitious people in more competitive jobs?

While Gilder seems oblivious to the economic forces operating on individual decisions, he is very effective in describing what society stands to lose if the caretaking roles are abandoned—essentially, the long-run health and prospects of our culture. Gilder's distinction between the short-term and long-term dimensions of sexuality is particularly definitive. In an economic context, the difference between the short term and the long term is the distinction between consumption and investment. Consumption is for immediate satisfaction, while investment is for long-run production and profit.

One need not be a Victorian moralist to rue the extent to which our culture seems to view sexuality as a short-term consumption good while ignoring and denying the long-term investment opportunities for caring, commitment, and procreation in sexual relationships. The so-called sexual revolution notwithstanding, any culture that becomes obsessed with sex as a short-term pleasure while denying its long-term potential for satisfying human needs is a sexually repressed society with a diminished future.

Why are the long-term dimensions of sexuality being devalued? Why are caring, commitment, and procreation apparently being given such low priority? Gilder would blame it entirely on a feminist consciousness that appears to discount the value of women's traditional roles. The hypothesis proposed here, however, is that it isn't women who have devalued their roles so much as an industrial and postindustrial market system that has made some of the traditional domestic functions obsolete, increasingly penalizes the rest, and has yet to recognize or deal with the problem. That isn't to say, however, that there isn't a feminist agenda.

THE FEMINIST AGENDA

Of course there is a feminist agenda. Of course women are refusing to accept subservient status in a technological environment in which they are perfectly capable of competing with men. Of course women want the right to make choices as free and independent individuals. To hear Gloria Steinem speak of the day she realized she didn't have to marry a writer because she could be one is to understand that the feminist movement is essentially about freedom and choice.

Just because women are born with the biological capacity to gestate and nurture doesn't mean they are obligated to do it. A boy born with the hormones to produce the husky build of a linebacker isn't required to play pro football, and he certainly isn't expected to do it cheaply. In the interest of simple fairness and respect for the individual, the "Jane Crow" system of arbitrarily restricting women's choices at birth has to go; but it has to be replaced by a system that can provide the caretaking functions that are vital to our culture and ultimately to human survival.

If society wants either economic man or the new economic woman to be more than just a competitor, it has to find a way to recruit and to compensate the caretakers fairly. Caring about children means caring about the caretakers of children—likewise the elderly, the needy, and anyone else that society wants protected. Those roles have never been as free or as cheap as they appeared; but now that the opportunity cost of women's productivity in alternative tasks is becoming increasingly and explicitly expensive, who is going to pay the cost? Again, how can society get "women's work" done when women no longer volunteer for their traditional jobs?

CARING ABOUT THE CARETAKERS: WHOSE PROBLEM IS IT?

FEMINISTS?

Some feminists would deny that society's need for women's traditional roles is any of their concern. In fact, the goal of equality is sometimes equated with escape from precisely those roles that have restricted women's choices throughout history. Given the length and arduousness of women's struggle to be recognized as free and equal human beings rather than inferior at best and mere property at worst, any feminist reluctance to worry about what happens to the traditional feminine roles is understandable. It may not, however, be very practical for several reasons.

In spite of many lingering prejudices about the ability of women to perform in competitive jobs, what has been described as the feminist backlash, the sexual static, and the general resistance to social change may be coming more from society's fear of losing its traditional caretakers than from any doubt about women's abilities to perform in nontraditional roles. "Who is going to take care of the children?" is a subliminal question in every discussion of the fight for women's equality in the marketplace. In that sense, it is likely that the Ayatollah Khomeini may have had a socially compelling reason for putting Iranian women back behind the veil; namely, that there was no visible alternative for getting women's traditional work done.

A scene in William Styron's *Confessions of Nat Turner* illustrates the point in the context of slavery in the American South when Uncle Ben, the brother of Nat Turner's plantation master, protests to Dr. Ballard, the local minister, that slavery is admittedly a wretched system but there doesn't seem to be any other way to get the work done:

> I am against the institution of slavery too. I wish to Jesus it had never come to these shores. If there were some kind of steam engine you could invent to plant corn or cut timber, another to pull suckers, still another big grand machine to set out in the field and chop tobacco, still another big grand machine to come chugging through the house, lighting the lamps and setting the rooms in order . . .
>
> Or a machine, I fancy, that when the mistress of the household prepared herself for an afternoon's outing, would harness up the mare and bring Old Dolly and the gig around to the front entrance, and then with its strange mechanism set the lady down on one seat and itself on another and prod Old Dolly into a happy canter through the woods and fields . . .
>
> Hey! Invent a machine like any of these, gentlemen, and I will say a happy adieu to slavery the moment I can lay my hands on the likes of such a machine.

We can always fantasize about ways of getting out of work; but in the absence of a lot of fantastical machinery, getting society's basic caretaking functions performed is everybody's problem. However unrecognized and underpaid jobs in the feminine economy may have been in the past, the value of that work and the essential nature of many of the functions performed in the traditional feminine economy are a significant hurdle to the economic emancipation of women. Any society is going to be reluctant to let go of the only caretaking system it has ever had as long as there is no viable alternative in sight. In that very pragmatic sense, taking women's traditional roles seriously is very definitely a feminist problem.

There is another even more basic sense in which the status of women's traditional roles is a feminist issue. The women's liberation movement will always remain unfinished until people are really free to choose among jobs and roles. How free is a rational person to choose between a career that provides economic support and independence and the role of housewife with all of its economic risks and drawbacks? (See, for example, Barbara Bergman's description of the economic penalties and risks of being a homemaker.) How fair and how socially productive is it that our economic system rewards production in the marketplace so much more than the caretaking functions on which our economy's productivity ultimately depends? The feminist movement really has to be about liberating the home as well as the marketplace as a choice.

ECONOMISTS?

Restructuring the feminine economy is also a problem for economists, though many might prefer to ignore it. It is economists who in many cases have laughed at the concept of comparable worth and charged that anyone proposing it just doesn't understand market economics. If the market says that a hospital janitor who dropped out of high school is worth more than a registered nurse with a college degree, then, the argument goes, that is the relative economic value of janitors and nurses to society according to the laws of supply and demand. By that reasoning, full-time mothers aren't worth one red cent to society.

People who have called the concept of comparable worth a "Looney Tunes" idea have missed the point, which is that as women increasingly acquire the attitudes and behaviors of *femina economica* (i.e., rational behavior in the economic marketplace), comparable worth is what society eventually will be forced to pay for women's traditional roles. Women with college degrees are going to be increasingly reluctant to enter fields that pay janitors' wages or to accept the risks of homemaking when it provides so little economic security. Society is eventually going to have to figure out a way to pay and to protect women's traditional roles more—*a lot more* — if those roles are to continue to be filled as competently as they were by our mothers and grandmothers.

Where a market already functions in a female dominated profession, as it does for secretaries and nurses, the problem will be taken care of by the laws of supply and demand. Employers will simply have to pay for what they want. It has, for instance, already been reported that some law firms now pay more for a legal secretary than for a new associate who has graduated from law school, that some corporations pay secretaries more than managers, and that some entrepreneurial nurses now earn more than some doctors. In other areas of the traditional feminine economy such as teaching, however, there is no system currently in place that enables parents or anyone else to get what they want from the system. There is no market system that allows the teaching profession to compete effectively in the labor market for the best college graduates.

Because of the implicit subsidy provided by over-qualified women (over-qualified in the sense that the same level of talent and education would command much more in a traditionally male profession), parents and taxpayers have naturally perceived public education as a bargain, which it clearly has been. The subsidy, however, is being progressively withdrawn as women increasingly become *femina economica* and follow the signals of the marketplace into more lucrative professions. The public generally seems to sense that something fairly drastic has changed in our schools, and almost everyone has a plan for school reform—school-based management, parental oversight committees, computers in the classroom, accountability measures, curriculum reform, a longer school year—all of which encourage the hope that we can somehow restore quality to the same basic system with approximately the same amount of money.

While many of the proposals for school reform may have merit, they tend to miss a major point about what has happened to the schools and why the system now needs fundamental change. Having lost their near monopoly on the market for the brightest and best-educated women, schools are faced with either paying salaries comparable to professions like law, management, and medicine or losing the level of talent that our mothers and grandmothers provided. Even if people could get past the idea that teaching is a traditionally female and therefore low-paid occupation, however, parents and taxpayers are never going to put the kind of money it would take to make teaching competitive with traditionally male professions into a system that can't be held accountable for the results. Paying market salaries is going to require market-type controls, a kind of control that is inherently beyond the capacity of an education bureaucracy, no matter how well intentioned or how many rules and procedures it may try to implement.

The most drastic proposal for school reform currently on the table is transferable vouchers that would give parents choices among schools both public and private. Such vouchers would indeed be a step toward changing the system by creating market-type controls on the demand side of the market. Parents with transferable vouchers are the people most likely to provide prompt, effective feedback on whether a particular teacher in a particular classroom in a particular school is meeting the needs of a specific child, which is the level at which a school needs to be held accountable.

Parental choice alone, however, isn't going to get the most talented people into the schools without paying them their comparable worth; that is, what their talent and education are worth in alternative professions. Any education reform that seeks to put quality back into the schools needs to deal with the facts of life on both the demand and the supply sides of the education equation. In the latter case, it means recognizing the enormous changes that are occurring in the feminine economy. Transferable vouchers can restructure the demand side of education, which is a prerequisite for becoming competitive on the supply side; but it's going to take real money to attract the level of talent that earlier generations could take for granted.

It isn't too difficult to imagine how a functional market can be created for talented teachers and effective schools. Once we face the fact that good teachers no longer come cheap and that schools are increasingly going to have to compete in the professional marketplace because women are no longer willing to subsidize the teaching profession, it becomes fairly clear that schools have to be reorganized on the demand side so they can be competitive on the supply side. Paying market salaries requires market controls, and the only real way to control the system is to put power in the hands of the individuals who have the most immediate concern and the most information for monitoring it. That would appear to be the parents and guardians of each individual student.

Paying teachers like lawyers and doctors and forcing schools to compete for students represent drastic changes, but they aren't beyond the realm of imagination. There are other areas of the traditional feminine economy, however, that are even more problematic. The most important area—the ultimate caring role of parenthood—would seem by definition to be beyond the reach of any market mechanism; and yet that is the role that more than any other needs support and reinforcement in the modern industrial economy. Reforming the schools and investing money in them will be relatively futile if families aren't producing teachable children.

At the same time that our whole society is wringing its collective hands about the problems of unguided youth, our economic system tells many responsible couples they can't afford to have children and tells many mothers and fathers they can't afford to let someone stay home with their children or to hire really good child care. Clearly, parents are getting some socially counterproductive signals that should be of considerable concern to economists who care about the integrity and rationality of our economic system.

In a capitalist economy, the market system is supposed to indicate what society values and what it doesn't. The marketplace is supposed to guide workers and investors to the most productive use of their resources. *An effective market system is supposed to support society's values, not sabotage them.*

THE SEARCH FOR ANSWERS

George Gilder has already been quoted as asserting that our culture won't survive unless women abandon their quest for liberation and equality and accept a "sexist . . . inefficient . . . and discriminatory" system of gender roles. Gilder argues that women's liberation is a tragic misunderstanding of the linchpin role that women have traditionally played and that by downgrading and deserting society's most important functions women are responsible for the breakdown of the family and the resulting social upheavals.

William Raspberry, a *Washington Post* columnist and a much more sympathetic and regretful critic of women's push for equality, comes to virtually the same conclusion:

> The growing presence of women in the workforce is not merely the outcome of the growth in female-headed households but also a product of our desire to succeed, not just as families but as individuals. Gender equality on the job puts pressure on mothers to return to work as soon as possible, lest their prolonged absence put them at a disadvantage with their male competitors.
>
> I would not want to return women to the second-class status they are only now escaping. But it does seem clear to me that we cannot have a workforce that equalizes opportunities for fathers and mothers—that eliminates the career costs of parenthood—and still do what we need to do for children.

The most radical feminists have approached the question from the opposite direction. Asserting that women's need for equality is a moral and social imperative, they hope for a technological and/or a social solution that will relieve women of any disadvantages whatsoever in connection with "the cruel institution of motherhood." The following quotes from Simone de Beauvoir, Juliet Mitchell, and Shulamith Firestone illustrate their line of argument:

> I think that the family must be abolished. I'm in complete agreement with the attempts made by women and indeed sometimes by men, too, to replace the family either with communes or with other forms which have yet to be invented.
>
> —Simone de Beauvoir

> It is woman's role in reproduction that has made her socially inferior, including not just the bearing and rearing of children but managing the family.
>
> —Juliet Mitchell

> Just as the end goal of a socialist revolution was not only the elimination of the economic class *privilege* but of the economic class *distinction* itself, so the end of the feminist revolution must be, unlike the first feminist movement, not just the elimination of male *privilege* but of the sex *distinction* itself: genital differences between human beings would no longer matter culturally . . . The reproduction of the species by one sex for the benefit of both would be replaced by (at least the option of) artificial reproduction: children would be born to both sexes equally or independently of either, however one chooses to look at it . . . The tyranny of the biological family would be broken.
>
> —Shulamith Firestone

More moderate voices have looked for compromises between the extremes of either returning women to the traditional sex-role caste system or abandonment of their reproductive roles altogether. The proposals of the moderates generally consist of advocating government and/or employer subsidies of child care, mandated parental leaves, and the expressed hope that men will assume a more equal share of the work at home.

Two prominent economists who have done very serious and comprehensive analyses of the conflict between economic equality and caretaking are Barbara Bergman in *The Economic Emergence of Women* and Victor Fuchs in *Women's Quest for Equality*. Both authors explicitly recognize what is at stake for individual freedom versus the general welfare, and both express a wish for a way out of the dilemma with varying degrees of pessimism. Fuchs summarizes the issue as follows:

> Women's weaker economic position results primarily from conflicts between career and family that are stronger for women than for men.
>
> It is only the extraordinary woman who can succeed in a demanding career while doing full justice to the needs of spouse and children. Most men have never even tried.
>
> Once we recognize the *legitimacy* of women's quest for economic equality, the problem of children becomes everyone's concern.
>
> Motherhood is different. Women make a higher investment in pregnancy, childbearing, and nursing—an investment that is crucial to the perpetuation of the species. The father's investment, in terms of time and energy is usually much smaller. Unlike other male primates, human fathers did become involved with their children, but typically in a patriarchal, hierarchical context. How to preserve that involvement in an egalitarian context is one of the great challenges of modern society.

Bergman poses the public policy issue succinctly:

> There are men and women who believe in equality but would like to find some way to reduce for women the attraction of opportunities outside the family. They believe a child needs a full-time mother. It is up to people who think this way to show us a new kind of partnership between mothers and fathers, with built-in guarantees of long-term sharing of financial burdens and long-term commitments to maintaining the relationship. Up to now, they have not done so.

Fuchs and Bergman have framed the issue—the basic conflict between the emerging economic rationality and competitiveness of *femina economica* and society's continuing need for the most basic functions of the traditional feminine economy. Is there another way? Is there a way to restructure the traditional feminine economy so that an economically rational person could choose the caretaking roles? Is there a way for society to take care of its caretakers fairly and justly; that is, to compensate them for their opportunity costs? Is there a way to liberate our culture from its tendency to repress the long-term dimensions of sexuality—the caring, commitment, and procreation potential of sexual relationships? Is it possible to reap the gains that can still come from specialization and division of labor between male and female within the family without exploiting anyone?

The answers to these questions need to have the same dimensions as the problem—Band-Aids won't suffice. The problem is the increasing economic imbalance between our society's need for family values as a social good and individuals' experience of family functions as a private cost—a basic incompatibility between the needs of society and the economic parameters of individuals. Choices for correcting the imbalance between public good and private cost consist, basically, of:

1. Trying to force women out of the marketplace and back into their dependent status in the home
2. Trying to shift the costs to taxpayers and employers by socializing more of the costs with government programs and mandates
3. Privatizing more of the benefits of family functions in a way that lets individuals choose their roles but rewards family investment more commensurately with its value to society.

The first alternative, it has been argued here, is neither a viable nor an honorable choice for several reasons:

- It requires an element of compulsion and exploitation of women that is incompatible with our cultural ideal of the inalienable rights of the individual and is, in any event, beyond the power of a non-totalitarian state in a modern economy.
- The economic base of the traditional double-coincidence model of gender roles has been greatly diluted by modern technology and by government programs (most notably, Social Security) that have transferred major wealth components out of the family.
- It isn't just women who are opting out of the traditional family system. Men appear to be no more willing to support women in their traditional roles than women are to assume them.

Rejecting the first alternative, however, means having to choose between the second and third alternatives. In making that choice it might be well to look at the historical precedents when other caste systems have disintegrated and had to be replaced. Feudalism broke down for men in Western Europe at the end of the Middle Ages as the Industrial Revolution progressed and as a capitalistic system evolved that provided the setting for the modern economic man. In retrospect, the changes were inevitable; but European statesmen spent a couple hundred years trying to use the powers of the state to block emerging market forces in order to retain the stability and security of the feudalistic order.

A school of thought known as *mercantilism* sought to use extensive government laws and regulations to "protect" whole nations from the forces of market competition. It was mercantilist thinking in England that produced the notorious Corn Laws that kept grain imports out of the country while citizens were starving. It was mercantilist policies in France that deliberately sought to keep the peasants poor and wages low so French exports could be competitive in foreign markets.

England's heavy-handed regulation of the economic affairs of its colonies under the guise of mercantilism was surely a contributor to the American Revolution, just as France's heavy-handed regulation of its peasants contributed to the French Revolution. Extensive government intervention ultimately proved to be neither a replacement for the safety and stability of a feudalistic caste system nor an effective block to the emerging forces of the marketplace and the activities of economic man. It was, instead, a futile and costly detour in making the transition from a feudalistic system to a market economy.

Unfortunately, much of what has been proposed as family policy seems likely to have the same fate as the mercantilist policies of Western Europe in the early years of the Industrial Revolution (or, to make another comparison, the Communist policies of Eastern Europe that attempted to replace the feudalism of Czarist Russia with a socialized system) in that it seeks to control things that are beyond the power of governments to control. While government is levying taxes to pay for extensive day care and mandating family-leave policies, employers may be finding more ways not to hire people with family obligations; or employers may simply move to Mexico. In today's international economy, the terms of exchange among individuals, families, and employers are even less amenable to centralized control than they were in Western Europe in the eighteenth century or in Eastern Europe in the twentieth century.

The alternative to trying to regulate and socialize the family is to use the market system to guide resources into the family. The pros and cons of trying to balance the family's cost/benefit equation either by socializing more of the costs and/or by privatizing more of the benefits are explored further in the following chapters, but whatever path is chosen, what seems clear is that:

> If we want a caring society,
>
> If we want a society with a future, one in which children can grow and develop and achieve their potential and carry on the best elements of our culture,
>
> If we want a culture that supports human wholeness, both the caring and the competitive needs of human beings,
>
> If we want a society that can take care of its elderly—
>
> If we want places where humans can feel safe—a womb, a family, sanctuaries from the competitive marketplace,
>
> We can't continue to penalize the caretakers, nor can we expect *femina economica* to bear the costs and risks alone.

4 WHERE DO BABIES COME FROM?

WHAT WE DON'T KNOW ABOUT THE FAMILY

Everybody knows that women's roles are changing in modern societies and that women have been entering the market labor force in increasing numbers. The media tell us frequently that families are in trouble, that our schools are failing, and that many children are at risk. We all know there were cultural shifts in the 1960s that significantly changed our society, and we are now being warned that our social-insurance programs are in trouble because of lowered fertility and declining productivity—families haven't produced enough workers who earn high enough incomes to support our dependents.

What we don't know is how to assimilate all of these social changes into the basic models of our culture. According to Senator Daniel Patrick Moynihan, the U.S. Senate's leading authority on family and welfare policies, there has been "a volcanic change in family structure, for which there is no comparable experience in human history," but "no one is near a hypothesis, let alone a general theory to explain it." Cultural models that guide how we understand our government and our economy haven't yet absorbed the enormous social changes of recent decades. We're still thinking about our late-twentieth-century economy with models based on seventeenth- and eighteenth-century assumptions.

The dominant intellectual models of social contract that serve as the basis for our economic, political, and legal systems are based on assumptions made by a group of philosophers generally known as Enlightenment theorists. Enlightenment philosophers postulated a social contract to which rational, independent men could be expected to agree. They explicitly denied any independent role for rational women and simply ignored the whole process of reproduction. Reproduction could be taken for granted by the formulators of social-contract theory because women were assumed to be restricted to the reproductive functions. The process of reproduction is still conspicuously missing from most discussions of economic affairs, as the following passage typifies.

WHAT IS MISSING FROM THIS PICTURE?

The following paragraphs are from the introduction to a special issue of *Business Week* entitled "21st Century Capitalism: The New Economic Era."

> Every once in a great while, the established order is overthrown. Within a span of decades, technological advances, organizational innovations, and new ways of thinking transform economies. From the 1760s to the 1830s, steam engines, textile mills, and the Enlightenment produced the Industrial Revolution. The years 1880 to 1930 were shaped by the spread of electric power, mass production, and democracy.
>
> On the eve of the twenty-first century, the signs of monumental change are all around us. Chinese capitalists. Russian entrepreneurs. Nelson Mandela President of South Africa. Inflation at 7 percent in Argentina. Internet connections expanding by 15 percent a month. Fiber optics transmitting 40 billion bits of data per second. From government dictators to assembly-line workers, everyone seems aware that unfamiliar and unusually powerful forces are at work. Says Shimon Peres, Israel's Foreign Minister: "We are not entering a new century. We are entering a new era."
>
> A great transformation in world history is creating a new economic, social, and political order. Communism's collapse and the embrace of freer markets by much of the developing world are driving huge increases in global commerce and international investment. The Information Revolution is forging strong links between nations, companies, and peoples . . . and so on.

Who is going to do the work of reproducing this magnificent culture? Where are the young people going to come from who will be capable of inventing, managing, and using the new technologies? Who is going to bear, rear, and educate all of tomorrow's engineers, scientists, managers, teachers, technicians, artists, and caretakers in this brave new capitalist world saturated by information technology that analysts are predicting? Who is going to take the time to instill the ethics and human values in the next generation that will be needed to make the twenty-first century livable? What kind of economic framework will the family need in order to function in the twenty-first century? *Business Week* is not alone in ignoring such questions. The question of where babies come from isn't as rudimentary as it sounds.

Children might as well come from cabbage patches as far as most political and economic theory is concerned. The fact that women's roles in procreation and their investment in human development (i.e., the feminine economy) have been omitted from virtually all recognized models of capitalist economies is neither an historical accident, an oversight, nor simply a problem of measurement. It is, instead, the result of a time-honored judgment by the most influential thinkers in the Western tradition, the same judgment that denied women the right to vote for so long. This judgment says that human activity is divided into two spheres: a natural, irrational, private sphere where biological functions occur and a civil, rational, public sphere where business is transacted. Since political and economic analysis has concentrated primarily on the public half of the equation, there is a very real sense in which social theorists don't know where babies come from.

THE DEAFENING SILENCE IN WESTERN POLITICAL TRADITION

How can the web of family that binds our society together be so pervasive in daily life and so invisible in intellectual theory? Why does an argument for taking the "feminine economy" seriously sound both weirdly radical and trivially obvious?

In order to understand where the debate about family values has been historically, it is helpful to recall how the most influential thinkers in our culture have viewed feminine roles in society. Although the Enlightenment writers cited previously go back to the seventeenth and eighteenth centuries, their cultural voices continue to shadow and constrain the modern debate about family issues. In her recent book, *The Sexual Contract*, Carole Pateman provides a very illuminating discussion of how it is that family functions have been so invisible in Western intellectual thought in the "Age of Reason and Enlightenment." The following summary is based on her analysis.

Rigid theoretical dichotomy between public and private spheres is deeply embedded in our intellectual traditions dating from the seventeenth century when political philosophers formulated the theoretical underpinnings of the modern democratic state. When thinkers such as Hobbes, Locke, Kant, and Rousseau postulated that democracy and the rule of law should be understood as being legitimized by a "social contract" mutually agreed upon by free and equal individuals, the individuals they had in mind were male heads of households. Their theories of a modern state based on individual freedom applied only to the public arena where each man could have one vote and where all economic agents (i.e., the economic men described in Chapter 3) could compete with each other and contract with each other on an equal basis.

Women and children were relegated to the private, natural sphere where different rules applied. Instead of being free like men to participate in public life, women were viewed by our intellectual founding fathers as too irrational and too disruptive to be allowed a public role. They were seen instead as being naturally subject to their husbands and necessarily confined to the private sphere. In Locke's words:

> Eve's subjection can be no other Subjection than what every Wife owes her husband . . . the Power that every husband hath to order the things of private Government in his Family, as Proprietor of the Goods and Lands there, and to have his will take place before that of his wife in all things of their Common Concernment; but not a Political Power of Life and Death over her . . .

Short of murder, whatever occurred between husband and wife was not considered by Locke to be of public concern. Rousseau was of a similar mind and denounced in scathing terms any woman who tried to enter the arena of public affairs by demonstrating rational intelligence:

> A brilliant wife is a plague to her husband, her children, her friends, her valets, everyone. . . . Outside her home she is always ridiculous . . . these women of great talent never impress anyone but fools.

Rousseau's scorn was matched by Kant's contempt in dismissing any intellectually serious woman who might try to be heard in discussions of public affairs:

> She uses her *books* in the same way as her *watch*, for example, which she carries so that people will see that she has one, though it is usually not running or set by the sun.

The principle of keeping women and their procreative abilities in their place (out of sight and out of mind) via the marriage contract reached its zenith with Sir William Blackstone's doctrine of coverture which, as an interpretation of British common law, was incorporated into the American judicial system. In Blackstone's words:

> By marriage, the husband and wife are one person in law; that is, the very being, or legal existence of the woman is suspended during the marriage, or at least is incorporated and consolidated into that of the husband; under whose wing, protection, and cover she performs everything; and is therefore called . . . a feme-covert . . . her husband [is called] her baron or lord.

"All *men* are *created* equal" as it was invoked in our Declaration of Independence literally meant what it said. Equality specifically applied to men (free white men, actually) vis-à-vis each other—not relative to women— and men were viewed for theoretical purposes as having been "created" full-blown like Adam and Eve rather than in any sense owing their existence and development to mothers and families, let alone having a family history going back many generations. Needless to say, such theories have great difficulty explaining continued survival of the human race, which is presumably why Hobbes was led to say that individuals should be thought of as simply "matter in motion," and on another occasion to remark that "we should think of individuals as springing up like mushrooms."

As Pateman vividly relates, Hobbes, Locke, and Rousseau all had substantive stories to tell about how the human race might have evolved from a state of nature in which it was every man for himself (in Hobbes's story, it was also every woman for herself). In such a state, they hypothesized that rational men would agree to a social contract that protected them from each other through rule of law. Women, it was assumed, must be subcontracted into a private sphere of womanly duties and submission to their husbands in return for personal protection. An independent economic woman was definitely and explicitly not part of the concept of our social contract as its formulators envisioned it.

John Rawls, the most noted and most frequently cited of our contemporary political philosophers, continues the Enlightenment tradition by taking the theory of social contract to a more abstract level; but he doesn't address the subject of gender roles. Although Rawls recognizes that the family poses a serious problem for any theory of justice, he doesn't have to tell a gender story because the "individuals" in his story are essentially genderless.

Pateman summarizes Rawls's human actors as follows:

> As reasoning entities (as Sandel has noticed), the parties are indistinguishable one from another. One party can "represent" all the rest. In

> effect, there is only one individual in the original position behind Rawls' "veil of ignorance." Rawls can, therefore, state that "we can view the choice [contract] in the original position from the standpoint of one person selected at random."

Rawls's representative agent is portrayed as a disembodied party devoid of any substantive human characteristics except rationality. At some points, Rawls does speak of his agents as being heads of families with descendants they care about, without ever indicating how his genderless rational agents could manage to reproduce. As Pateman notes, parthenogenesis would seem to be the only possibility.

Hobbes, Locke, Rousseau, Kant, and, most recently, Rawls are generally considered to be intellectual giants in the theoretical development of our individualistic Western culture, and deservedly so. Their concept of a social contract that gives every man natural rights as a moral person was an emancipatory doctrine par excellence as it dismissed in one fell swoop all claims that men had traditionally used to justify domination over each other—divine right, custom, force, tradition, nature, superior attributes, and so on. Government could derive its right to exist only from the consent of the governed.

Social-contract theory was brilliantly designed to break the bonds of feudalistic male caste systems and to undercut pretensions to unearned power by all manner of monarchs, dictators, and tyrants in the public arena; and it has served that purpose admirably for 300 years, especially as the concept of equal personhood is being extended to include racial and ethnic minorities. What social-contract theory has been woefully unprepared to deal with, however, is the breakup of the female caste system within the family, the emergence of *femina economica* in the public arena, and the concept of women as also having inalienable rights to their own persons.

As long as women have stayed in their traditional roles, the feminine economy and its functions could be ignored in discussions of public affairs, which is why there has been such a void in political and economic theory with respect to women's contributions. The absence of a feminine voice in the intellectual vocabulary of our culture (what Stephanie Coontz, author of *The Way We Never Were*, describes as "a deafening silence about women and the family in political theory") makes it exceedingly difficult, however, to deal with some of the most basic facts of life when we can no longer take the family for granted.

Extending "the rights of man" to women is not just another expansion of the social contract to include another excluded group. It is instead a major revision of the contract as its original formulators understood it because it means that women's investment in reproduction can no longer be assumed —we are actually going to have to *talk* about it. Unfortunately, not only do we lack statistics and models for dealing with the reproductive facts of life, we hardly even have the words—"parthenogenesis," "mushroom men," and "matter in motion" hardly suffice.

CHILDREN AREN'T MUSHROOMS: THEY DON'T JUST POP UP

As the traditional family contract disintegrates, the most important, vulnerable, and problematic part of the feminine economy is the parenting role. As noted in the previous chapter, men and women increasingly have the option of surviving and earning a living independently of each other because gender roles have lost much of their economic imperative. Gender independence breaks down, however, when it comes to the project of reproduction. Unlike other social activities, reproduction fundamentally requires cooperation between male and female, at least at the level of sperm and egg; and conception is hardly the end of the story.

The human child requires an enormous amount of care and attention in order to become a healthy, responsible, and productive citizen, a degree of care and attention that depends on the kind of cooperative environment traditionally provided by families. The author Erica Jong describes our basic need for families as a cooperative institution:

> One thing has always been true of us big-brained, slow developing mammals; it takes us two decades to reach maturity. This is both the glory and the curse of the human race. We cannot survive without thinking of ourselves as tribal, communal animals, without promoting cooperation among the generations and between the sexes.

Jong goes on to say that the cooperative family relationships necessary for human development are being stretched to the breaking point:

> In our time cooperation among the generations and between the sexes has diminished almost to the breaking point where it can barely sustain life. We have gone from the three-generation family, to the two-parent family, to the single-parent family in less than a century. Relationships between men and women have never been more problematic. Nor has there ever been less consensus about what constitutes civilized sexual behavior or sound child-rearing. . . . The single-parent family is a travesty of human needs.

Unfortunately, the travesty Jong sees in single-parent families isn't the lowest point to which cooperation between the sexes and among the generations can sink. Children shuffled among foster homes, living in the streets, or mistreated by abusive or neglectful parents don't even have one adult taking responsibility for them.

Organized cooperation among various levels of producers and consumers is the essence of what economic systems are supposed to contribute to civilization. Development theorists are increasingly emphasizing the importance of a society's ability to coordinate extensive and complex forms of cooperation in the marketplace as being the key factor in economic growth and development. Gender cooperation and intergenerational cooperation within the family, however, are rarely mentioned as being an important part of the economic story.

When political leaders, social analysts, and media commentators plead for "family values," they are essentially asking family members to cooperate with each other for a social purpose. What society presumably wants from families is increased investment of time and resources in the process of intergenerational cultural transfer and child development. There is no shortage of voices in the media and elsewhere suggesting what parents ought to be doing for their children.

In a recent conference at Brown University entitled "Growing Up in a Changing World," a group of social scientists, educators, and policymakers attempted to define the goals of child development:

Amitai Etzioni, president of the American Sociological Association, described the goal as developing an effective and ethical person with the capacity for judgment and self-discipline.

Jacquelynne Eccles, psychologist at the University of Michigan, emphasized life skills and mental habits such as planning, managing time, and discipline.

Ronald Gallimore, professor of psychiatry at UCLA, emphasized four domains of competence that children need to learn—health and mortality, subsistence, relationships, and morality.

Robert A. LeVine, a professor of education and anthropology at Harvard, has identified three universal, cross-cultural goals of parental care in order of importance as follows:

1. survival and health
2. acquisition of economic capabilities
3. attainment of whatever other cultural values are locally prevalent

One particularly notable statement (which achieved best-seller status) of what society wants parents to instill in children is William Bennett's *The Book of Virtues*. There are 10 virtues on Bennett's list that he suggests need to be instilled in the next generation: self-discipline, compassion, responsibility, friendship, work, courage, honesty, perseverance, loyalty, and faith. Since virtues are character traits that aren't very amenable to classroom instruction, the job of developing such traits falls heavily on the adults with whom children have their primary contacts; that is, in most cases, parents. Such demanding agendas represent very tall orders for today's harried parents. How are parents supposed to accomplish these things?

PARENTAL REQUIREMENTS

The energy it takes to raise a child is comparable to climbing the Pyramids in heels every day carrying a bucket of ice to the top before it melts.

—Erma Bombeck

You know the only people who are always *sure about the proper way to raise children? The people who never had any.*

—Bill Cosby

If we want to understand the reasons for family dysfunction and why the family as an institution isn't performing up to society's demands, we have to be as clear as possible about what it is parents are supposed to do. What, specifically, *are* parents supposed to do and what are the costs of doing it?

As every involved parent knows, there are no formulas that guarantee the production of virtuous children. What works for one family doesn't necessarily work for another, and what works for one child within a family may not work for another child in the same family. There are no generic families and no generic children. Each is unique. The fact that there are also many factors beyond a family's control that impinge on a child's development makes childbearing and childrearing to some extent a roll of the dice—it takes some luck. Nevertheless, there are some basic necessities involved in every family's efforts to improve a child's chances for developing into the healthy, self-sufficient, socialized adult society wants. A list on which most parents and professionals probably could agree would include the following:

◆ *Healthy parents:* Healthy children start with healthy parents. At a minimum, both parents need to be free of sexually transmitted diseases and free of exposure to environmental factors that cause birth defects. Pregnant mothers need to avoid drugs, alcohol, nicotine, and malnutrition for a child to have a fair start in life. Basic reproductive health involves constraints on lifestyle that our "do your own thing" culture tends to devalue.

◆ *Provisions:* Food, clothing, shelter, transportation, education, medical care. Rearing a child to maturity requires large expenditures on the basic necessities of life. According to the Family Research Group of the U.S. Department of Agriculture, a family in the middle third of the income distribution ($35,500 to $59,700) spends an average of $201,909 on provisions for the first child from birth to age 18 (in 1997 dollars). Similar estimates for families with incomes under $35,500 and over $59,700 are $148,180 and $294,252, respectively. Second and third children are estimated to cost 19.6 percent and 38 percent less per child respectively. There are, apparently, some economies of scale associated with the number of children in a family; but the provisioning aspect of childrearing necessarily involves a substantial amount of financial resources.

◆ *Love, care, and guidance:* One way to illustrate the value of love is to note what happens to children when love is missing from a home. The evidence is necessarily anecdotal, but it is very compelling. Many of society's most noted psychopaths have spoken of loveless childhoods. A child can be physically healthy, well-fed, clothed, housed, disciplined, and so on and still fail to thrive because the emotional connections necessary for human development are missing.

Love alone isn't sufficient. Babies and small children can't consume food, clothing, and shelter or even stay out of harm's way by themselves. Someone has to take care of them 24 hours a day. Even if child care is provided totally within the family, it is still very expensive because the family caretaker could be earning a wage or salary outside the home instead. Opportunity costs and/or out-of-pocket costs of 24-hour-a-day child care are a major item in the childrearing equation.

In the teenage years, parental care takes different forms. In today's society with its loss of extended family; its shaky educational system; and its adolescent peer culture of sex, drugs, and unguided youth, parents frequently find it necessary to serve as teacher, tutor, motivator, counselor, and soccer coach just to get kids through adolescence without falling into the cracks. The fact that so many parents in a neighborhood aren't home after school makes some parents feel they have to be there at all costs to provide an adult presence. If a child has physical or emotional problems, parents may also have to serve as nurse and therapist.

There is a critical difference between child care and childrearing. Families can hire child care for the purpose of feeding, diapering, tutoring, and generally tending a child; but childrearing involves taking ultimate responsibility for a child's growth and development. That responsibility has to include physical, emotional, mental, and social development in all its dimensions. Parental guidance is a job that is arguably tougher now than it has ever been for conscientious parents. Whereas earlier parents considered it to be their job to reinforce the prevailing culture, modern parents frequently feel they have to fight the dominant culture. The numbers of dysfunctional families whose kids run loose in their peer culture, the perverse and pervasive messages of our mass media, and the absence of institutional supports increase the difficulty of, as a *Reader's Digest* article puts it, "raising G-rated kids in an X-rated world."

Advice books for parents on how to deal with child-development problems at every age level fill many shelves in bookstores and libraries. While there are many philosophical and practical approaches to child-rearing, instilling virtues generally requires a lot of on-the-spot examples, explanations, illustrations, models, and reinforcement by people who know a child very well and who are there consistently enough and who have sufficient motivation and insight into a particular child's mind to convey an integrated value system effectively. As Penelope Leach, author of an award-winning book on parenting, states:

> However much they may delegate to other caregivers and to educational institutions, parents and parent figures are crucial to every phase of this long human childhood, not least because it is individual parents who most passionately want to meet the needs of their own children, and passion is part of what is needed.

Given that Mary Poppins is a fictional character, it is hard to imagine any kind of hired help (teacher, tutor, or babysitter) who could take the ultimate responsibility for instilling character in someone else's children, although devoted nannies and institutions such as church, school, and community can provide substantial reinforcements. Childrearing is frequently a tough, time-consuming, nail-biting job for parents these days; and even with the best parental effort, things sometimes go wrong.

The major cost of love, care, and guidance is time—primarily parental time—which also has an implicit monetary cost in that the same time and effort could earn a financial return doing something else.

◆ *Safety and stability:* Many parents find it necessary to accept long commutes so their children can live in safe neighborhoods or near good schools or close to trustworthy caretakers. Parents often feel compelled to constrain career moves in order to keep the family together and to minimize the amount of disruption in their children's lives. Every college professor who does advising is familiar with the problem of college seniors whose fellowship offers are in Boston while their fiances' law-school admissions or job offers are in Chicago or Denver. In the next century, the economic pressures on families are likely to be global—the spouse's job offer may be in Mexico or Thailand. Just keeping a family together geographically in today's increasingly mobile society can inflict enormous costs on an individual's economic opportunities. Providing the safety and stability that children need can mean major financial and personal sacrifices.

◆ *Acceptance of risk:* While many of the items on this list are more or less predictable from the time of conception, parents also face considerable risks from the unpredictable. Beginning with pregnancy, there are significant physical risks. Few women die in childbirth in modern countries, but pregnancy complications are always a threat, and many women experience permanent physical effects ranging from stretch marks and varicose veins to various gynecologically caused disabilities. Pregnancy and birth aren't trivial undertakings, but they are just one of the risks that people take in becoming parents.

A child may, for instance, be born with serious handicaps or developmental problems requiring extended periods of care. A family whose wage earners are without medical coverage can lose everything when a child becomes seriously ill. In addition to the physical and financial risks of being a parent, there are also emotional risks. The parent-child relationship sometimes brings heartache.

◆ *Parental cooperation in all of the preceding:* There are many heroic single parents who do their best and who frequently succeed in producing healthy, well-adjusted children. Children must count themselves lucky to have one dedicated parent; but the practical logistics of bearing and rearing children suggest that two heads, two hearts, two pairs of hands, two sets of grandparents, friends, and relatives, and frequently two paychecks have a considerably better chance of covering the parental bases working as a team than one parent trying to do it all alone. Many psychologists and sociologists would add more intangible considerations concerning gender polarities in human development, considerations that translate as differences in paternal and maternal forms of love, and the importance to children of having both male and female role models.

Marriage frequently requires heroic compromise on the part of one or both spouses. Keeping a marriage together for the sake of the children when adults are having trouble getting along sounds old-fashioned in these days of no-fault divorces. Any partnership that runs into problems, however, has to weigh the value of staying in a relationship versus the value of getting out of it. There are valuable assets and the viability of the business to be considered—considerations that place a value on compromise, if at all possible. In the case of parental partnership, the "business" involved is that of providing a suitable environment for the growth and development of very vulnerable human beings who are attached biologically and emotionally to both parents. The social value of the "assets" involved is estimated in the following chapter.

PERSONAL STORIES

Career/family trade-offs aren't just an issue for working mothers, nor is it just children of single parents and poor families who are at risk. Some very prominent fathers have gone out of their way to share lessons acquired through family tragedies. In a personal memoir about a daughter who had an abortion at 15 followed by recurring depression and alcoholism that ended with being found frozen to death in an alley in Madison, Wisconsin, former Senator George McGovern speaks poignantly of the conflicts between his career and "being there" as a parent:

> Nor can I escape regret over the ways in which my political career and personal ego demands deprived Terry and my other children of time, attention, direction—and fun with their father . . .

> If I were to do it all over again, I would insist on more times of riding with my children, camping with them, engaging in sports with them, teaching them to ski and play tennis, taking leisurely strolls and trips, and just listening to them at home. This is no guarantee of a more secure and happy life for one's children. There are peer pressures and other circumstances beyond the parents' control. But the kind of activities and involvements I have suggested might have been a better way to fortify my children against the heavy pressures and temptations of adolescence . . .

Many stories reported in recent years have illustrated the practical effects of what parents of both genders do or don't do at all income levels and in all social strata. Mickey Mantle's story was one of the most dramatic. Mantle's family story came to public attention when he received a liver transplant in June of 1995 after years of alcoholism and, by his own description, spending more time with his drinking buddies than with his sons.

Mantle publicly blamed himself for the death of his son, Billy, who died of a heart attack in a drug-treatment center in 1994. "'I wasn't a good family man,' Mantle wrote in *Sports Illustrated*. 'I was always out, running around with the guys . . . They [his sons] all drank too much because of me . . . If only I'd gone to Betty Ford sooner, Billy might be here.'"

Of his eldest son, Mickey, Jr., who had a brief minor-league career, Mantle said Mickey, Jr. "could have made the majors" if he [Mantle] had pushed and encouraged him as Mantle's own father had done.

Where do the healthy, productive citizens society needs come from? They come from the parents who sacrifice sufficient fun and fortune to keep children alive and to give them the help and support they need to achieve their potential.

IN SUMMARY

In contrast to the mystical connotation that generally surrounds the concept of "family values," family values in real life translate as very tangible restraints on lifestyle, large investments of time and money, restrictions on mobility, considerable risk, and, preferably, the ability to work as a parental team—requirements that are at least as demanding and complicated as the effort, investment, risk, and compromise involved in operating any business partnership. While families are in many ways a unique form of enterprise, in some important ways they also function as a business in the sense that they require large amounts of economic resources and result in a product in which society has a substantial interest. The theoretical dichotomy between business and family that has excluded reproduction from economic models for so long is in many ways a false dichotomy. The following chapter analyzes the question of where babies come from, economically speaking, as a prelude to suggesting a way of assimilating the family's role into the basic models of our political and economic culture.

5 THE FAMILY ENTERPRISE

THE BUSINESS MODEL

It is time to attach some dollars and cents to the preceding generalizations about family costs and responsibilities. This is a part of the analysis that many people understandably might prefer not to see or even to think about. Reluctance to quantify family values is a very natural reaction because it invades our private space with the crassness of the marketplace.

The following analysis is in no way intended to suggest that money can measure many of the important dimensions of family. But thinking about the family in a business context sheds considerable light on where the stresses are on the modern family and what might be done to alleviate some of them, because commitment to family requires individuals to invest substantial resources and to make many of the same kinds of decisions that business managers and investors have to make.

As a basis for comparison, consider the operation of a typical business enterprise such as a wheat farm in the Midwest owned by the Jones family. The quickest way to get a picture of how the Jones farm operates is to look at its profit-and-loss statement as in Table 5.1.

Like all businesses, farmers must purchase inputs to produce a marketable output. A farmer's inputs include such things as land, equipment, seed, fertilizer, pesticides, wages for hired hands, insurance, and so on, which would be listed on the expense side of a P and L statement. Typical farmers who devote their own effort to the

51

Table 5.1: *Farmer Jones's Profit and Loss Statement*

Revenues	Expenses	
Wheat Sales $200,000 (80,000 bu. @ $2.50/bu.)	Land Equipment Supplies Services Time	$ 50,000 40,000 30,000 30,000 40,000
	Total	$190,000
	Profit	$ 10,000

operation should also count the value of their time as a cost. The opportunity cost of the Joneses' time (i.e., what the same time and effort could earn doing something else) is an expense of producing the product.

As a matter of fact, all of the Jones farm's expenses are opportunity costs for the economy because the same resources (land, labor, capital) could be used to produce other things consumers want. The reason farmers have to pay the going price for land, for instance, is because if they don't someone else will. Whoever is bidding against them presumably has a profitable use for it. If the farm's expenses add up to $190,000, it is using resources that consumers value at $190,000 in the hands of some other potential producer.

In order not to take a loss on the wheat-farming operation, the producer must transform the resources used into a product the consumer will value at at least $190,000. The market therefore serves as both information system and taskmaster. It tells potential producers what wheat is worth to consumers and what the resources it takes to produce wheat are worth to society in alternative uses and also forces producers to yield something that is worth its resource cost or get out of business.

The market is a taskmaster, but it isn't a slavemaster. If the Joneses want to run an unprofitable horse farm because they really love horses, they are free to do so as long as they are willing to bear the cost. Producers can put love on the revenue side of a P and L statement if they want to do so.

CONVERGENCE OF SOCIAL AND PRIVATE VALUES IN THE MARKETPLACE

The essential argument for the efficiency of capitalism is the convergence of a producer's profits with society's welfare that occurs under ideal conditions. If a social profit-and-loss statement were constructed for what society gains and loses from the Jones operation, it ideally would have the same numbers on it and a farm's profit would also be society's gain.

In Table 5.2, which is an extension of Table 5.1, columns 1 and 4 compare the social gains and losses of this operation. Since $190,000 worth of resources have been converted into $200,000 worth of wheat, it appears that there is a net social gain of $10,000 worth of wheat. The economic engine that performs this transformation of resources into product is contained in columns 2 and 3 where producers are guided by what they see in their expense and revenue accounts.

Table 5.2: *Social/Private Profits and Losses from Farmer Jones Operation*

Social Benefits (1)	Private Revenues (2)	Private Expenses (3)		Social Costs (4)
$200,000 worth of food	Wheat Sales $200,000 (80,000 bu. @ $2.50/bu.)	Land Equipment Supplies Services Time Total Profit	$ 50,000 40,000 30,000 30,000 40,000 $190,000 $ 10,000	$190,000 worth of resources

If column 2 exceeds column 3, a producer will continue to produce wheat. If column 3 exceeds column 2, the Jones Enterprise would be better off doing something else with its resources. When the market does its job of putting prices on things so that a producer's expenses equal society's costs and a producer's revenues measure society's benefits, a producer's profits and society's welfare converge to the same decision—produce a product as long as the price covers the cost. If not, produce whatever it is that society values more.

The market system is the major venue through which our capitalistic economy indicates to individuals what society wants done at the point "where the rubber meets the road," so to speak; that is, where actual decisions about resource allocation are made. Consumers tell the farmer how much they value wheat by the price they are willing to pay for it (in this case, $2.50 per bushel). Market prices also tell farmers what the land, labor, and capital it takes to produce wheat are worth to other producers who are bidding for them in the marketplace. It is market prices that signal to farmers that they should produce wheat when consumers value wheat more than any alternative goods or services the same resources could produce.

Economists know full well that there are many ways in which a market's performance in serving society's wants can be distorted and compromised, but this is a bare-bones outline of the way markets generally work.

MARKET THEORY AND THE FAMILY

So what does production economics have to do with the family? If we use the production framework to think about the family enterprise of bearing and rearing children, it quickly becomes apparent that our economic system is sending some very inconsistent signals with respect to families. The market sends one signal to society about the value of families and a very different signal to parents. Conceptualizing a profit-and-loss statement for the family may seem like an exceedingly blunt way of looking at the problem, but financial statements are just ways of arranging information on paper. Arranging information on paper doesn't change in any way what is actually happening, but it can help us understand it.

Although there are many intangible aspects of parenting such as love, risk taking, and parental cooperation that are virtually impossible to cost out, provision costs are tangible and time costs can be estimated. Table 5.3 is set up as a partial profit-and-loss statement estimated for a hypothetical family at three different income levels: low, medium, and high as defined by the Family Economics Research Group of the U.S. Department of Agriculture. All of the estimates in this table are in 1997 dollars. Explanations of how the numbers have been computed are given in the notes following the table.

Table 5.3a: *Family Profit and Loss Statements*

Low-Income Family
(Income < $35,500, Average = $22,100)

(1) Social Benefits	(2) Private Revenues	(3) Private Expenses		(4) Social Costs
Workers (Human Capital) **$639,000**	**Personal** Love, Pride, Parental Instinct	**Provisions** Housing Food Transportation Clothing Health Care Educ. & Child Care Misc.	$ 47,852 29,748 22,097 12,065 10,639 10,602 15,178	A family's provision and time costs are also social costs because economic resources are consumed.
		Total	$148,180	$148,180
	Family Labor?	**Time** 	$283,500	$283,500
	Old-Age Insurance	**Education**	?	$ 84,500
		Total	$431,680	
$97,767				

Social Security Transfers

LOW

Table 5.3b: *Family Profit and Loss Statements (continued)*

Medium-Income Family (Income $35,500 – $59,700, Average = $47,200)			
(1) Social Benefits	(2) Private Revenues	(3) Private Expenses	(4) Social Costs
Workers (Human Capital) $1,390,500	Personal Love, Pride, Parental Instinct	Provisions	A family's provision and time costs are also social costs because economic resources are consumed.
		Housing $ 66,303	
		Food 35,675	
		Transportation 30,628	
		Clothing 14,223	
		Health Care 13,801	
		Educ. & 18,600	
		Child Care	
		Misc. 22,680	
		Total $201,909	$201,909
	Family Labor?	Time $657,000	$657,909
	Old-Age Insurance	Education ?	$ 97,500
		Total $858,909	
$ 212,746	Social Security Transfers		

Table 5.3c: *Family Profit and Loss Statements (continued)*

High-Income Family
(Income > $59,700, Average = $89,300)

(1) Social Benefits	(2) Private Revenues	(3) Private Expenses		(4) Social Costs
Workers (Human Capital) $2,655,000	Personal Love, Pride, Parental Instinct	**Provisions** Housing Food Transportation Clothing Health Care Educ. & Child Care Misc.	$ 108,704 44,293 40,908 18,340 15,847 28,921 36,940	A family's provision and time costs are also social costs because economic resources are consumed.
		Total	$ 294,252	$ 294,252
	Family Labor?	**Time**	$1,291,500	$1,291,500
	Old-Age Insurance	Education ?		$ 117,000
		Total	$1,585,752	
$ 406,215	Social Security Transfers			

EXPLANATION OF TABLE 5.3:

On the Expense/Social-Cost Side

Provisions. Average provision expenditures by parents for a first child to age 18 are based on estimates by the Family Research Group of the U.S. Department of Agriculture, which uses the 1990-92 Consumer Expenditure Survey—Interview Portion (updated to 1997 prices) administered by the Bureau of Labor Statistics. The USDA estimates that second and third children cost 19.6 percent and 38 percent less per child, respectively, than first children. These average figures obviously conceal large variations among individual families as between, for instance, those who send children to public school and those who pay private-school tuition. Excluded from the USDA estimates are all costs prior to birth. In 1991, prenatal care and delivery averaged $4,720 for a normal delivery and $7,826 for a cesarean delivery.

Time. The USDA estimates are just for the direct costs of provisions for one child through high school—they make no allowance for the cost of parental time, which is likely to be by far the larger cost. Given that people tend to marry those of similar educational backgrounds and aspirations (social scientists call it assortative mating), differentials in spousal incomes can be attributed to the costs that one spouse incurs due to being the more flexible partner with respect to job commitment for the sake of family responsibilities. The figures listed in Table 5.3 for Time are based on hypothetical assumptions about the costs of being the more flexible parent as follows:

For a low-income family with, for example, an average annual income of $22,100, if one parent averages $14,200 per year as a janitor and the other parent averages $7,900 as a nurse's aide by working part time and/or intermittently during a working lifetime of 45 years, the cost of being the flexible parent is $6,300 × 45 = $283,500.

For a middle-income family with an average income of $47,200, if one parent earns $30,900 as a sales representative and the other parent averages $16,300 as a computer consultant working part time and/or intermittently, the flexible parent's income loss is $14,600 × 45 = $657,000.

For a high-income family with an average income of $89,300, if one parent is a manager who averages $59,000 per year and the other parent is a teacher who averages $30,300 working part time and/or intermittently, the cost of being the more flexible parent is $28,700 × 45 = $1,291,500.

Time costs, of course, vary considerably among individuals according to personal circumstances; but on the average, these estimates probably aren't exaggerated. If anything, they are more likely to be understated because both parents frequently make job compromises. Parents who pass up overtime or promotions in order to have more family time or who turn down advancements involving relocation so their families can have more stability incur additional costs. Parents who pass up jobs requiring travel and/or long hours or who take teaching jobs rather than administrative jobs so someone can be home with children after school and during summers and vacations can incur very large costs as do people who elect to be nurses rather than doctors or social workers rather than lawyers in order to have more time and energy for family. Spouses who forgo opportunities in our increasingly mobile society just to stay with each other may pay a high price for their immobility.

Several statistical studies confirm the likely costs of being the flexible parent who has primary responsiblility for children. One comprehensive analysis of lifetime earnings costs due to childrearing is a study by Heather Joshi. Her estimates are derived from econometric models based on the nationwide "Women and Employment Survey" conducted in Britain in 1980 with numbers converted to 1990 prices. Joshi calculates the lifetime earnings losses due to child care for a junior secretary who, if she were childless, would start working at age 17 and by age 22 earn a salary of £9,000 in 1990 prices and retire at age 59. At an exchange rate of £1.65/$1.00, £9,000 is approximately $14,850. Income losses due to caretaking consist both of lost wages due to time away from the job market and loss of position on the career ladder when the caretaker returns.

If the secretary leaves her job at age 25 and stays home for eight years to care for two children until they start school, then works half time for 12 years until her younger child is 15, at which point she begins working full time until retirement at age 59, her income losses are computed as follows, adjusted to 1997 prices:

Loss while not working	$164,389
Loss due to part-time work	$149,168
Loss due to re-entry at lower-level job	$ 97,416
Total	$410,973

Lost pension benefits aren't included in these numbers, nor is lost leisure for mothers who give up more than just their working hours to be on call 24 hours a day.

Studies of the American labor market also find significant negative effects on women's wages associated with having two or more children. The costs are attributed primarily to losses of tenure and experience in the labor market. A study by Korenman and Neumark suggests an additional effect of children on mothers' wages. Their study is quite complicated but seems to suggest that children lower a mother's productivity and therefore her wages and that lower wages cause mothers to be less interested in continuing to work. In other words, a caretaker's commitment to the job market serves as both cause and effect in determining the costs of childrearing.

It is difficult to measure statistically all of the ways in which constraining one's participation in the labor market for the purpose of childrearing can inflict costs on parents, but the opportunity costs of time spent on family constitute both private and social costs. Income forgone by choosing, for example, to be a nurse rather than a doctor in order to have more time and flexibility for family represents both a loss of income to the individual and a loss of the doctor's more expensive services to society.

Education.   The USDA figures listed in Table 5.3 for Education and Child Care are for parental expenditures (private-school tuition, books and supplies, tutors, SAT prep, etc.) to age 18. Education expenditures by parents beyond high school are additional costs. As with other parental costs, parental expenditures on education are also social costs because they absorb economic resources. No attempt is made here to estimate parental expenditures on post-high-school education because of the degree of variability of such expenditures among families.

In the substantial portion of our education system that is publicly financed, costs are shared by parents and nonparents. Parents who buy larger houses or houses in neighborhoods with better schools pay additional property taxes. Although the property taxes paid by parents are counted by USDA as housing costs and thus listed under Provisions, much of what parents pay in property taxes is actually expenditure for education. Parents also pay substantial portions of state and local taxes that support public schools and universities.

Social costs of education include all of the economic resources spent on education by parents and nonparents, both publicly and privately. The cost estimates for public expenditures on education are computed here as follows: the estimate for the low-income family is for kindergarten through 12th grade (13 years) at $6,500 per year. The estimate for the middle-income family is for kindergarten through two years of post-high school education (15 years), and the estimate for the high-income family is for kindergarten through one year of post-college education (18 years) at the rate of $6,500 of public subsidy per year.

Total Costs (?)   Because of the hypothetical nature of parental time costs and the absence of any estimate of what typical parents spend for college education, the total cost figures must be regarded as incomplete and hypothetical. No inferences are made concerning these numbers except that they are likely to be very large for most families. (A March 10, 1998, cover story in *U.S. News and World Report* starts with the costs outlined above, adds some likely costs that have been conservatively omitted here, and estimates the total lifetime cost of one middle-class child at $1.4 million!)

On the Revenue/Social Benefit Side

Parental Love. No attempt is made here to put a price on parental love, but that is in no sense to discount its value in the family equation. To the contrary, in the context of family accounting, parental love is shown to be an extremely valuable asset given that modern parents incur such enormous costs for so little financial return. This is another way of saying what many people from fundamentalist conservatives to evolutionary biologists assert—that parental love is an extremely precious thing.

Human Capital. Sons and daughters who become productive members of the labor force are a valuable resource to society. The market value of a person's capacity to produce goods and services is a measure of what economists call "human capital." Lifetime contributions of a worker to economic output are estimated in Table 5.3 for three different income levels. The low-income janitor who averages $14,200 a year for 45 years has a lifetime value of $14,200 × 45 = $639,000. Similarly, a middle-income sales representative who averages $30,900 for 45 years has a lifetime value to the economy of $1,390,500; and a high-income manager who averages $59,000 for 45 years has a lifetime value of $2,655,000. The child of a low-income family may, of course, become a medium- or high-income worker and vice versa. The numbers assigned here are simply to illustrate the likely magnitudes of value to society when parents succeed in reproducing themselves in terms of marketable human capital.

Social Security Transfers. The value of old-age, disability, and Medicare insurance transferred out of the family by Social Security is computed as the 15.3 percent rate that workers currently pay in payroll taxes (workers' + employers' FICA contributions) applied to lifetime earnings computed as the value of human capital of a low-, middle-, and high-income worker, respectively.

CONCLUSIONS FROM TABLE 5.3

Cost of Children

The first point that Table 5.3 makes clear is that family doesn't come cheaply. The sheer quantity of economic resources that pass through one family in the process of rearing one child qualify the family as a major economic undertaking at all income levels. When time and provision costs alone are added together (not to mention costs of college tuition or the various risks and constraints parents incur), the cost of producing one child comes to $431,650, $858,909, and $1,585,752 respectively for the hypothetical low-, medium-, and high-income families defined in the table.

The economic magnitudes involved in the family enterprise call into question the basic models of social reformers, which suggest that the family can be accommodated around the margins of the capitalist system. The numbers in Table 5.3 aren't marginal. There is no practical amount of government assistance that can begin to match more than a small fraction of the costs of bearing and rearing a child in today's economy.

Hidden Costs of Time

Table 5.3 also makes clear what is likely to be most expensive about child-rearing in the modern environment—it's primarily time, the resource that for most Americans is currently in shortest supply (see, for example, Julie Schor's *The Overworked American*). Provision costs aren't small, but by far the larger expenditure for most families is likely to be parental time, especially when both parents hold jobs. The fact that people can't be in two places at once frequently requires at least one parent to preserve some family flexibility by making sacrifices in terms of market wages and career development. There are, of course, some successful two-career couples with children who are able to work double shifts at home and at work and make few career compromises; but that requires luck and stamina and is still much more the exception than the rule.

It is the relative invisibility of time costs and forgone opportunities that has obscured the dimensions of the family's economic functions from public view. That invisibility can be surmised to be responsible for much of the frustration people are now feeling about their overextended lives that is chronicled in Schor's book. We can wonder why it is that when *both* parents now work we feel so stressed and seem to have so little extra to show for it because we never counted what our mothers and grandmothers did when "Mother didn't work."

The fact that children are time-intensive projects is the major reason given by economic theorists to account for declining fertility in developing countries. Simple economic theory suggests that people would have more children when rising incomes make children more affordable; but in fact, the opposite happens rather dramatically, due, apparently, to increasing parental investment per child and to increasing opportunity costs of parental time.

Both time costs and provision costs tend to increase with economic development. As economies become more complex, the period of physical dependency increases as does the need for parental time to train and guide children in a more complex world. As anthropologist Wanda Minge-Klevana noted in a survey article about how people spend their time in different stages of economic development:

> During the transition from preindustrial society to industrial society, the family underwent a qualitative change as a labor unit—from one that produced food to one whose primary function was to socialize and educate laborers for an industrial labor market. To understand this, one must understand that childhood changed so radically that the cost to the family was not merely the money paid for education per se. What put a burden on the family in industrializing European countries and the United States was the extension of childhood from age 5 or 6 to age 15 or 16 for the middle class and to age 22 or 23 for those families that could send their children to a university. Whereas previously children had worked when they became old enough to do so, now their parents found themselves supporting adolescents.

Nor does parental support necessarily end with college graduation. An increasing number of parents are experiencing a phenomenon known as "boomerang kids"—children who return home after college and require continued parental help until they get sufficiently established in a career or profession to support themselves. As one father quoted another in a *Washington Post* article, "Don't think you're done supporting them when they graduate. You'll be subsidizing them for years."

It isn't just the length of dependency that changes with economic development. Anthropologists have also noted that the intensity of parental interaction with children increases as societies become more complex. Whereas in agrarian societies babies are slung on the backs of field workers and small children are cared for by siblings, in industrial societies children are tended primarily by adults. Parents in complex societies are more likely to carry their children in front, talk to their children more, play with them more, and take them more places.

While the period of dependency lengthens and the intensity of interaction increases, opportunity costs of parental time spent in the home also increase as wages for work outside the home increase with economic development. This is especially true for women because jobs in advanced economies demand more education, intelligence, and personal skills and therefore offer more rewarding opportunities for women. Parental time has thus become increasingly more important for children and, at the same time, more expensive for parents to supply.

WHERE OUR ECONOMY'S OUTPUT COMES FROM

It is customary in economic models to measure investments in human capital as the costs of formal training and schooling. What Table 5.3 makes clear, however, is that expenditures on formal schooling are likely to be a small fraction of the total cost of producing one worker and that a much larger share of the cost occurs within families.

The table is an incomplete listing of the costs of childrearing that many families incur; but even so, the costs of public education pale beside parental costs for provisions and time. Given that parents also pay school taxes, even the public schooling listed in the table is paid substantially by parents. If parents pay half of the public-school taxes, then the parental share of the total costs of producing one worker for the hypothetical families in Table 5.3 is approximately 91.8 percent for the low-income family, 94.9 percent for the middle-income family, and 96.6 percent for the high-income family.

If parents bear 95 percent of the costs of producing a worker and if workers generate 2/3 of our national output (as they have consistently for over a hundred years), then parental investment is the source of over 60 percent of the income-producing wealth in our economy. These are "back-of-the-envelope" calculations, but they reinforce what some anthropologists have hypothesized: namely, that contrary to popular belief, industrialization didn't put the family out of business as the center of economic production. As Minge-Klevana suggests, the family's economic role has evolved from being the primary producer of food and necessities in agrarian societies to being the primary producer of the labor force in market-based economies.

CONNECTION BETWEEN THE NATURAL AND THE RATIONAL

In contrast with the separation between the natural and the rational spheres of life dictated by our philosophical forebears, Table 5.3 suggests that neither the natural instincts of reproduction and parental love nor the rational calculations of economic costs and benefits can operate independently of each other within the family. No conceivable amount of economic benefit from children is likely to offset all of the costs to parents in any family. On the other hand, parental love, no matter how strong, can hardly afford to ignore the cost side of the family equation.

Contrary to most political and economic models, parental love is generally recognized by biologists to be a very precious evolutionary asset. The basic lesson of evolutionary biology is that the genes of organisms that don't reproduce or don't care adequately for their young don't survive. Nature programs every successful species to engage in gender and intergenerational cooperation to the extent that is necessary for reproduction. In the case of Erica Jong's "big-brained, slow-developing mammals" of the human species, however, virtually all cultures until very recent times have reinforced parental instincts with substantial economic incentives for parental investment.

Although reproduction is generally seen as part of nature and thus not within the scope of economic analysis, no discussion of family economics can afford to ignore the natural feelings, drives, and instincts involved in reproduction. As a noted anthropologist stated, ". . . the theory of culture must take its stand on biological fact. Human beings are an animal species." On the other hand, parental feelings, drives, and instincts can't operate independently of economics either because reproduction is such an expensive process. In the context of family accounting, the traditional dichotomy between the natural and the rational dissolves because the natural and the rational are inextricably linked together within the family.

DIVERGENCE BETWEEN PRIVATE AND SOCIAL FAMILY VALUES

The family accounts illustrated in Table 5.3 closely resemble the accounts of the Jones farm in Table 5.2 with one conspicuous exception. There is a large financial hole in column 2 of the family's private account, where a producer's revenues normally appear when a business enterprise succeeds in doing something useful to society. The revenue side of the family's P and L statement has been deteriorating in recent decades to the point that the only thing left on the revenue side is love. Parental love is surely a significant asset in most families, but no society until recent times has expected love alone to support the family enterprise. To put it another way, parental love has never cost so much. In financial terms, net parental profit has never been so negative.

The family's economic imbalance is due to the fact that although it may succeed in producing a very expensive and valuable product (our labor force), unlike most producers, the modern family has no socially recognized claim on the wealth it produces. That hasn't always been the case. Children in simple economies routinely serve as valuable labor on family farms and in small shops at a relatively young age, but those opportunities tend to disappear in modern, urban economies. Children also took care of their parents in old age.

Prior to the institution of our Social Security system, parents had a recognizable claim on their children's resources in old age. In fact, children were viewed by many families as their major form of old-age insurance. Socializing old-age insurance has removed that claim from the family balance sheet. No one has a claim on the Social Security system by virtue of being a parent, even though the system is just as dependent on the future earnings of children as the family used to be. As was noted in Chapter 1, people who never have children, parents who abuse, neglect, or abandon children, deadbeat parents who don't pay child support—all have as much claim (in many cases more) on the earnings of the next generation via the Social Security system as does the most conscientious parent.

The magnitude of wealth transfer involved in effectively disinheriting parents from their children is not a trivial number; 75 per cent of American taxpayers now pay more in Social Security taxes than they do in income taxes. *The present value of what the Social Security system expects to pay to people currently in the system (i.e., workers and retirees) is over $21 trillion—an amount that is roughly comparable to the total tangible wealth in our whole economy. No other economic institution has ever been subjected to that kind of negative transfer and expected to survive.*

What if we told farmers they were expected to invest in land, plow the field, fertilize, weed, and water the crops, guard against pests, and do the harvesting, but when the crop came to market they would have no claim on the proceeds? If they wanted to eat, they would have to hold a job in a factory as well. How much difference would it make if we offered farmers unpaid leave from the factory at planting time and perhaps even supplied a caretaker to watch the farms while the farmers work in the factory but also told them that the risk, expense, labor, and responsibility for producing a successful crop still rested with them?

We would never think of treating any other producers the way we now treat families. Economics is, to be sure, only one dimension of the family; but it is a critical dimension. To ignore the economic dimensions of family and the economic crunch that the modern family is experiencing is to abandon our most cherished institution to an increasingly stressful fate.

6 TELLING THE TRUTH ABOUT FAMILY VALUES

THE POLITICAL ARENA

It is liberals who seem to understand and acknowledge the moral right and human need of women as well as men to participate fully in the social contract, to be free economic agents, and to have the inalienable right to their own persons that democracy claims rhetorically for all individuals. It is conservatives, on the other hand, who seem to realize that caretaking roles aren't optional for society, that the work needs to get done and done well if our society is to prosper, and that government programs and mandates are poor substitutes for what our mothers and grandmothers did. On these counts, it would seem, both sides are right; and there is little room for compromise.

The question is: How can we get the necessary work done for the family without repressing or exploiting individuals in roles they would not freely choose if they had a full range of alternatives? Surely, society needs families as desperately as it needs farmers.

A MARKET APPROACH TO FAMILY VALUES

There may be a way to depolarize the social warfare that family issues have become, an approach that preserves both the liberal insistence that individuals should be free to choose their roles in life and the conservative

67

position that family roles aren't optional. The suggestion is that we apply basic investment theory to the family. To do so would require that:

1. We recognize and respect the family as the major investment institution that it is.
2. We think of the family as embedded in our capitalist system with many of the same needs as other investment institutions that have to compete for resources in a market economy.
3. We let people make their own choices about whether to invest in family, but also find a way to let the market system reward family choices more in accordance with their social value.

THE BASIC INVESTMENT EQUATION

The argument for applying investment theory to the family rests on the following assumptions:

- Family members are rational.
- Individuals (including women) are free economic agents and their time is a marketable asset.
- People may have a natural instinct to reproduce and to care for their young, but they are forced to balance their instincts against the costs of indulging them—we don't live in the Garden of Eden.
- Even when many of the costs are of the opportunity variety and most of the benefits are subjective, people still have to evaluate the investor's basic equation; that is, they have to ask:

    Do benefits equal costs?
    More correctly, given the lags and uncertainties involved in most investment situations, do expected benefits equal expected costs?

LET'S GET REAL

Liberals and conservatives have both approached family issues with policies aimed at the cost side of the investment equation. Liberals have tended to advocate government subsidies and mandates that would transfer a portion of family costs to taxpayers and employers, while conservatives have leaned toward advocating traditional family roles for women that have the effect of hiding costs because no money changes hands when women aren't in the workforce. The sheer size of the numbers in Table 5.3 suggests, however, that it is going to be increasingly difficult either to transfer or to hide the enormous costs of family. In any event, neither approach really gets at the essence of the economic problem.

It isn't the expense side of the equation that doesn't tell the truth to families. The expense part of the market's message to families is, unfortunately, pretty close to reality in terms of reflecting actual resource costs. Except for the share of public education paid by nonparents, families outside the welfare system take on themselves most of the social costs associated with their children.

The major distortion of family values from an economic perspective is on the revenue side of the ledger. A market system that says a dollar invested in the stock market has economic value but a dollar's worth of time invested in a child has no economic significance is a gross distortion of reality. An economic system that says time is worth $200 an hour as a lawyer and worth nothing as a parent simply isn't telling the truth. Is it possible to make our market system tell a more truthful story to families?

PARENTS AS SHAREHOLDERS IN THE FAMILY

One way to put a portion of family-produced wealth back on the family balance sheet would be to declare a parental dividend. As unromantic and outrageous as this may sound at first, if we want to deal realistically with what has happened to the family's economic base, we need to restore some economic equity to the family balance sheet. If we want to retain the family as an economically viable institution in our postindustrial economy, we need to put our money where our sentiments are. The family needs an economic infrastructure that is consistent with the conditions under which it now has to function. Obviously, such a radical restructuring of the caretaking economy would succeed or fail on the details of implementation; but stated very simply, we need an economic system that tells the truth to parents about the value of what they do.

A parental dividend could be instituted by putting a tax on children's incomes and giving the proceeds to their parents. This conceptually simple but far-reaching step would have two dramatic results:

- Requiring children to pay dividends to their parents based on their success in the marketplace would have the effect of visibly retying the generations together economically and making parents shareholders in their own families.

■ A parental dividend would send a message at ground level where parental decisions are made that society values parental investment in children.

How large could a parental dividend be? Given the current tax load on wage earners, most of any such dividend would have to be diverted from the payroll tax that children (workers) at large are already paying to the older generation through the Social Security system. If the current Social Security taxes were transferred directly to the wage earner's parents (perhaps in the form of a retirement trust fund), it would immediately apply one of the core tenets of capitalism to our social policy; namely, that you reap what you sow. It would restore the quantities of wealth designated as Social Security Transfers in Table 5.3 *to the families that produce the wealth*.

The Social Security transfers computed in Table 5.3 ($97,767, $212,746, and $406,215 for low-, medium-, and high-income families, respectively) are modest relative to total parental costs. The same numbers, however, are quite large relative to the average wealth of households. The Federal Reserve Board's most recent analysis of its Consumer Finance Survey estimates median household net worth at approximately $56,400. The median financial net worth (excluding home equity and employer pension accruals) is reported to be about $13,000 for all U.S. families.

Declaring a parental dividend in the neighborhood of 15 percent of children's incomes, which is what younger generations are already transferring to the older generation via Social Security and Medicare, would create a family asset of significant size relative to the total financial wealth of most families. It would *not* make childrearing profitable for anyone who didn't put a large value on parental love; it would just make parental love less expensive by restoring a portion of the family's historical economic base. As the numbers in Table 5.3 indicate, even if all Social Security transfers were returned directly to parents, anyone who doesn't truly want the experience of rearing children would still be much better off financially to save the expense and invest it in the stock market (see Tables A.3 and A.4 in the Appendix for specific comparisons).

Children will never replace Merrill Lynch because, first and foremost, children can't be owned like property. Saying children can't be property, however, isn't to say that parents shouldn't have any claim whatsoever on their children—who has a better claim? At the very least, parents should have a preferential claim on any social-insurance system that is based solely on the earnings of the next generation of children.

Family investment has become a "we lose, you win" situation for parents versus society in the sense that the economic costs of family are privatized while the economic benefits of successful parenting are mostly socialized. To put the family in touch with economic reality, it is necessary to balance revenues against costs and have a stake (what Wall Street calls "shareholders' equity") in the operation; that is, something both to gain or to lose from the enterprise. Again, this would not be a new or unprecedented arrangement. It would simply be the family's traditional intergenerational arrangement in a new format.

QUESTIONS ABOUT INVESTOR STATUS FOR FAMILIES

WHO IS FAMILY?

Obviously, many things would have to be considered before anyone would conclude that restoring parental equity to families is a workable and benign concept in a market economy. One of the first questions to be dealt with would be "who is family?" The courts are already struggling with the definition of family and questions of parental rights in connection with abuse cases, stepparents, adoption, in vitro fertilization, artificial insemination, surrogate motherhood, and so on, issues in which biological parenthood is separated from social parenthood. As difficult as these issues are, they have to be adjudicated. Society has to decide who is responsible for a particular child.

Creating an economic asset in the form of a parental dividend would obviously up the ante in these kinds of contentious issues. A new area of family law would have to be developed to deal with who is entitled to what in cases of dispute. It isn't possible to spell out a whole new legal code overnight—it would have to evolve over time the way the rest of our legal system has evolved. The legal infrastructure needed for adjudicating parental claims could prove to be as extensive and complex as the legal infrastructure we provide for the business economy, which is certainly a daunting prospect. Given the amounts of wealth produced within the family, though, family rights are surely worth as much legal attention as the kinds of property rights to which our legal system already assiduously devotes itself.

Rather than initially trying to settle all of the questions of who is family, it would be more practical to start by defining who *isn't* family. Parents who abandon children, parents who are convicted of abusing or neglecting children, parents who don't pay their child support, for example, would seem to be candidates for exclusion from the economic benefits of family. Denial of parental dividends to grossly irresponsible parents would be a practical way to start putting teeth into society's demand for parental responsibility.

As this branch of our legal system evolves, parental dividends would be much more than just a stick to hold over negative forms of parental behavior—they would also be a carrot for positive behavior. Compared with the operative sanctions for responsible behavior in the business sector of our economy (profits and losses), we have only the crudest tools for discouraging neglect, abuse, and irresponsibility with respect to children. The legal system currently punishes the most egregious forms of child abuse and neglect, but such crimes are difficult to prove. Abuse and neglect have to be extreme before the criminal justice system can deal with them, and remedies such as foster care and termination of parental rights are heavy-handed solutions that the state is very reluctant to administer. Introducing a form of market discipline would supplement the "sticks" of the justice system with a much more extensive, subtle, and flexible system of "carrots" for responsible parental investment.

After suffering large increases in juvenile crime, many states and cities have recently attempted to introduce more sticks into their legal systems for enforcing parental responsibility. According to the National Conference of State Legislatures, about half the states have passed laws in the last few years that provide or strengthen sanctions against parents of offenders. According to a *New York Times* report:

> In 1995 alone, at least 10 states from New Hampshire to Louisiana to Oregon passed so-called parental responsibility laws calling for fines or sometimes imprisonment.

> An Idaho law, for example, authorizes courts to require parents to pay detention costs for a juvenile. In West Virginia, parents of a child caught defacing a public building can be liable for up to $5,000 in fines. In Louisiana, which passed the most severe parental responsibility law last year, parents can be found guilty of "improper supervision of a minor" and fined up to $1,000 and imprisoned for up to six months if their child associates with a convicted felon, drug dealer or members of a street gang.

Whether or not such laws can withstand a constitutional challenge, society has a compelling need to hold someone responsible for taking care of children; but if parents are to be held substantively responsible when their children do something wrong, it is only fair to allow them to share in the tangible rewards when their children do things right. The legal system has no means of punishing parents for not being very nurturing or supportive, for not going to PTO meetings and teacher conferences, for not enforcing reasonable rules on their children, for not helping with homework, for not being willing to help with college tuition, and so on. Our economic system, however, has the flexibility to reward positive behavior by giving parents a claim on the results.

WOULD TREATING PARENTS AS INVESTORS HAVE A PRONATAL EFFECT?

A parental dividend that enables parents to recoup part of their childrearing costs would be less antinatal than an economic system that tells parents that children have no economic value. It would be considerably less pronatal, however, than various forms of family assistance that are paid on a per-child basis. Unlike most family-assistance policies, a parental dividend based on future earnings of adult children would not reward fertility per se. It would instead reward effective parenting—effective at least to the extent that parents are successful in rearing children who are neither criminals nor economic dependents. Such a dividend would call attention to the economic trade-offs involved in doing more for a smaller number of children versus doing less for a larger number.

Regardless of the size of a parental dividend, having children just to reap a monetary reward wouldn't be a very good bet. As most parents know, children have minds of their own that don't respond very well to parental demands that don't make sense or don't "feel" right. In addition to all of the normal risks of childrearing, any parents who were just in it for the money would be even more likely than most to have rebels on their hands. Anyone who couldn't bring a reasonable amount of love, care, and commitment to the parental relationship would be unlikely to profit even in the most crass sense, let alone in the all of the emotional ways that parents benefit from children.

The major message that a parental dividend would send would be that a wise investment of time and resources in children has social and economic value. No dividend of any imaginable percentage could make parenting profitable—it would just make parental love less expensive. Giving parents a claim on returns from their investment could help parents invest more resources in their children in situations where a choice has to be made between working harder or saving more to put money in their 401(k) plans versus spending more time with children or investing money in children's health or education.

It is impossible to know for sure what the fertility responses to a parental dividend would be—beginning with Malthus, economists have frequently guessed wrong about fertility. Given that fertility is below replacement levels in most industrialized countries, however, there would seem to be no particular reason to worry about a modest increase in fertility in the modern economies that are looking for ways to support family functions.

Given the message that they have to do something right if they want to collect a return in old age, people not really committed to parenting might be nudged toward the alternative of saving money instead. It is estimated in the appendix (see Table A.3) that if all of the income that the average poor family (as defined by USDA) sacrifices for two children were saved and invested instead, parents would have a retirement fund between $1.3 million and $3.5 million in 1997 pretax dollars at age 67. For the middle-income family, the amount would be between $2.1 million and 4.8 million, and for the high-income family it would be between $3.4 million and $8.1 million.

But, would a parental dividend cause parents to invest more in a child with more economic potential at the expense of those with less potential? Suppose, for instance, that one sibling has the potential to be a brilliant scientist while the talents of another sibling are more appropriate for a trade. Given the much longer period of education and the greater amounts of college tuition required for the scientist, the rates of return on the investments required from the parents for both children to achieve their potentials may be more or less comparable. The scientist will cost much more to educate and will take considerably longer to produce an income. If the goal of parenting is to help each child achieve his or her potential, there is no economic reason for the less-talented child to be slighted.

Clearly, there are limits on the ability of the marketplace to reinforce all of the parental attributes that might be considered ideal, but making parents shareholders in their own families would directly support parental encouragement of most of the virtues on William Bennett's list (see Chapter 4). Compared with many kinds and degrees of parental neglect, any system that encourages the rearing of healthy, productive, honest, and hard working citizens would be a considerable improvement.

WHAT ABOUT REALLY BAD PARENTS?

There are surely some parents who, it could be argued, don't deserve any rewards for their parenting. Short of the kind of neglect for which parental rights can be terminated, however, children are expensive even for bad parents. No child is likely to make it to productive adulthood without costing parents considerable amounts of money. A parental dividend would return to parents part of the money they have spent on their children, but money is all some parents would get. Really bad parents are likely to have a lonely old age devoid of the love and affection that a good relationship with their children could provide.

WOULD A PARENTAL DIVIDEND BE FAIR?

This question has to be considered from several angles. Giving parents a claim on a portion of the wealth they succeed in producing through their children is both fair and unfair in all the ways that capitalism is fair and unfair to investors. Capitalism is in many ways an unattractive, even repulsive, system for the way it rewards self-interest, commercialism, competition, and just plain luck at the expense of altruism, esthetics, and the more impractical virtues. It isn't a question of whether capitalism is a totally benign system, however, but rather which of the known economic systems can best serve our society's needs with respect to the family. The major argument for capitalism is its relative efficiency in getting work done while giving people freedom to make their own choices about what they do.

This Isn't a Welfare Program

A parental dividend would be the reverse of welfare in that it would distribute wealth to people who produce it at the expense of people who don't. The argument for rewarding parents as investors is basically an efficiency argument. The object is to institute a practical and effective way of signaling to individuals at ground level what society wants done by tying family decisions to economic consequences. It's hard to beat the efficiency of a market system for performing that kind of task. Efficiency arguments, nevertheless, are always accompanied by questions of fairness. Proposals of this magnitude inevitably raise serious equity and class questions that need to be addressed.

Fairness to Investors

The major argument for the fairness of rewarding parents when their children are economically successful is the substantial unfairness involved in expecting families to bear all of the economic costs, risks, and sacrifices of childrearing while the rest of society gets a free ride from having a well-reared younger generation. We don't treat any other investors that way. Why should successful stockholders and speculators be treated so much more favorably than parents? Fairness to parents as investors, however, is just one of the fairness questions that comes to mind in connection with families; many others need to be asked.

Fairness to Children

Children don't ask to be born. Is it fair to attach a string—a payback in the form of a tax on future earnings—to parental investment before the beneficiaries can agree to the deal? There are several ways to think about this question. Our Social Security system has already attached a very long string to generations of children for support of their parents' generation. If attaching strings to future generations without their consent is wrong, the Social Security system is indefensible. A parental dividend would simply tie the string in a more direct and arguably fairer way.

Another angle on the question is provided by the concept of social contract that inspired the framers of our political and economic systems. Social contracts are strictly hypothetical—no one has ever actually signed one—but they provide a useful way of thinking about social arrangements. Philosophers have found it useful and credible to ask what kinds of agreements free, rational, and equal adults would be willing to sign if they could. Unborn children obviously can't sign prebirth contracts, but it is not unreasonable to hypothesize what kind of contract children would be willing to sign with parents for quality care if they could understand the terms.

A more appealing argument for the fairness of attaching parental strings to children is that children don't stay young forever. We all aspire to get old and to be cared for when we need to be. If we care about our children, we want them to be cared for in old age also. There are numerous conflicting interests in our society, but the need for an intergenerational system to provide for the elderly isn't one of them. Barring early death, everyone involved eventually benefits.

Reducing Cultural Warfare over Reproductive Issues

Recognizing parental contributions in a tangible way would help clear the air around some of our most divisive cultural battles—issues such as the tension between mothers who stay home versus mothers who enter the workforce, a war that pits women who should be allies in family causes against each other. A feature article in *Newsweek* describes some of the tensions:

> Elaine Cohen, an executive with a New York television company, moved to suburban Westchester County when her son was 3 years old. Although she had a full-time babysitter while she worked, she wanted to find a play group for him. It should have been easy, but it wasn't. "I called everywhere," she says. But the mothers she spoke with made it very clear that children with babysitters weren't welcome. "As soon as I said that I was a working mother, it was as if I had a disease."

Seven hundred miles away, near Chicago, Joanne Brundage ran into very different problems. Brundage quit her job as a letter carrier to take care of her two children. After a few weeks, a friend telephoned and, busy with the baby, Brundage didn't pick up the phone until the fourth ring. "Oh . . . sorry," drawled her friend. "Did I interrupt a crucial moment in your soap opera?"

Every so often a feud erupts that helps to define an era. In the '60's, it was hippies vs rednecks. In the '70's, the decade of the women's movement, it was women against men. By the the mid-'80's and now into the '90's, it's mothers who stay at home against mothers who work. This conflict is played out against a backdrop of frustration, insecurity, jealousy and guilt. And because the enemies should be allies, the clash is poignant.

As a teacher quitting her job to stay home with her children because "I can no longer cope with the physical exhaustion of holding down two full-time jobs" wrote to Ann Landers, "For generations women have been fighting for the right to choose. Too often, the ones who make us feel guilty for the choices we made are OTHER WOMEN." Ann Landers agrees: "You wouldn't believe the mean-spirited letters I receive from women lambasting their sisters who choose to stay at home with their children," and begs, "Women, give sisters a break." It's hard for sisters to sympathize or cooperate with each other, however, when the apparent rewards for employees versus mothers are so unbalanced. Explicitly acknowledging the contributions of individuals both as parents and as employees could go a long way toward clearing the air.

The abortion issue is an even more divisive issue between sisters. Surely part of the social tension around abortion concerns the price paid by a woman who sacrifices her prospects to an unwanted pregnancy in order to bear and rear a child versus her sister who preserves her career and lifetime earning capacity with an abortion. A parental dividend can't resolve the philosophical issues of abortion, but it can make the decision to bear a child or not to bear a child fairer by directing more of the benefits of reproduction to those who bear the costs.

Dimensions of Fairness

Amartya Sen, a prominent Harvard economist who has written extensively about fairness, notes that it is inevitably defined as some form of equality. The question then becomes, "equality of what?" Sen claims it is essentially a matter of which variable is given priority that separates the major ethical systems and ideologies. Libertarians stress equal liberties while other forms of egalitarianism stress equal opportunity, equal means, equal income, equal welfare, and so on.

John Rawls has constructed a particularly powerful and influential argument for defining the prerequisite of justice as a distribution of "primary goods" that would be considered fair by a rational individual behind a "veil of ignorance" as to what his own station and status in life might be. Rawls defines primary goods as goods that are necessary for achieving human goals. His list of social primary goods includes rights and liberties, powers and opportunities, income and wealth.

Parents Are the First-Order Condition of Fairness

A major problem with the way ethical theorists since Aristotle have defined fairness and equality is that none of the things on which ethicists tend to focus is of any use to helpless infants who don't have responsible adults taking care of them. No society can distribute to children either tangible things such as income and wealth or intangible things such as rights and liberties without first passing them through the hands of parents and guardians, who then may or may not pass them on to children. However fairness, justice, and equality may be defined in the abstract, the really primary good (the "preprimary good" that necessarily precedes all others) for a fair chance in life is responsible parenting. The unkindest and most unfair thing any society can do is to contribute, deliberately or inadvertently, to the deprivation that the absence of parental care represents for children.

In feudalistic times, poverty was primarily a function of being deprived of land. In the Industrial Age, the crucial resource was tangible capital. In the postindustrial age, more and more income has been going to human capital in the form of wages and salaries than to either land or tangible capital in the form of interest, profits, and dividends. Accordingly, it is the civilizing and educating effects of parental care (investment) that now determines the bulk of income distribution in our economy.

The Conflict between Equality and Freedom

It is undeniably true that middle-class and upper-class parents have more resources to invest in children than poor parents, but the issue isn't just money. As Bill Cosby says in *Fatherhood*, the main role of parents is to be there. No family is too poor to turn off the boob tube and make kids do their homework. With or without a parental dividend, there is an inherent conflict between equal opportunity for all children and the freedom of parents to invest time in their own children.

It would be an extremely impractical and counterproductive version of fairness to say that no parent should turn off the TV set or read bedtime stories to their children unless all children get TV supervision and bedtime stories, and yet it is just such supervision and parental interaction that give children enormous advantages in life. As James Fishkin, a professor of philosophy at the University of Texas, has noted in his book on issues of equality and the family, the only way to give everyone equal chances in life at the moment of birth would be to assign newborn babies to parents at random.

There are other aspects of the class issue about which it is possible to speculate. The numbers in Table 5.3 suggest that in some ways a parental dividend would benefit the middle- and higher-income classes most because their children are likely to make higher incomes and therefore to pay higher dividends. In those same classes, however, the costs of child-rearing are also generally higher because of the higher costs of schooling and the opportunity costs of parental time. Computed as a rate of return on investment, there would be no particular advantage to the higher-income classes of a parental dividend based on children's incomes. (Some specific computations of this point are illustrated in the Appendix.) There would simply be the same kind of advantage any potential investor has who commands more resources in our economy. The question is whether we want children of all classes to be in a better position to compete with other forms of investment into which people can put their time and money, be it mutual funds or lottery tickets.

The Role of Bequests

Another class consideration is the fact that middle- and upper-class families tend to depend less on their adult children financially in any case. The upper classes are more likely to leave bequests. It is the lower-class family for whom returns from children are most likely to be significant and for whom the disappearance of the family's economic base has been most devastating. Middle-class families are still likely to value the insurance of having a claim on their children's earnings if they need it. It would be the truly rich who live off inheritances and pass substantial family wealth on to their children who would have the least to gain by establishing a parental dividend.

Children Are the Poor Man's Capital

While it is certainly a disadvantage for any potential investor to be poor, poor people have a better chance of producing capital through their children with their love, caring, and time than they do of producing capital in other areas of the economy where financial requirements are even more prohibitive. Climbing the economic ladder through your children and grandchildren is the part of the American dream that has always been the most realistic and the most achievable. In the interest of fairness, we should at least not rob poor families of the one asset they have.

Even the poorest unemployed father can help his children by being there, staying sober, and pitching in. He can walk his children to school through the projects past the gangs and drug dealers, share the routine work of child care and housekeeping, limit television watching and supervise homework, and help enforce discipline and responsibility, especially when boys become too big physically for their mothers to handle them.

Our economic system currently has no tangible, substantive way of saying to individuals that such parenting work is a valuable contribution to society. If our economy validated the work of people as parents, even the poorest fathers could once again have a respected role in the family. This is not glossing over the problems of poverty or saying that people living in oppressive conditions just need to pull up their socks and "act" middle class and their children will be fine. It is saying that there is plenty of parental work to be done wherever families are and that our economic system needs to have some way of rewarding those who do the work. The idea that men who can't get good jobs are inherently worthless to their children is a cruel and self-fulfilling prophecy.

What if a Son or Daughter Is an Artist?

Another equity question concerns how fair it would be for parents whose children become doctors and lawyers to collect so much more than parents whose children become, for instance, artists or social workers. The fact that our society provides such miserly support for the arts is a valid social issue, but it's a different issue. However misguided society's treatment of the arts and various other occupations may be, people who go into low-paying jobs generally have to accept the consequences of their choices. Many people who would like to be artists go into other things because money is important to them or to their families. Changing our society's priorities for art versus expensive cars or for social workers versus bond traders is a worthy agenda, but there is a limit to the number of agendas that can be laid on the family.

A Parental Dividend Doesn't Preclude a Safety Net

As will be noted in the discussion of the welfare system in Chapter 10, declaring a parental dividend doesn't preclude providing a safety net for people in need; but that, too, is a different issue from trying to figure out a way to provide appropriate incentives for parental investment. Wealth has to be produced before it can be redistributed. Somebody has to produce the doctors, lawyers, engineers, managers, clerks, teachers, plumbers, and mechanics whose incomes will enable them to buy art and to help the unfortunate.

CONCLUSIONS ABOUT FAIRNESS

While making parents shareholders in their own families certainly wouldn't solve all of society's fairness questions or even all of the equity questions associated with family, it would make major contributions to fairness and equality in several ways:

◆ Providing economic returns for effective parental investment would create incentives for parents to invest more time and resources in their children and result in fewer children falling behind due to parental deprivation. It wouldn't redistribute resources to the poor for being poor, but it would provide incentives for producing fewer deprived children and therefore fewer poor adults. As William Raspberry notes in a slightly different context, it's better to fix the boat before it leaves the shore than to have to bail it out once it's afloat. It's better, if possible, to prevent poverty than to have to try to remediate it.

◆ A parental dividend would send a message to parents in "the coin of the realm" that their work as parents is valuable and that they have an important role in society regardless of their status in other areas of the economy.

◆ Rewarding parents for their investment in producing society's human capital would alleviate some of the conspicuous unfairness between double-income, childless couples who can indulge in luxuries while parents struggle to support the future workforce.

◆ Some of our society's most divisive social issues from abortion to the "mommy wars" are essentially about who pays the costs of reproduction. As the costs increase, the battles intensify. The costs aren't going to go away, but some of the resentments could be alleviated by a fairer distribution of the benefits of reproduction; specifically, by directing more of the benefits to the people who incur the costs.

◆ Because many poor people have a better chance of creating wealth within their families than they do in other forms of investment, returning a portion of wealth to the family economy would help reconstitute the most viable (although still very difficult) way poor people have for climbing the economic ladder in our society.

Will restoring some economic equity to the family guarantee that every child will have responsible and caring parents? Obviously not. As heartbreaking as it is to acknowledge, no system can guarantee that. As Amartya

Sen notes, the powerful rhetoric of our culture that "all men are created equal" tends to deflect attention from reality. One aspect of that reality is that society can't deliver equal parenting to all children without breaking the biological ties between parents and their offspring, which isn't generally a viable or desirable option; but we can at least try to make the economic incentives for responsible parenting point in the right direction. The people most likely to be affected by economic incentives are those who are the most economically vulnerable.

IS A PARENTAL DIVIDEND TOO RADICAL?

What is really radical by historical standards is what has happened to the family in recent decades in modern economies and the extent to which parents have been disinherited from the economic value of family. As a practical matter, establishing an explicit parental claim only seems radical because such ties never have had to be openly discusssed. Declaring a parents' dividend would be an essentially conservative move in that it would restore a kind of economic tie between generations that traditional families in most cultures take for granted. Economic ties between parents and children have simply been taken for granted for most of human history.

Combining the theory of economics with the natural process of reproduction is an admittedly radical approach intellectually in that it attempts to bridge the chasm between the natural and rational dimensions of life decreed by our philosophical forebears (see Chapter 4). Biologists and anthropologists have been bridging the chasm from the natural side of the fence for several decades and have made a strong case that rational human behavior can't be separated from its natural base—that humans are biological animals and the human brain is a biological organ. They have amassed considerable evidence that human behavior shares significant characteristics with other primates and that while human culture exhibits enormous diversity much of our behavior is substantially guided by biological needs, drives, and constraints.

The argument developed here approaches the intellectual chasm from the opposite direction; specifically, from the perspective of economics, which claims to be the most rational of the social sciences. Economists have taken major steps across the bridge by modeling fertility as an economically and rationally determined variable in household consumption decisions and by acknowledging the investment value of children both for the family and for the economy. This analysis suggests that we take one more step and recognize that if we want families to continue to act like investors we need to treat them like investors in a way that will be viable in the next century.

Because we don't live in a Garden of Eden where resources are unlimited, even such natural functions as reproduction and parental love are necessarily constrained by rational decisions about how to allocate scarce resources. It isn't a question of whether family decisions are subject to the calculations and constraints of an economic system—they clearly are—but rather which economic incentives are best suited for the job of guiding such decisions. Unlike the dismissive treatment accorded in most social-science models, the natural dimensions of life aren't consigned in this analysis to a peripheral role. Parental love and parental instinct are specifically included in the family-investment equation and accorded a value too large to be ignored. Economic considerations notwithstanding, parental love will always be the most important asset in the family equation.

What are the alternatives for dealing with the basic fact that society is going to have to pay dearly for time invested in the feminine economy one way or another? One liberal/feminist model for dealing with the changing circumstances of the family is to classify children as public goods like national defense and environmental protection and assign major responsibility for children to the state. Compared with that idea, reprivatizing some of the economic wealth produced by families surely qualifies as a modest and conservative approach to dealing with economic stresses on the family.

The basic idea of the children-are-public-goods model as defined by Nancy Folbre, a leading feminist economist, is that competitive capitalism is for people who can take care of themselves and socialism is for people who can't and that we can make the family an altruistic refuge from capitalism by requiring the state to support our dependents. Such a model assumes that:

1. We can run the production economy as a capitalistic war zone where competent, consenting adults compete with each other while
2. We operate the caretaking economy as a kind of socialistic ant hill where we all sacrifice for each other if
3. We collectively transfer enough resources from the war zone to the ant hill to support the young and the elderly.

This model has considerable intuitive appeal because it extends the caring image of family to the whole community and seeks to create an oasis of relief from the nonstop competition of the marketplace. There are, however, several problems.

◆ The sheer quantity of resources required by the family economy is too large for the war-zone economy to transfer without compromising the incentives that make it function. Such a model may have been more viable when children were less expensive and the elderly didn't live so long, but the quantities of resources currently required to rear productive children (see Table 5.3) and to care for the elderly (more than the total tangible wealth in the U.S. economy by current Social Security formulas) aren't manageable by any conceivable transfer program that the competitive economy could sustain.

Variations of this model suggest that we only partially subsidize the care of dependents so that the taxes and transfers wouldn't be unduly burdensome on the production economy. While many families would undoubtedly say that some help is better than none, any subsidy of manageable size is going to have only a marginal effect on the family's economic equation.

◆ To the extent that we try to socialize care of dependents, we inevitably impose conformity on families. Using taxes to support such things as day-care centers on a large scale would put pressure on parents to use the services their taxes are paying for and penalize other kinds of arrangements that may be better for a particular family.

◆ Such a polarized model of human personality doesn't seem very realistic and probably isn't functional even if it could be financed. Is it really the case that people are totally altruistic and uncompetitive with respect to their families and the opposite on their jobs? Amartya Sen, among others, argues that family is best characterized as a situation of "cooperative conflict." In any event, it would be rash to lock into a specific reproductive model without asking whether it really meets our human needs.

◆ Human beings are going to resist cultural dictates that are too inconsistent with their innate desires. As E.O. Wilson, quoting Lionel Trilling, notes in *Beyond Culture*, "'Somewhere in the mind there is a hard, irreducible, stubborn core of biological necessity, and biological *reason*, that culture cannot reach, and that reserves the right, which sooner or later it will exercise, to judge the culture and resist and reverse it.'" As an example of biological resistance to cultural imperatives, Wilson cites the inability of societies to maintain slavery indefinitely. Unlike ants, Wilson asserts, humans are incapable of fully adopting a slave culture because slaves persist in being human.

Kinship ties among humans aren't a trivial matter either. To paraphrase Robert Frost, relatives are people who, when you go to their door, they have to let you in. As Wilson notes, the human species didn't evolve as ants or any other species that reproduces collectively—humans evolved as primates. Primates have a strong individualistic bent to take care of their young, a primal instinct to fight for their offspring, and a fierce tribal loyalty to their own kin. Social-science research on stepparent families has underscored the point that biological ties are surprisingly difficult to duplicate.

Substitutes for a missing parent may not be any better for children than no parent. Several studies have found that children who live with stepparents frequently fare no better and sometimes do worse than children living in single-parent families. The element of passion in the "family values" lament could be interpreted as a primal cry for parents and kinfolk to reclaim their young. The lesson of most sociobiological research is that it would be easier to collectivize the production economy in the manner of the communist experiment in Eastern Europe than it would be to socialize the biological instincts involved in reproduction.

By defining reproduction as an irrational function and women as irrational beings who would tend to it, the formulators of social-contract theory were conveniently able to forget about biological instincts altogether and to concentrate solely on the rational and social aspects of human behavior. As a result, the Enlightenment story of rational choices omits the most basic component of all life—the biological drive to reproduce and the accompanying behaviors that while not biologically *determined* are biologically constrained. It is certainly true that human civilization manages to do many things that chimpanzees don't do, but we have to think very hard about how far our primate nature can be stretched with respect to something as primal as reproduction.

Whatever social system we set up to replace the female caste system has to take into account our human nature in all its dimensions or it is inherently doomed to failure. This basic fact may require considerable rethinking of the modern welfare state as we attempt to deal with problems such as the insolvency of our Social Security system, a problem which, as discussed in the following chapter, is tied much more directly to families and the process of reproducing our labor force than any of the major proposals for Social Security reform take into account.

7 SOCIAL SECURITY FROM THE SUPPLY SIDE

Social Security has done a number on every country that has tried it.

—Laurence Kotlikoff, author
of *Generational Accounting*

LIBERTÉ, EGALITÉ, AND UTTER GRIDLOCK

"Liberté, Egalité, and Utter Gridlock" was the headline of a *New York Times* article about a massive strike that paralyzed France over a government proposal to trim social benefits in December 1995. France, like most industrial countries, has promised its citizens a high level of caretaking services of the kind that families used to provide. Also like most industrial countries, France is experiencing a demographic crunch in its family-replacement system as its ratio of workers to retirees has declined to such a critical level that there aren't enough wage earners to pay the pension and medical bills.

France's situation is a precursor of what is in store for most of the Western world as populations age and the supply side of social insurance fails to keep up with the demand. Governments are being forced to recognize that, while the demand for social insurance is stronger than ever, the supply of such insurance can no longer be taken for granted. For the first time in the history of the modern welfare state, governments (meaning all of us) will have to focus on the *tangible* things that are required to provide pensions and medical care in old age.

WHERE DOES OLD-AGE SECURITY COME FROM?

Social Security checks essentially come from the same place that babies come from: parental investment. It is families who produce the workers who earn the salaries to pay the taxes that support the system. The Social Security system is both part of the cause and part of the effect of what is happening to the family.

By way of suggesting how a parental dividend might actually be implemented, it is necessary to look at the system that already collects massive taxes from the young and transfers them to the elderly. We could hardly afford two large intergenerational transfer systems, so parental dividends would have to be considered as a substantial replacement for the existing system. Given the amount of misunderstanding and controversy that tends to surround discussions of Social Security, it is important to be as clear as possible about what it is that a parental dividend would replace and to be as specific as possible about how such replacement could work in practice.

THE DEMAND SIDE OF SOCIAL SECURITY

Like all systems involving economic resources, Social Security has the job of matching the supply of services with the demand. The demand side of Social Security is very compelling. Growing old is something to which we all aspire, and it is something that we are achieving in increasing numbers. (Life expectancy in the United States at age 65 is now 17.3 years, and a third of the population will live to 85 and beyond.) Just as the lengthening period of childhood dependency is creating unprecedented economic challenges for parents, the lengthening period of old-age dependency is confronting modern societies with unprecedented needs for support. Social Security is therefore our most popular social program for some very compelling reasons:

- As the life span has lengthened, the need for old-age support has increased.
- Old age is haunted by uncertainties, what AARP calls "the great terror of life." It is impossible for individuals to predict what their economic needs will be after retirement without knowing how long they

will live or what the state of their health will be; hence, the need for a very reliable old-age insurance system.

- Increasing mobility and various social changes have made the traditional family an unreliable source of old-age support.
- People have a strong desire for personal independence. Receiving a pension and medical insurance on the basis of past contributions is more dignified than being dependent on children or charity.
- Collectively taking care of our elderly provides a sense of community in our otherwise competitive economy. A sense of community is a source of satisfaction that appeals to many.
- Social Security has reduced substantially the number of our citizens living in poverty.
- Last but certainly not least, Social Security and Medicare have been very good deals for participants. People haven't had to live very long to get back what they paid in plus a profit far above what could be obtained in any other pension system.

Any program that can satisfy so many wants at such a bargain price is guaranteed a very loyal constituency. Something has happened, however, to the bargain that Social Security and Medicare have been. Our peace of mind about being taken care of in old age by a system that has seemed to work so well for 50 years was blasted by some very unsettling '90s headlines:

"THE CASE FOR KILLING SOCIAL SECURITY"
TIME cover story, March 20, 1995

"SOCIAL SECURITY: APOCALYPSE SOON—OR SOONER"
Business Week, May 1, 1995

**"SOCIAL SECURITY'S FUTURE:
CONGRESS FAKES THE LEDGER"**
Martin Mayer in *The New York Times*, January 30, 1995

"WE ARE A NATION IN DEEP DENIAL"
Newsweek, March 13, 1995

"CONGRESS WARNED OF PERIL TO MEDICARE FUND"
Washington Post, April 3, 1995

**"DEBATE SHOWS SOCIAL SECURITY IS SIMPLY BIG BUNDLE
OF IOU'S"**
William Raspberry, syndicated columnist, February 28, 1990

WHAT WENT WRONG WITH SOCIAL SECURITY?

The answer is that Social Security (and Medicare) were disconnected from the family investment required to support them. Social Security is a system that is all demand and no supply. Legislative acts that levied taxes and defined benefits have never contained any provisions for investing in assets to provide future benefits. The system has, instead, *assumed* that the workers needed to pay the taxes would be there—they would somehow pop up like mushrooms—the mushroom theory again!

WHO LET SOCIAL SECURITY DOWN?

You could say that families have let the system down by not producing enough workers who are sufficiently productive to support the system, but it's unfair to blame the Jones family or the Smith family or any other family when nobody told them that our major social-insurance system depended on their parental investments in children. Even if someone had told families that the system depended on them, the message that families must spend enormous amounts of resources (see Chapter 5) on childrearing so someone else can collect Social Security is hardly compelling.

You could say, then, that politicians have let us down. With a few heroic exceptions, political leaders generally have avoided telling the public that Social Security isn't the savings system most people have thought it was. Politicians haven't been anxious to admit publicly that Social Security is an intergenerational pyramid scheme that depends on the appearance of a new generation of taxpayers to pay the claims of the preceding generation.

Politicians could defend themselves by saying they simply made the same assumptions that most economic models make; namely, that parental investment can be taken for granted. Economists, in turn, would say that economic theory (especially investment theory) is primarily about the market economy, not about the family. Our cultural concepts of democracy and capitalism have been developed for rational, independent adults, not for dependents such as children or the elderly.

You could say, then, that it was those Enlightenment philosophers who, in Professor Kotlikoff's words, "did a number" on our political and economic systems by omitting reproduction and the caretaking functions from all of their theories and models on the assumption that women would naturally tend to it. The problems of the Social Security system essentially result from our cultural confusion about where babies, children, and ultimately workers come from and who is responsible for making the necessary investments in the next generation. The current gridlock in our present system is a prime example of what can happen in a culture that refuses to discuss the costs of reproduction in any realistic way, to consider what kind of parental investment is needed to produce the workers necessary to fund a retirement system, or to give any thought to providing compensation for the requisite investors. The question has to be asked: Why did Social Security and Medicare seem to work so well for so long?

SOCIAL SECURITY THEN AND NOW

When the Social Security Act was passed in 1935, it was defined initially as a savings system that would require workers to accumulate wealth for their own retirement. The taxes collected were to be put into a trust fund that would accumulate over time to pay each retiree's benefits, but operation of Social Security as a savings system didn't last very long. Politics and depression economics moved Congress to start paying full benefits to retirees out of current revenues in 1940, and Social Security was thereby converted to a transfer system.

Although the initial tax rate was quite low (2 percent on the first $3,000 of annual earnings), the first groups of beneficiaries received large windfalls. The first retiree, Ida Mae Fuller, a librarian in Vermont, received more in her first month's check than the total amount she had paid in taxes. Windfalls for the first retirees were easy to finance in the early years because there were many workers paying into the system relative to the number close to retirement. In 1950, there were 16 workers for each beneficiary.

Every year, as more retirees were added to the group of beneficiaries, the worker/retiree ratio declined and the windfall rates of return decreased because each new cohort of retirees had been paying into the system longer before collecting benefits. It would take a long time (essentially a working lifetime) for the system to mature, as the actuaries say. Maturity wouldn't occur until new retirees had been paying into the system their entire working lives and the windfalls were eliminated.

The system received a large shot in the arm when baby boomers began pouring into the labor force in the mid-1960s, swelling tax rolls and flooding the system with cash. Medicare was added to the system in 1965, a cost-of-living provision was added in 1972, and substantial increases in benefits were implemented in 1972, 1975, and 1976. Once the baby boom was absorbed into the workforce, however, the relentless maturing of the system resumed and worker/retiree ratios progressively deteriorated.

Initially, Social Security included only about half of all workers; but it was gradually extended to include most of the workforce. Since the ratio of workers in any new group to those in that group about to retire is large, bringing in previously uncovered groups tended to stave off maturity. Bringing in new groups of workers, increasing payroll tax rates, and raising the caps on income subject to tax have been the strategies used to keep the system going as it matured. People retiring in the 1980s could still expect to collect from two to four times what the same contributions to a private insurance plan would pay.

By the 1990s, however, system gridlock was on the horizon. Few groups of workers remained outside the system (primarily state workers) to be annexed, tax rates had reached the maximum level of public tolerance, the baby boom was approaching retirement, fertility was below the replacement rate, life expectancy was increasing, and the productivity of our workforce was lagging behind historical trends. By 1995, newly retired, single, maximum-earning workers could expect to get back *less* than what their contributions would have earned in a bank savings account; and AARP was estimating that the same workers retiring at age 66 in 2015 would have to live 47.1 years to get back what they paid into the system even if benefits aren't reduced as they are, in fact, likely to be.

U.S. workers in 1998 were paying a payroll tax of 15.3 percent on wages and salaries up to an annual income limit of $68,400. The system was supposedly generating a surplus for the anticipated retirement of the baby boom, but the surplus was being put into government bonds that would need to be redeemed by many of the same taxpayers already paying 15.3 percent of their wages in payroll taxes. Should people have seen the gridlock coming? Could they have seen it?

THE ILLUSIONS OF SOCIAL SECURITY

Many policy makers and professionals as well as the general public have been confused about the financial aspects of Social Security. For the average voter and taxpayer, anticipating the '90s crunch would have required a keen perception of the mechanics of the system and accurate forecasting of demographic and economic trends. What seems obvious now was hard for individuals to detect only a few years ago. People naturally tend to believe what they see. People who saw their grandparents living comfortably on Social Security and being taken care of by Medicare were led to believe that the system would work the same way for them. Unfortunately, there were serious illusions hidden in the system, illusions that, despite all of the media attention to Social Security's problems, have still not been articulated clearly.

ILLUSION 1: WE CAN TAKE CARE OF THE ELDERLY WITHOUT TAKING CARE OF CHILDREN

The biggest illusion of Social Security is that it is possible to take care of the elderly over time without investing in the next generation of children. There has been an implicit assumption that children will somehow take care of themselves, then grow up to pay Social Security taxes (the mushroom theory again).

Socializing old-age insurance has appeared to be the answer to a problem as old as the human race—the desire of parents to be independent of their children and vice-versa. Social Security has made people *feel* as if they aren't dependent on their children and made children *feel* as if they're not responsible for their parents. In fact, nothing has really changed with respect to who it is that must support the elderly—it's still our children. The illusion of intergenerational independence could be maintained for approximately the working life of the youngest initial taxpayers and even longer by raising tax rates and taking in more workers, but eventual exposure of the truth was inevitable from the beginning. *Somebody has to produce healthy, productive children to support a system that depends on workers' earnings.*

ILLUSION 2: WE HAVE PAID FOR OUR BENEFITS

It is a form of doublethink to assume that we can somehow pay for our own retirement by supporting the retirement of our elders.

The traditional family used to do two things: it took care of the elderly and it took care of children, and the two forms of caretaking were tied together within one structure—the family. Active adults had to take care of both their elderly relatives and their children. Social Security has seemed like an enormous bargain because it has said, in effect, that we only have to pay half of the caretaking bill—and that is what we have paid.

Social Security *feels* like a funded insurance system. If we pay our taxes the way people pay annuity-insurance premiums, we should be able to collect annuity benefits—and we have certainly paid our taxes. Approximately 75 percent of taxpayers are now paying more in Social Security and Medicare taxes than they pay in income taxes. Even though it feels like a funded insurance system, however, it isn't. We are paying for taking care of our predecessors, but we aren't paying for the children who are needed to take care of us.

ILLUSION 3: THE SYSTEM WAS FIXED IN 1983

When payroll taxes were raised to generate a surplus for baby-boom retirement, the Social Security system started generating a surplus in the 1980s that was invested in government bonds for the expressed purpose of covering retirement needs of the baby-boom generation. U.S. government bonds are generally considered to be the safest of all investments, and normally they are because they are backed by the full faith and credit of the U.S. government. The U.S. government has never defaulted, but money received from the sale of bonds is spent on the current expenses of government. The bonds that the Social Security Trust Fund holds are the same kind of unfunded debt as the rest of our large national debt.

For most of our history, our government has been confident of its ability to redeem its bonds by selling more bonds to the same types of investors. As a group, bond investors generally don't want cash, they want bonds, so the government's maturing debt is usually refinanced by "rolling over." The Social Security Trust Fund, however, is not a typical investor. It is an investor with a very specific, time-limited purpose: namely, to have assets it can redeem for cash when the baby boom starts retiring.

The only way a government can redeem the bonds in the Social Security Trust Fund is by raising taxes or selling more bonds to general investors. Taxpayers will have to ante up or the government will have to raise interest rates to make bonds more attractive to general investors. Raising interest rates would increase the costs of refinancing the rest of the large national debt that our government continuously rolls over. Accordingly, there are no easy ways for the government to redeem the bonds held by the Social Security Trust Fund.

KILLING THE GEESE THAT LAY THE EGGS

There is a certain amount of logic in Social Security. As family ties were weakened by industrialization, children increasingly defaulted on the implicit family contract that required families to take care of their own dependents. Too many children left their parents to be burdens on society. It seemed to make some sense, then, for a government to say, as governments of virtually every industrial country did: OK, if children aren't taking care of their parents individually, they will have to do it collectively. Unfortunately, the same logic that says that children should collectively take care of society's elders disconnects all individuals from responsibility for taking care of the children on which the system relies. It says, in effect, that people who invest in children will be making gifts to the system.

There isn't any way to say it politely, so it has to be said bluntly: large socialized retirement systems that depend on the next generation of workers are a form of expropriation from the family on a massive scale. Social Security wasn't set up with the intention of robbing parents, but that has been the effect. By way of illustrating this point, consider some hypothetical stories that illustrate how families are treated by the system.

The Yuppies' Free Lunch

David and Dianne are a "power couple" who devote their lives to their careers. They work long hours at jobs they love and have no time for children. David and Dianne's joint incomes support a comfortable lifestyle. They live in a condominium with many amenities, drive "his and her" sports cars, play golf at the country club, go to aerobics classes at a spa, and take skiing trips or cruises when they can get away from their jobs. They both earn lifetime average incomes of $70,000 (in 1997 dollars).

Ruth and Robert are blue-collar parents who split shifts between home and work. He works nights as a security guard and she works days as a convenience-store clerk so someone can be home with their two children most of the time. Robert also works a part-time job on weekends to help make ends meet. Together, they earn about $27,000 a year. Ruth and Robert have to worry every month about how to pay the bills for basic necessities for their children—food, clothing, shelter, transportation, medical insurance, and so on. Almost all of their free time when they aren't working at their jobs, sleeping, or doing housework is spent with their children. Ruth and Robert's investments in their family pay off. Their children finish high school, go to a state university while living at home, get better jobs than their parents have, and start paying 15.3 percent of their incomes into the Social Security and Medicare systems.

When these two couples retire, what do they collect from the Social Security and Medicare systems supported by taxes on Ruth's and Robert's children? In 1997, David and Dianne would each collect close to the maximum of $15,912 for a total of $31,824 per year. They also would be entitled to Medicare benefits worth about $10,250 a year while Ruth and Robert together would collect a total of approximately $14,974 a year from Social Security along with about $10,250 worth of Medicare.

Dianne and David would probably argue that they deserve their larger pension benefits—more than twice Ruth's and Robert's—because they paid more taxes. David's and Dianne's taxes, however, simply provided for the retirement of their parents' generation. With the exception of the subsidy of Medicare Part B that comes out of general revenue (approximately $1,459 per person per year in 1997, which must also be paid by the next generation of taxpayers), the only source of Social Security and Medicare support for David, Dianne, Ruth, and Robert is the payroll taxes paid by Ruth's and Robert's children.

Jim and Janet

Jim and Janet married after graduation from college. He worked as a sales representative and she stayed home to have a family. They had three children in nine years, at which point the marriage ended in divorce. Janet got custody of the children. Jim moved to another state, defaulted on child-support payments, and proceeded to live the life of a carefree bachelor. Janet reared three children with a combination of part-time jobs (approximately half-time at $6.00/hour in 1997 dollars) and assistance from relatives.

Life for Janet and her children was tough. Janet gave up most of her personal interests and many of her chances at a social life in order to hold things together economically and to be there for her children. But Janet's parental dedication paid off; her children turned out well in terms of being productive citizens. When Janet's children started working, they began paying 15.3 percent of their wages into the Social Security and Medicare systems. When the last child left home, Janet was 52 years old and at last able to take a full-time job; but the only job she could get with her 30-year-old college degree was a retail clerk's job paying $7.00 an hour. She worked until age 67 and then retired.

At retirement, who deserves to collect the larger share of the Social Security and Medicare taxes that Jim's and Janet's children are paying? Who actually collects the bigger share? If Jim was a successful salesman and earned an average income of $70,000 (in 1997 dollars) over his working life, he would collect close to the maximum of $15,912 per year from the Social Security system. If Jim has remarried, he may also collect a spouse's benefit for a total of $23,868 along with $10,250 worth of Medicare insurance for him and his wife. Janet, on the other hand, because she has a much lower earnings record, would collect approximately $6,184 per year from Social Security along with about $5,125 worth of Medicare insurance. It is even possible that Jim could remarry two or three times before retirement and that all of his additional wives (if the marriages each last 10 years) could collect spouse's benefits and

Medicare—paid by the children that abandoned caretakers like Janet rear and support.

Susan and Sharon

Susan and Sharon are college roommates. Both discover they are pregnant. Susan opts to have an abortion and stays in college. Sharon drops out of college to bear and rear a child. There are numerous possible endings to this story, but it is likely that Susan's lifetime earnings and opportunities will be considerably better than Sharon's. Susan may, of course, later marry and start a family and give her children a better life than she could have if she had dropped out of college. Susan has the option, however, of going on to a potentially lucrative career and/or marriage unimpeded by family responsibilities, while Sharon's options are likely to be severely constrained. If Sharon succeeds in rearing a productive worker, her child's earnings will be taxed more to support Susan in old age than to support the mother who sacrificed her lifetime prospects for motherhood.

Lucy and Lorraine

Lucy and Lorraine are both single mothers living on public assistance. Lucy is a conscientious mother of two who stays on welfare because she has a chronically ill child and can't afford to risk losing Medicaid. Lucy works extremely hard at keeping her children clean and healthy and at encouraging their development. She teaches discipline, manners, values, and self-respect. She is active in school and church and succeeds in the incredibly hard job of rearing independent, successful children under conditions that would cause many people to give up. When Lucy's children leave home, Lucy is 43 years old and in poor health. She takes a part-time job at $6.00 an hour and earns an average of $8,000 per year until she retires at age 62.

Lorraine is a mother who gives up. She has a drug habit and puts her personal wants first. She has a succession of boyfriends who abuse her children, and she pays little attention to where her children are or what they are doing. Her children tend to live in the streets, have trouble with the law, drop out of school, and become criminals and drug addicts. When she is no longer eligible to collect AFDC, Lorraine also takes a part-time job at $6.00 an hour and earns an average of $8,000 per year until she retires at age 62.

Against all odds, Lucy has succeeded in rearing two children who are paying Social Security taxes to support other people's parents; but Lucy has no more claim to the taxes her children are paying than does Lorraine, who made relatively little effort to take care of children who are now a burden on society. How will the system reward Lucy and Lorraine? Both will get approximately the same shares of the Social Security taxes paid by Lucy's children.

SOCIAL SECURITY AND THE ECONOMY

The financial community has grasped the fact that Social Security is a deteriorating bargain for taxpayers because the system doesn't reward investors for investing in any assets capable of producing the income necessary to meet the system's obligations. As a result, there have been numerous calls by analysts and commentators for "privatizing" the system:

"IT'S TIME TO PRIVATIZE SOCIAL SECURITY"
Paul Craig Roberts, columnist in *Business Week*, February 27, 1995

"HOW TO SAVE SOCIAL SECURITY: ALLOW WORKERS TO PUT TAXES INTO AN IRA"
Senators Bob Kerrey and Alan K. Simpson,
The New York Times, May 23, 1995

"HOW TO SECURE SOCIAL SECURITY'S FUTURE: A Privately Managed System . . ."
Gary Becker, columnist in *Business Week*, July 12, 1993

"PUT SOCIAL SECURITY IN PRIVATE SECTOR"
James Kilpatrick, syndicated columnist, February 11, 1990

Privatizing is understood to mean putting Social Security taxes into financial intermediaries such as IRAs that will invest the funds in stocks and bonds. The proceeds of stocks and bonds are generally invested by their sellers in real capital such as factories and equipment. By adding to the economy's productive capacity, the theory of privatization says, we would create the real wealth needed to support us in old age.

THE KING MIDAS APPROACH

Certainly, it would be progress to recognize that if we want to consume goods and services in our later years we have to create assets capable of producing things when we no longer can; but concentrating solely on investment in stocks and bonds (factories and equipment) is a narrow and ultimately self-defeating way of dealing with the problem. Given the degree of mobility in world capital markets, factories and machines financed through workers' IRAs would be spread around the world. Even if all new investments stay at home, factories and machines alone won't do much more for our economic security than a world full of gold did for the mythical King Midas who (loosely speaking) didn't understand the law of diminishing returns. To think that we can finance all of our pension wealth solely by investing in machines is to replace one set of illusions with another.

There is a long history of chasing illusions in this area. Economists have tried to measure a "wealth-illusion" effect of Social Security on individual incentives to save and invest in assets such as factories and machines. Because Social Security creates an illusion of pension wealth where no real wealth exists, researchers have expected to find that Social Security has discouraged saving and therefore been a drag on investment in our economy. Extensive analysis by very notable researchers, however, has failed to find any clear-cut evidence of such an effect. Failure to find a wealth-illusion effect on investment is still considered a puzzle. As Henry Aaron, a Brookings Institute economist, has noted, it is hard to believe that such a large transfer of resources wouldn't have an effect somewhere in our economy.

In view of the perspective outlined here, it seems likely that economists have been looking in the wrong place for the wealth-illusion of Social Security. What Social Security primarily replaced for its working-class beneficiaries was the need for parents to invest in children, not in factories and machines. The illusion of Social Security is that the necessary *workers* will be there to pay the taxes to support the system. Given that the wealth-illusion of Social Security has been a "human-capital effect" rather than a "tangible-capital effect," it has probably influenced incentives for parental investment much more than it has influenced incentives for financial investment.

The truth is that our economy needs *both* labor and capital to produce very much of anything and that not enough of one reduces the usefulness of the other. People need machines and machines need people. Given that over time labor has consistently produced about two-thirds of our national output, it would be a serious distortion of investment priorities to force families to put most of their pension investment into business capital at the expense of investing in their children. It is both inhumane and economically counterproductive to tell parents that giving money to Merrill-Lynch is economic investment for old age but helping children with college tuition is just private consumption with no long-run payoff. It is true we need to be investing in *something*, but it is foolish to think that buildings and machines alone can take care of us in old age unaccompanied by investment of parental time and resources in producing our labor force.

One analyst implicitly recognizes this fact by suggesting that funded pension systems (funded in the traditional financial sense) won't be any more reliable than unfunded systems if succeeding generations are too small or too unproductive to buy what a retiring generation needs to sell:

> But this consensus [the desirability of funding pension systems with financial savings] never broaches the gnawing doubt of whether funded regimes are more successful at bridging the demographic transiton to higher dependency ratios. Greater savings may indeed lead to larger economies in the future. But what will happen when the holders of all those assets outnumber the buyers?

A STRATEGY FOR ECONOMIC SECURITY

Social Security has been described as a con game with redeeming social virtues. The challenge of Social-Security reform is to retain the virtues, the most important of which is our society's formal commitment to care for our elderly, while replacing the con games with a system that ties the demand for old-age security to its real sources of supply.

The only realistic strategy for achieving the economic security we desire is a system that tells the truth about what it takes to provide security. It takes real resources (labor and capital) capable of producing goods and services. Doctors need hospitals and equipment in order to be effective. Hospitals and machines need doctors in order to be useful. *No economic-security program is real unless it invests in the necessary labor and capital in approximately the right proportions.* Historically, about two-thirds of our economy's output has come from labor and about one-third from capital. That should be a rough guideline for effectively privatizing Social Security. (It is estimated in the Appendix that a parental dividend held in trust-fund investment until parents retire would effectively invest about one-third of Social Security taxes in tangible capital and pay out about two-thirds to parents who have produced the labor force—see Table A.2.)

Would-be reformers have already proposed various programs for channeling Social Security taxes into investment plans such as IRAs that would then invest in factories and machines. What is missing from the various reform proposals is any recognition of the importance of investing in human capital as well. Hospitals and machines won't do us much good without doctors, nurses, technicians, and administrators to operate them. To assume that the workers needed to operate the machines will be there is to make the same mistake that has haunted Social Security from the beginning.

Simply put, the supply side of our economic security also requires a labor force. Several possible strategies have been proposed for dealing with this necessity:

REVERSE COLONIALISM

Just as European colonial powers exported surplus populations to their colonies, countries could import young people to make up for their reproduction deficits. Inasmuch as there is considerable demand by foreigners to immigrate to the richer countries, those countries could exploit the parental investments of poorer countries by taking in the youngest, healthiest, and best-educated immigrants to support their aging populations. Despite the current nativist backlash, using immigrants to replenish worker/retiree ratios is undoubtedly a strategy that both the United States and Europe will employ to some extent to support their aging populations in the next two or three decades.

Immigrants presumably want to migrate because it is advantageous for them to do so. It may also be advantageous for their families back home if immigrant workers are able to send their families remittances they couldn't earn at home. In some sense, it is possible for everyone involved to gain from such a transaction. People in richer countries who prefer not to invest very much in children can support themselves in old age with the children of foreigners who have more well-reared children than their economies can absorb.

The key assumption in such an arrangement is that people are making the investments in children they really want to make and that they prefer to get their old-age security by bequeathing their capital and culture to other people's children rather than to their own. If an economic system is telling the truth to people about the trade-offs involved, letting foreigners subsidize our reproductive deficits is perhaps a reasonable alternative. It is a perverse distortion of reality, however, for an economic system to tell prospective parents that their children have no value to the economy for retirement support or anything else when industrialized countries are, in effect, having to buy children to support their elderly.

The frequency and intensity of anti-immigrant sentiment expressed in countries to which most immigrants want to go suggest that resorting to reverse colonialism as a solution for taking care of intergenerational business doesn't satisfy some of society's deepest desires. The French want to remain French, the Germans want to be German, and so forth. Cultural pride can degenerate into ugly forms of zealotry, racism, and xenophobia; but one need not be a cultural bigot to think there is something wrong with a society that can't take care of its own dependents and can't manage to reproduce itself. In any event, the fact that the populations of most developing countries are now aging considerably faster than those of the developed countries suggests that the current supply of young, productive immigrant workers won't last forever. *To survive, cultures have to be willing to pay the costs of reproduction and caretaking*.

PUBLIC INVESTMENT IN CHILDREN

One way to try to make it easier for families to produce the necessary workers is to subsidize the costs of parental investments with various kinds of transfers such as family allowances; subsidies of housing, food, and medical care; requiring employers to institute family policies such as parental leaves; and providing public education. These things are the focus of most discussions of family assistance. However helpful such forms of assistance may be to families, the analysis of Chapter 5 suggests they don't go very far toward covering the costs that a typical family incurs.

France and Sweden have gone further with providing social assistance to families than most other countries, but such largesse hasn't solved their basic family problem. An additional problem with such approaches is that they treat responsible, effective parents such as Lucy and irresponsible, ineffective parents such as Lorraine exactly the same way. Society might feel generally better about helping with the costs of parenting if there were substantive incentives in place for promoting responsible parental performance.

LAISSEZ-FAIRE

Given that the family is where most of the investment in children has to occur, and given that children are the major resource required to take care of the elderly, we could dismantle the Social Security system and return to letting families handle both parts of the transaction as they once did. A variation of the laissez-faire approach would be to require workers to pay a fraction of their current payroll taxes into IRAs to be invested in tangible capital, dismantle the rest of Social Security, and leave to individuals the job of collecting old-age support from their children.

The problem with the laissez-faire approach is that the traditional family contract for taking care of elderly dependents had already deteriorated by the 1930s for reasons that have only intensified as our economy has continued to industrialize, urbanize, and internationalize. Social Security was begun for the purpose of doing what a significant number of families weren't doing very well. Elderly indigents were becoming burdens on society because children were defaulting on their end of the deal.

Today, in order for families to handle the role of investing in sufficient human capital to take care of themselves in old age in a modern economy, the family needs a more formal contract that provides some protection for return on its investment. Families in traditional societies have such a contract. The family contract isn't usually written on paper, but it is understood that parents take care of their children and that children take care of their elders. Close-knit communities have ways of enforcing such agreements. Individuals who don't do the right thing can be shamed and shunned by people they care about in communities where social standing is important to earning one's livelihood. In modern societies, enforcement of implicit social contracts is much weaker for at least two reasons:

◆ *Mobility*: Children who no longer live near their families can't be embarrassed or penalized by their neighbors and business associates for the way they take care of their parents. Nobody around them even knows their parents.

◆ *Inheritance*: In rural societies, even relatively poor parents who own a little land can hold inheritance over their children as a way of controlling behavior. Money inheritance can also serve the same purpose for parents who have significant amounts of wealth. In modern economies, however, except for the very wealthy, the crucial inheritance that parents give their children is devotion to childrearing and investment in their education, usually expended before a child reaches the age of 25.

The flexible parent(s) in a family who sacrifice a half million dollars or more in lifetime earnings and savings for family commitments (see Chapter 5) may have relatively little more to bequeath in the form of financial inheritance. The social and financial strings that tend to enforce intergenerational contracts in traditional societies become increasingly irrelevant in economies where children need to receive their primary inheritances from their parents during their developmental years and then, frequently, move long distances to find their niches in very mobile societies.

A SOCIAL CONTRACT FOR THE MODERN FAMILY

The modern family needs a contract with society that explicitly recognizes the contribution that parental investment makes to economic welfare in general and to old-age security in particular. It was suggested in the previous chapter that the most straightforward way to recognize parental contributions would be to declare a parental dividend from children's earnings. Much of the bureaucratic mechanism needed to administer such a dividend is already in place. The payroll taxes that the Social Security Administration collects could be paid into a retirement fund for each worker's family, and the retirement fund could be administered in the way that IRAs and 401(k) plans are administered now.

Younger generations undoubtedly would object that converting Social Security to a parental dividend would cause them to have to pay twice—once for their parents' retirement and again for their own. *True*. Working adults would have to repay a portion of the investment their parents made in them and create future assets for themselves by investing in their own children and/or by saving for their own pension funds. Requiring people to pay twice, however, would simply be a return to economic reality. Taking care of *both* the young and the elderly is what families have always had to do. *It has been a seductive but misleading illusion to imagine that a social program can do the family's traditional job at half the price—that we can somehow take care of our dependents at both ends of the life cycle by paying for only one of them.*

THE FAMILY CIRCLE

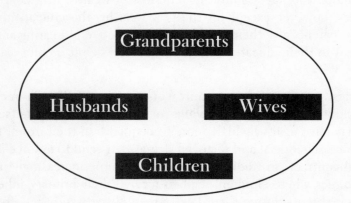

Parents and children are inevitably tied together at the beginning and end of life because there is no way to take care of either the young or the elderly without the other. As dependency lengthens at both ends of the life cycle, it becomes increasingly important for a society to be honest about the intergenerational facts of life. The facts are that the generations need each other and their primary nexus is within the family. Any policy that seeks to provide security in either childhood or old age has to deal with that reality.

Childrearing, retirement, and health care are all essentially generational issues. Much of the stress on health-care systems is attributable to the same demographic arithmetic that threatens Social Security. Given that the need for medical services tends to increase with age, medical-insurance rates inevitably rise for everyone when the average age of the insurance pool increases. By some estimates, men in their late 60s spend almost five times as much on health care as men in their early 30s: and men over 60 spend more than six times as much as children under 15. All of the arguments about Social Security outlined thus far, therefore, apply to the health-care system as well. Collective pay-as-you-go systems don't work much better for health care than they do for retirement and for the same reason—they don't invest in producing the next generation of young and healthy rate payers or the next generation of doctors, nurses, and technicians needed to carry the load.

While business-minded reformers correctly argue that what is needed is investment in real resources that can actually produce the things we need in old age, they miss a major point about what is wrong with Social Security and Medicare. All of the plans publicly proposed for converting Social Security to an investment system focus single-mindedly on one kind of investment—that which is financed by stocks and bonds. Stocks and bonds finance tangible assets such as factories and machinery. They don't invest in the people required to make the factories and machines productive.

Such proposals are typical of the tunnel vision that has characterized most of our economic models. As Robert Solow, an MIT economist who won the Nobel Prize in 1987, states, "What we normally measure as capital is a small part of what it takes to sustain human welfare." Solow's comment was made in support of a recent pioneering effort by the World Bank to measure national wealth in a nontraditional way. In a 1995 study entitled "Monitoring Environmental Progress," the World Bank attempted for the first time to combine estimates of both human capital and natural resources with the usual measures of business capital in assessing a country's economic prospects. Although the resulting profiles of national wealth are necessarily rough, they are a major step toward realism in measuring the sources of national economic security and progress.

According to the World Bank estimates, wealth in developed economies such as the U.S. consists of 25 percent natural resources, 16 percent manufactured capital, and 59 percent human and social capital. By definition, investment can't create natural resources. Of the producible forms of wealth, manufactured capital constitutes 16/75 or 22 percent while human capital contributes 59/75 or 78 percent. Apparently, the main purpose of the World Bank study was to focus attention on the economic significance of natural resources; but it makes an even stronger case for the importance of human and social capital. Given the dominant role of human resources in our economy and given that human resources are created primarily within the family, family investment can hardly be overlooked in any realistic attempt to convert Social Security to a privatized investment program.

Intergenerational effects take several decades to materialize, and correlations over such long periods of time are difficult to prove statistically. Nevertheless, it seems likely that the economic devaluation of family ties that has occurred over the past 50 years in modern economies has contributed significantly to the problems that both the family and our social-insurance programs are currently experiencing. It has been the ultimate conceit of modern economies to assume that a family's generations can function independently of each other with the help of the state and/or that the feminine economy would subsidize the dependency phases of life free of charge.

LIBERTÉ, EGALITÉ, FRATERNITÉ

"Liberté, egalité, fraternité" was the slogan of the French Revolution. It is both ironic and appropriate that a newspaper headline about a French strike over social benefits would replace "fraternité" with "gridlock" because in a very real sense fraternité has caused the gridlock. As a statement of Enlightenment philosophy and democratic ideals, liberty, equality, and brotherhood has been enormously influential, inspiring, and compelling, nowhere more so than in France. As noted earlier, however, the Enlightenment interpretation of brotherhood explicitly excluded sisters from the right to vote, to own property, or to enter into contracts—excluded them, in fact, from the whole scope of political and economic analysis. Our persistent cultural blind spot on the effects of such exclusion is now proving to be very problematic.

The modern welfare state has with the best of intentions attempted to supply an unprecedented degree of liberty, equality, and brotherhood while effectively ignoring the role of sisters in providing the first-order conditions of human welfare. As was argued in the previous chapter, none of the dimensions of freedom, justice, and equality discussed by modern philosophers has much relevance for helpless infants and dependent children in the absence of parental care. Only by taking the feminine, caretaking economy for granted is it possible to interpret liberty as freedom from the ties and obligations of family and equality as equal entitlements to the economic benefits of family regardless of contributions to family investment.

Given that the feminist revolution is now claiming liberty and equality for sisters as well as brothers and given that brothers also have new choices for obtaining many traditional family services without having to support families, our social security in the future will depend on the ability of a modern culture to develop new ways of supporting the caretaking roles that are vital to security and progress. Any *real* reform of Social Security must tie the demand for goods and services in old age to real sources of supply; that is, to real labor and real capital. Converting Social Security to a parental dividend based on children's earnings would be the most direct way of reconnecting the demand for a productive labor force with its primary source of supply.

8 THE MARRIAGE CONTRACT

I don't like to put this in moral terms, but I do believe that having children out of wedlock is just wrong.
—Donna Shalala, Secretary of Health and Human Services

Marriage is the most politically social contract there is. It's about power and status and a lot of things. Jane Austen understood that.
—Emma Thompson, actress and script writer

You know, people think that at the end of the day, a man is the only answer. Actually, a fulfilling job is better for me.
—Princess Diana

In this day and age, marriage is not the big thing it once was. You can shake it off like a flu bug.
—a literary character

THE STATUS OF MARRIAGE

Economic ties between parents and children aren't the only part of the family's social contract that has come unglued in modern society. The marital relationship is equally problematic. Since the relationship between parents is a critical link in the family's ability to perform its functions, the state of marriage has to be a matter of concern in any analysis of family issues. What does marriage mean in our culture at the end of the twentieth century? What should it mean? Who decides what it means?

Marriage is the relationship within which the feminine economy has performed most of its caretaking work. In the words of one family therapist, "the marital relationship is the axis around which all other family relationships are formed. The mates are the architects of the family." Marriage appears, however, to have lost much of its appeal to the baby boomer and X generations who, according to statistics, have become increasingly casual about entering and leaving this once hallowed institution.

It isn't just welfare recipients who are cohabiting and bearing children out of wedlock. The reason illegitimacy rates have risen so dramatically in recent years (from 5.3 percent of all births in 1960 to 30 percent in 1995) is not because the fertility rate of single women has increased but rather because fewer people in all economic classes are getting married and because the people who do get married are having fewer children.

The family's social infrastructure has had both *inter*-generational and *intra*-generational components; but whereas the contract between parents and children has been mostly informal, societies have generally attempted to formalize the contract between mothers and fathers. Getting married usually involves explicit legal procedures—obtaining a license, taking vows, and being governed by the laws of the land—and ending a marriage requires judicial approval. Ritual and formality notwithstanding, the legal weight of marriage vows and the effective terms on which conjugal obligations can be terminated in modern societies have changed as much as the rest of the family's social contract. Far from being the binding commitment "until death do us part" that couples vow at the altar, the modern marriage contract lasts only "until one of us changes our mind;" and people change their minds quite often.

As a *Wall Street Journal* article notes:

> With either spouse able to cancel a marriage at any time for any reason, the marriage contract has become easier to break than one involving a home, car or job.

Given that the willingness of people to enter a contractual relationship is linked to the terms on which the contract can be terminated, it could be that younger generations have downgraded marriage as a priority because it represents *too little* obligation rather than too much. When violating marriage vows carries less legal weight than defaulting on a car loan, why should people bother?

The decline of marriage is viewed by many social scientists as a dangerous deterioration of society's cultural infrastructure and destruction of the bridges of social connectedness. As with the issue of parental investment in children, however, there appears to be a significant difference between social and private perspectives on the value of marriage. Rather than focusing on the social aspects of the decline of marriage as analysts tend to do, it may be more enlightening to examine what marriage means for the individuals involved. Romanticism aside, what exactly *are* the benefits of marriage to individuals? What are the costs? What are the risks? What, since this is an economic analysis, has happened to the cost/benefit ratio of making and legalizing personal commitments between male and female?

THE CENTER OF THE FAMILY CIRCLE

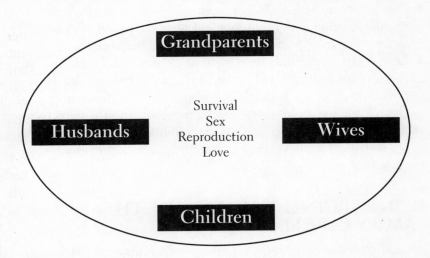

The family web is woven together with two kinds of threads: the long, continuous threads that tie generations together and the linear cross-threads that bind couples together. Intergenerational threads are the warp and intragenerational threads the woof of the family fabric. Ties that have traditionally bound couples together include:

◆ *Survival:* As was noted in the discussion of gender roles in modern economies (Chapter 3), physical survival needs are no longer a major reason for marriage between male and female. Women no longer require husbands to plow fields, hunt game, or bring home paychecks; and men no longer need wives to cook, sew, can, or preserve.

◆ *Sex:* It wasn't very long ago that sex was a compelling motive for getting married and for staying married. Prior to the late 1960s, nonmarital sex was a strong taboo in American culture. However often the taboo may have been breached, the social sanctions weren't trivial. Violaters felt compelled to sneak around, pregnancies usually resulted in shotgun weddings, and whole communities remembered for generations which couples "had to get married" if a baby was born within nine months of a wedding date. In contrast, it is likely that few people in today's younger generations have ever heard the term "had to get married" because such marital compulsion no longer exists. Outside of some religious communities, there are no longer any effective social sanctions that require people to marry either before or after having sexual relations.

◆ *Reproduction:* As has already been explored at length, much of the economic value of reproduction has been transferred out of the family by urbanization and by the Social Security system.

◆ *Love:* Virtually the only tie remaining between husbands and wives is the love and affection they feel for each other and for their joint project of rearing children. Unfortunately, love alone isn't a strong enough force to hold many couples together; and the costs to society when the center of the family doesn't hold can be significant. Numerous statistical studies find negative effects of family disruption on outcomes for children.

REINFORCING THE CORE OF THE FAMILY CIRCLE

What can a society do to send a message to parents that putting up with the irritation of a less-than-thrilling marriage until children are reared is, in many cases, something that benefits society? How can society convey the importance of meeting the emotional needs of one's partner in childrearing? How can society make people understand that marriage is a socially significant undertaking and that marital partners need to be chosen carefully? How can the cross-threads of the family web be strengthened?

It isn't going to happen by repressing women, reversing technology, or reviving old-fashioned community sanctions—in those respects, "the good old days" are surely gone. Neither the economic independence of women nor the technological changes that have moved production of food, clothing, and shelter out of the family and into the marketplace are going to disappear. Effective community sanctions against nonmarital sex aren't likely to return either. The degree of mobility in modern economies generally precludes local communities from exerting effective sanctions on anything. As Judith Martin explains in her book, *Miss Manners Rescues Civilization:*

> Sanctions imply the existence of a community in which a violator *must* [emphasis added] live. Sanctions have an effect because the person is grounded in that community and relies on it.

In addition to romantic love, the major tie that is still operative between male and female is the project of reproduction. There *are* ways to reinforce a couple's joint interests in reproduction. A parental dividend would appear to be one of them. Giving back to parents the $21-plus trillion worth of wealth that Social Security currently transfers out of children's earnings in the life span of one generation would be a major step toward rewriting the marriage contract with respect to the project of reproduction. In situations where getting married or staying married is problematic for the parents but better for the children, the children's interests would be represented in a tangible way; but there are other aspects of the marriage contract in its current form that need attention before such a policy could be implemented.

WHO NEEDS A CONTRACT?

People involved in any long-term relationship generally need some form of contract. Cooperative relationships by their very nature involve interdependence; and because dependence is accompanied by risk of default, people need enforceable agreements that specify the obligations of the parties and the terms on which the relationship can be terminated. The ability to make and to trust long-term agreements is probably the second-most distinctive characteristic (the first being verbal communication) of human social organization. It is certainly a key component of economic organization.

Since the business aspects of marriage, childrearing, and old age involve very substantive, long-term relationships, family members have many of the same needs for contract enforcement that business relationships do, the major difference being a question of who writes the contract—the individual parties or the state? Because it is physically impossible for parents and babies to negotiate with each other for their periods of dependency, intergenerational contracts have to be social contracts. Is there still a need for the state to write a contract for two consenting adults? Should it be a matter of social concern that the formal marriage contract has increasingly become a contract that can't be trusted, that while marriage vows promise lifetime commitment the legal system enforces something very different? .

Even though marriage involves consenting adults, the romantic and erotic nature of sexual relationships makes it difficult for individuals to bargain rationally with each other at the beginning of marriage. In many traditional societies, relatives do the bargaining for a betrothed couple with little regard for the wishes of the bride and groom—it is a deal between families. In modern societies in which the feelings of the bride and groom for each other are supposed to be paramount, it is difficult to mix romance and business in the same conversation. When partners are in love with each other and emotionally committed to each other, there is no need for a formal contract; and once love breaks down, it is too late to bargain. Divorce law is the prenuptial contract our society falls back on when romance falters.

The legal system obviously lacks the power to force two people to love each other or to live together when they are no longer so inclined, but society has a substantial interest in the consequences of marital breakdown. Marriage has social and economic consequences that extend beyond two people. Marriage tends to create two types of dependency, both of which have long-term consequences:

- ◆ Spouses who begin as independent individuals become dependent on each other in various ways within the marriage.
- ◆ Children who begin life as physical, economic, and emotional dependents need to be transformed into independent persons while their parents move toward a second stage of dependency.

The business dimension of family is essentially about cooperation between adults and between generations in dealing with the dynamics of dependence. The kind of dependence that marriage creates between adult spouses raises substantive questions of status and power.

FEMINIST CRITIQUE OF MARRIAGE

Even very moderate feminists will object to reendowing the family economically unless additional protection can be provided for family caretakers. If implemented crudely, parental dividends could have the effect of devaluing daughters in the eyes of their own parents simply because daughters tend to earn lower lifetime incomes than sons by becoming mothers and caretakers and by being paid lower wages when they work. That kind of female devaluation in traditional societies is blamed for the infanticide and neglect of female children that has resulted in 40 million missing females in India and 38 million missing in China. No one should doubt that the wrong kinds of social contracts with respect to the family can be dangerous to the health and well being of vulnerable parties.

Feminist critique of the practical terms of marriage has a long history. From the Marxist-oriented contempt for marriage as a form of exploitation to social-reformer Eleanor Rathbone's description of the "Turk complex" of some husbands to feminist-economist Barbara Bergman's critique of the occupational characteristics of a housewife, feminists and social analysts have worried about issues of justice and equality within the family. "I do" has frequently had a disproportionate price for women and men, a price that many women are now reluctant to pay. In the words of a recent *Economist* article entitled "The Bargain Breaks," "women increasingly see marriage as a bad bargain."

Marriage has tended to be an unfair and sometimes dangerous form of liaison for women because of its unequal distribution of power and status. Given the extent to which money is economic power, the primary cause of power imbalance within marriage in modern economies is the economic power that comes from specialization by one partner in market work that earns money while the other partner specializes in nonmarket work that doesn't involve money explicitly. Another source of marital injustice is the power of a physically stronger partner to commit violence, abuse, and intimidation (women are five times more likely to be murdered by their husbands and boyfriends than men are to be killed by wives and girlfriends). Lack of economic power, however, is a major hindrance in escaping abuses of physical power; so marital injustice of various forms tends to be closely linked to economic power.

CONSEQUENCES OF UNBALANCED POWER

Unequal power in any relationship creates opportunities for abuse. Like all partnerships, marriage sets up a situation that inherently combines cooperation with conflict. Partners have mutual interests in cooperating to maximize the total welfare of a partnership and conflicting interests in distributing the benefits of partnership. Distributive conflicts have to be resolved by some form of bargaining process. In a bargaining situation, each party's bargaining power is proportional to his or her perceived contributions and to the credibility with which each party can threaten to withdraw from the partnership.

If "fair distribution" is defined as a distribution of benefits proportional to what each partner contributes, fairness requires accurate perceptions of individual contributions and equal freedom for partners to withdraw their contributions. Bargaining power that is disproportional to contributions because of either inaccurate perceptions of value or unequal barriers to exit will tend to produce unfair outcomes. Partners who are both unable to leave and unable to claim their share of the benefits of the partnership, however, are likely to be less than totally cooperative in promoting the partnership's interests; so fairness in distribution is inherently a condition for maximizing partnership productivity. Fairness and efficiency are tied together in cooperative arrangements, a point that was well understood by the great classical economists who opposed the kinds of forced cooperation imposed by imperialism and slavery on grounds of economic efficiency, although they never thought to ask how the principle might apply to families.

The dynamics of partnership bargaining are hardly propitious for the specific kinds of cooperation that marriage and family require. Human reproduction being the arduous, complex, and expensive process that it has become (see Chapters 4 and 5), parents frequently find it physically impossible to avoid specializing in either breadwinning or caretaking to some degree; but such specialization almost inevitably leads to disproportionate bargaining power between marital partners.

Harvard economist and former president of the American Economic Association Amartya Sen, has noted several ways in which nonmarket specialization by one partner tends to result in weaker bargaining power:

- Having an inferior breakdown position gives one less bargaining power.
- *Ceteris paribus*, attaching less value to one's own well being, weakens one's bargaining position.
- Underestimation of a partner's perceived contributions to the cooperative arrangement reduces that partner's bargaining power.

Sen's first point refers to the fact that because a person who has less ability to earn money in the marketplace is likely to suffer more economically when marital cooperation breaks down, the nonmarket specializer has a weaker bargaining position within the partnership. The second point is that if those who specialize in caretaking are inclined or conditioned to care more about others in the family and less about themselves than those who specialize in competitive market work they will tend to demand less for themselves in conflict situations. Third, the lack of explicit monetary value placed on one's work tends to reduce both partners' perceptions of the value of a caretaker's contributions to a partnership and therefore reduces a caretaker's ability to make claims upon on it.

JUSTICE BEGINS AT HOME

In an extensive critique of modern political philosophy, Susan Moller Okin makes several telling points about the role of justice in family relationships:

1. Modern theories of justice and equality have never been carried to their logical conclusions with respect to the family. Philosophers have instead either ignored the family or treated it as:

   (a) an institution *outside* society's system of justice on the assumption that only adult males have the capacity to be full citizens in the sense that Western political theory has understood the term "citizen" (being born female is essentially viewed as a congenital birth defect that disqualifies individuals for full participation in any system of justice) or

   (b) an institution *above* justice because family members have such fine sentiments and altruistic feelings for each other that applying the principles of equality to families would degrade an institution that is better than justice.

2. Okin argues that marriage should be viewed neither as a union of congenital unequals nor as an association of saints and that it is a blind and/or hypocritical distortion of the principles of justice to ignore the power relationships within families.

3. Families, Okin further argues, are society's basic training school for citizenship. How just can a society be if individuals learn their first lessons about freedom and equality in an institution that allows one adult to systematically dominate another? How fair can a society be in which children learn their first lessons about fairness from parents who are allowed to abandon children and their caretakers to destitution and neglect while retaining substantial resources for themselves? How wise can a society be with respect to family issues if most of the people making the policies have little hands-on experience at nurturing children?

leaders aren't caretakers.

HOW FAMILIES FUNCTION

Family therapists make many of the same points as economists and political philosophers about the ways in which power, fairness, and efficiency are related. In her book, *Intimate Worlds: Life Inside the Family*, Yale psychologist Maggie Scarf provides a psychotherapist's inside view of the different ways in which families make and enforce or fail to enforce rules and how power relationships affect a family's ability to deal successfully with life's problems. According to Scarf:

> It is now widely recognized that *the family is a rule-governed system.* That is, family members interact with each other in a highly repetitive, orchestrated fashion; what happens to families on a daily basis is by no means random. . . . People living in a family need to know, generally speaking, who will do what and when it will happen.

By way of evaluating the success with which families function, Scarf relies on a scale devised by psychiatrist W. Robert Beavers. The Beavers Scale defines five levels of family competence, ranging from least successful to optimal, as follows:

Level 5—Dysfunctional, chaotic, and incoherent
Level 4—Order maintained by a tyrant
Level 3—Order maintained by internalized rules
Level 2—Order maintained by cooperation reinforced by rules and/or tyranny
Level 1—Order maintained by egalitarian cooperation

The Level 5 family is described as a severely disturbed family. "This kind of family is comparable to a nation in a state of civil disorder; nobody seems to have authority; no one is able to enforce rules or effect needed changes; real leadership is totally lacking." Chaotic "anything goes" families are the antithesis of the kind of stability that is needed to provide developing children with a firm grip on reality.

The next level of family functioning on the Beavers Scale is one in which a degree of order is maintained by a strong leader in a tyrannical way. A family sheriff who maintains order, draws boundary lines, and enforces rules is, Scarf makes clear, a definite improvement over anarchy; but the order achieved is of the nature of an armed truce. Individual feelings and complexities are repressed and there is a constant threat of mutiny among family members.

Moving up the scale of family competence, Level 3 refers to families that have eliminated both chaos and despotism and solved the problems of order and control by obeying internalized rules. Instead of being policed by a sheriff, everyone in the Level 3 family does what they are supposed to do as though ruled by an invisible referee. Gender stereotypes tend to be quite strong—women "should" do this and men "should" do that, and there is a basic distrust of the capacity of individuals to behave lovingly and cooperatively toward each other because they really want to rather than out of blind adherence to the rules.

At the top of the scale, Level 1 and Level 2 families differ only in the extent to which they achieve a balanced and flexible form of cooperation.

> The most competent family systems are egalitarian ones, in which *equal overt power is shared by the parents* in a manner that is mutually attentive to and respectful of each other's sometimes different viewpoints. In purely political terms, one would call the optimal family a democratically organized group, with strong, clear, joint leadership at the head of its government, and a citizenry (the younger generation) with a voice that will be heard and responded to reliably.

Needless to say, the rate of marriage breakdown in recent decades has contributed significantly to pushing families off the chaos end of the Beavers Scale. As Scarf states:

> In these disjointed, emotionally disconnected families, so many different people—ex-husbands and ex-wives, children of other marriages and liaisons, casual girlfriends and boyfriends, grandparents and other substitute parents—seem to drift onto the family stage for a time and then drift off into obscurity again.

Scarf describes a particular Level 5 family encountered in therapy because a teenage son had been expelled from school for disruptive behavior and had aimed a gun at his sister. A barely acknowledged illegitimate son of the father's and the father's surreptitious support of the son and his mother were causing enormous stress on the whole family's sense of its boundaries:

> In this family, it was hard to say which people were actually in the emotional system and which were outside it [is an illegitimate son to be thought of as a sibling?] and this is, it should be said, a frequent characteristic of the severely disturbed and emotionally distanced Level 5 system. . . .The entire extended emotional system seemed to be permeated by the sense that expendable infants and discardable children, partners, parents, and entire families, for that matter, could be banished somehow, shipped off to some parallel universe that was paradoxically both within the family's orbit and outside its boundaries completely.

DIVORCE HURTS

As the preceding example illustrates, parents don't have to get a divorce to fracture a family's emotional boundaries and its members' sense of security. Family members can be emotionally divorced without being legally divorced. Divorce is a legal formality; nevertheless, it is a convenient focus point for trying to deal with the consequences of marital breakdown. The legal process of divorce has been simplified considerably in recent years by conversion of state divorce laws to the no-fault concept, but streamlining the mechanics has left a vacuum in the judicial process for dealing with the consequences. As critics have noted:

> No-fault necessarily eliminated the fault system's principal justification for post divorce adjustments: the guilty spouse's continuing responsibility for the well-being of the family left behind.
>
> No-fault divorce did more than simply eliminate abandonment, adultery, and extreme cruelty as prerequisites for divorce; it dismantled the traditional provisions for childrearing without agreement on a new system to take its place.
>
> The combination of the changes in the grounds for divorce, support, and custody amounted to a wholesale withdrawal of legal recognition and financial support for the childrearing role.

Mary Ann Mason writes in *The Equality Trap*:

> No-fault is more than just a legal transformation, it is a state of mind. One of the most difficult experiences for me during my own no-fault divorce was that everyone, including my parents, made careful remarks such as "couples grow apart" or "these things happen nowadays." No one said it was a terrible thing to happen to a family, but it was.

> It is with spousal support (alimony) and child support that women and children have been most damaged by the deadly combination of no-fault divorce and egalitarian attitudes. Although the divorce laws in the individual states don't insist upon it, judges have taken the position that women with children can support themselves as well as men can support themselves. It is as if every time the media announces that a woman has been appointed to a judgeship or a high corporate position thousands of women lose spousal support.

WHEN PRINCE CHARMING DOESN'T WORK OUT

When even Princess Diana, one of the most glamorous and (by some standards) well-married women in the world concludes that marriage doesn't guarantee women very much of anything and that a woman is better off relying on herself for security and identity, the institution of marriage and the role of family caretaker are clearly in trouble. The statistics are now familiar concerning the extent to which primary breadwinners can walk away from families and improve their standard of living (an average of 40 percent by some accounts) while forcing children and their primary caretakers into poverty (an average decline of 30 percent in standard of living by some estimates).

In an all too common scenario, a woman who marries and compromises her own career potential in order to live in the same place as her husband, to help him through school or build a business, and/or to bear and rear children can find herself divorced in middle age with:

relatively few marketable skills
minimal child support
large parental responsibilities
a pressing need to retrain herself
a simultaneous need to support herself and her children
facing old age with few assets or pension rights

while her husband takes most of the economic resources with him and goes on to a new life, a new wife, and a new family.

There is even some risk of losing custody of children for having devoted oneself to being their caretaker. "The best interests of the child" standard currently invoked in custody cases can be interpreted as favoring the best breadwinner even when the breadwinner's superior financial position is a product of lack of involvement with the children. If a Florida judge can decide that a convicted murderer and accused child molester is a better custodial parent for an 11-year-old girl than a lesbian mother who was by all accounts devoted to the child, it's not hard to imagine that a judge could decide that the best interests of a child are with the parent with more financial resources and with a new wife able to stay home with the children, as opposed to a mother who is being forced into the workplace full time with poor job prospects. A parent who compromises career options in the market economy to invest in the family economy of producing well-nurtured children takes a risk of losing everything.

The prospects for children of divorce can also be dismal. The majority of children living in single-parent households are there because of separation or divorce, not illegitimacy. Single mothers are six times more likely to be poor than married mothers. Children who grow up in single-parent families are more likely to drop out of school, marry during their teens, have a child before marrying, and experience a breakdown of their own marriages. According to a 1988 National Health Interview Survey of Child Health, individuals from single-parent families or stepfamilies are two to three times more likely to have emotional or behavioral problems than those who have both of their biological parents present in the home. Military officials attribute significant differences in behavioral attributes of recruits from broken homes:

> These days, drill instructors say they are contending with the children of the 1970s, a passive generation raised by babysitters and day-care centers and one unaccustomed to accountability. "The broken-family kids are one of the biggest problems we have," says Sgt. Charles Tucker.

A RETURN TO FAULT DIVORCE?

One need only listen to a few divorce stories to understand why the courts were glad to get out of the business of adjudicating fault in marriage breakups. *The Wall Street Journal* quotes a husband divorced against his will who, while admitting he was dictatorial and financially irresponsible, claims that because he doesn't drink and was never physically abusive or adulterous his wife would have had no grounds for divorce under a fault-based system. The article leaves one wondering how dictatorial and how irresponsible the abandoned husband may have been.

When do personal idiosyncrasies become "fault" in a marriage? How dictatorial and how irresponsible would a spouse have to be for the legal system to find "fault?" Probably more dictatorial and irresponsible than many husbands and wives could bear, given that even the most egregious faults such as battery and adultery are frequently difficult to prove in court. In the words of columnist Jane Bryant Quinn:

> Forcing people to stay in marriages they hate would only cause more problems. It would also bring back poisonous lawsuits charging "fault." You have to have been there before to remember how awful it was.

The fault system of divorce was based on a concept of marriage (essentially Blackstone's doctrine of coverture—see Chapter 4) that no longer prevails. Prior to the 1960s, a married woman virtually ceased to exist in the eyes of the state. In practice if not always in law, a married couple became one person, that person being the husband. On the day of her marriage, a wife's legal residence was automatically changed to her husband's residence, her name was changed to her husband's name, and she could get credit, own property, or register to vote only under her husband's name.

Until very recently, marital rape was considered by most states to be a theoretical impossibility because in marriage two bodies became one—a wife's body belonged unconditionally to her husband. Marital union was defined as so complete it could be torn asunder only by an egregious act of a guilty party against an innocent party. If both parties committed abandonment, adultery, or extreme cruelty, the union was still held to be inviolate. Underlying this almost immutable definition of marriage was the assumption that people had to stay married because a woman couldn't survive by herself. If a husband didn't support his wife, she and her children would become a burden on the state.

Things changed in the 1960s:

- Statutes began to address child abuse and family violence. What went on within the household was no longer considered a totally private matter of the husband's discretion.
- Married women began to achieve legal status as individuals in their own right.
- The assumption that a woman couldn't support herself was reversed almost 180 degrees to a presumption that she could.

Thus, while the ritual and ceremony with which couples are joined together have remained virtually unchanged, legal interpretation of the marriage contract has changed rather drastically. Sanford N. Katz, professor of law at Boston College, notes that:

> . . . divorce laws and policies have consistently moved toward a view of marriage as an economic partnership and away from the concept of marriage as a status totally regulated by the state and dominated by the husband.

In legal terms, marriage has evolved from an almost irreversible merging of a woman's identity into that of her husband to an economic partnership between theoretical equals that can be dissolved at the request of either partner. Few women, presumably, would want to return to the assumptions on which the old system was based. Nevertheless, in response to the dismal stories and statistics of divorce, several states are considering reinstating "fault" in order to put more pressure on couples to stay in existing marriages.

Divorce is, unfortunately, sometimes the best alternative for everyone involved and sometimes necessary for the health and sanity of at least one of the parties. Assuming that people are basically rational and aware of their own interests, divorce represents an improvement for at least one of the parties. Given that much of what the other partner in a contested divorce wants from the marriage is likely to be irretrievable, decreasing the acrimony of divorce probably benefits everyone, especially the children. As one professional noted in a discussion of the proposed changes in Michigan divorce law:

> "No law, no matter how well intentioned, can force people to stay together," said Michael Robbins, a suburban Detroit lawyer who heads the family law section of the state bar association. "Before no-fault, there was a lot of perjury, a lot of fabrication, just so people could legally separate. And if we go back to that, we'll be spending more time on who's to blame."
>
> He added: "That means more litigation, more expense, more adversarial behavior. And for children, it means being subjected to character assassination between the parents. That's a heavy burden for a kid."

Sponsors of repealing "no-fault" argue that it would give innocent parties in divorce the upper hand in getting better economic settlements:

> "Let's say a homemaker has a husband who cheats on her," said Dan Jarvis, the director of public policy for the Family Forum. "Under the proposed law, she would have the upper hand. She can say: All right, you want your divorce? You can have it. But it's going to cost you."

It's not readily apparent, however, why the courts should have to adjudicate personal fault to hold a spouse responsible for the economic consequences of divorce for dependents or what practical difference it makes in the enforceability of child support and spouse support. Why does no fault have to mean no responsibility?

With or without judging fault, why can't the state say automatically and unequivocally, "All right, you can have a divorce; but first you have to show how you are going to provide fairly for the dependents you are leaving behind. Your current dependents are 'preferred stockholders' who have first claim on your resources." If one party can leave a marriage at will, both parties should be able to leave on equal terms—one party should not be left holding the bag for the mistakes made by both. While there may be little point in trying to trap people in their mistakes forever, there *is* a point in holding people responsible for the consequences of their mistakes.

TAKING CARE OF FAMILY BUSINESS

People aren't allowed to walk away from business deals without taking care of their contractual obligations. Short of bankruptcy, business creditors can go after debtors with the full force of the law. As the writer of a *New York Times* Op-Ed article asks:

> What would happen if courts treated business contracts as they now treat the marriage contract? . . . Under such circumstances, the economy would collapse.

The courts have long held that partners in private partnerships have greater obligations to each other than do shareholders in public corporations. In the words of Justice Benjamin Cardozo, "partners owe each other 'not honesty alone,' but something much greater: 'the punctilio of an honor the most sensitive.'" Considering what is at stake, no partnership could be more in need of an honor most sensitive than the partnership between husband and wife. Family debts and obligations are at least as important as auto loans. Consistent with the modern definition of marriage as an economic partnership, divorce is a time to call in the auditors for a full accounting of marital assets and liabilities.

FAMILY ASSETS

In modern economies the primary source of value is human capital; that is, the ability of human effort to earn income. Partnership income is generally derived from an efficient merging of human capital that allows individuals to specialize in some things while relying on their partners for other things. One partner may provide the technical expertise, another may manage production, one may do the accounting and record keeping while another is responsible for sales and marketing. Only the salesperson actually brings in money directly, but each partner's contribution is defined in the partnership agreement that allocates shares as claims on the distribution of profits. If the partnership dissolves, partnership assets are distributed on the basis of ownership shares.

In poor families, the ability to work and to earn income is usually the only asset people have. In middle-class families, assets are likely to consist primarily of human earning capacity supplemented by relatively small incomes from tangible property or from stocks and bonds that represent claims on tangible assets. In rich families that have substantial inherited wealth, assets may be primarily in the form of claims on tangible assets.

A definition of family property that is restricted to claims on tangible property is weighted heavily toward the concerns of rich families. It has little relevance to middle-class families, and virtually no relevance to poor families. (In a sample of 1,800 divorce cases in Wisconsin between 1980 and 1984, the median value of tangible assets at disruption was $12,049 in

1997 prices.) The tendency of courts to restrict the definition of community property in a marriage to tangible things such as real estate or claims on tangible items such as stocks and bonds ignores the reality of the middle- and lower-class family economy.

FAMILY LIABILITIES?

The liabilities of a marital partnership consist of what the partners owe each other and what they owe society as a consequence of their marriage. One interpretation of marriage is that it is a couple's covenant with society to take care of each other and to take care of their dependents. Family dependents include:

Dependent Children

Dependent children are a social debt for which both parents are generally considered responsible.

Semi-dependent Spouses

As with any true merger, marriage produces dependency between partners. Marital dependency can take various forms, but economic dependency between spouses traditionally has derived from the disproportionate investment of women's labor in family caretaking. One feminist model advocates trying to eliminate caretaker dependency completely by urging spouses to share work inside and outside the home equally and by requiring employers to accommodate family obligations for all employees. It is a theoretical model that may work well for some families and for some employers; but it is frequently easier said than done, even with the best intentions by all concerned.

Regardless of their preferences, not every couple is lucky enough to find two equal jobs in the same community. Not everyone has the stamina to work double shifts at home and at work. Not everybody wants to be part of a two-career family in which both spouses work 40-hour weeks, let alone 70-hour weeks. Some couples have backup from grandparents or other family members and some don't. Not all children at all ages thrive in day care or in surrogate care. Not every employer is able to accommodate every work/family conflict and stay in business.

Sometimes the balancing act can be worked out and sometimes it can't; but even if it can, not every couple wants an androgynous marriage—many people still cherish a degree of gender specialization. In any event, it is surely presumptuous to try to tell all families in our very complex economy how they should arrange their divisions of labor in marriage when we don't dictate the division of labor in any other kind of partnership.

There is certainly reason to hope (in fact, to insist) that both employers and employees will continue trying to find better forms of work/family accommodation and that some of the ways in which things are currently organized both at home and at work will be found to be unnecessarily arbitrary or technologically obsolete. The hard reality, however, is that parents often find that their family's personal needs have a dismaying tendency to occur on a schedule that conflicts with the workplace in terms of time, energy, and/or location. If one adult in a family is required to be highly specialized just to earn a living, the other adult may have to be more specialized in caretaking if there is to be a family life. Even if spouses earn equal incomes outside the home (as almost half of all couples currently do), it doesn't solve the problem of spousal vulnerability in the event of divorce. A spouse earning equal income who is left with dependent children to both support and to care for can be seriously disadvantaged.

Dependent Parents

Aged parents are inevitably dependent on the next generation. As was argued earlier in the context of Social Security, there isn't any way to take care of an older generation without a younger generation. If the major economic tie between parents and children is to be retained within the family, dependent parents must also be a responsibility of the marital partnership.

CAN THE FAMILY BE MADE SAFE FOR CARETAKERS?

The women's movement is understandably wary of the risks of marriage and very doubtful of the social will to treat the traditional feminine roles fairly and equitably. Some feminists argue that the only way power can be balanced within a marriage is if both parties have equal economic power outside the marriage, meaning that both husband and wife need to spend equal time and effort in the marketplace. Such arguments are compelling, given that marriage law has gone from a system of divorce based on the assumption of inherent female inferiority and subservience to a blindly egalitarian definition of economic partnership that ignores the sacrifice of economic potential that family caretakers make.

Is earning an equal income in the marketplace the only way our society can think of for a spouse to have an equal claim on family resources in the event of divorce? Is the only way a woman can protect herself from the threat of destitution over a lifetime to bear few children (preferably none) and meticulously avoid any specialization within a marriage in order to compete on an equal basis with men in the marketplace? Does equality have to mean sameness for spouses in order to have equal power and status in our most basic family relationships?

If the answer to these questions is yes, then the most radical feminist points about marriage and family have to be conceded. Katha Pollitt submits the view that marriage is an outdated institution for protecting women and children:

> There isn't any way in our modern, secular society to reconnect marriage and maternity. We'd have to bring back the whole nineteenth century. Restore the cult of virginity and the double standard, ban birth control, restrict divorce, kick women out of decent jobs, force unwed pregnant women to put their babies up for adoption on pain of social death, make out-of-wedlock children legal nonpersons.
>
> None of this will happen, so why not come to terms with reality? Instead of trying to make women—and men—adapt to an outworn institution, we should adapt our institutions to the lives people actually live. Single mothers need paid parental leave, day care, flexible schedules, child support, pediatricians with evening hours. Most of all, they need equal pay and comparable worth. What they don't need is sermons.

Some feminists would deny any relevant gender differences beyond the anatomical plumbing that enables a woman to conceive and bear a child and argue that all women who aren't socially conditioned to accept gender roles would want to share childrearing and breadwinning equally, as would men. Other feminists don't insist on sameness of gender roles for either theoretical or practical reasons, and many feminists celebrate what they perceive as natural gender differences. All feminists, however, demand dignity and autonomy as self-evident truths in the finest tradition of Western social theory.

Autonomy within marriage requires a balance of power; balanced power requires equal exit positions; equal exit positions mean equal claims on combined marital assets beyond divorce for support of all dependents. If our political and economic systems can't enforce a marriage contract that provides fairness and equity for its investors in the event of dissolution, then all individuals will be compelled to seek their economic security by fully investing their efforts outside the family. Is that the social arrangement we really want?

Surely the students at Wellesley who protested the choice of Barbara Bush as commencement speaker because she was "only" a wife, mother, grandmother, and volunteer were misguided. Barbara Bush was a partner in a very substantial family enterprise: wife of a president, mother of five children, grandmother to a brood of grandchildren, and an active volunteer in worthy causes. It could hardly be said that Mrs. Bush had led a frivolous or unproductive life.

What the Wellesley students seemed not to understand was the extent to which their lives were literally built on their own mothers' contributions. Many of the protesting students probably wouldn't have made it to Wellesley, or even have been born, if their mothers and grandmothers hadn't done the kind of work that Barbara Bush did; but as Mrs. Bush herself said at the time of the controversy, she signed on to her role in life at a time when it wasn't considered a choice. Now, it is a choice. Fortunately for Mrs. Bush, her marriage lasted and delivered the kind of lifetime security that marriage vows imply. If society wants anyone in the future to invest their time and talents in family, however, we have to find ways of protecting that investment in the all-too-likely event of marital dissolution.

Some mothers want to work full time outside the home and are as committed to professional careers as any father. By the same token, plenty of men would love to disconnect from the killer career track and invest more time in their families—and some are even doing it. Many women work full time for the same reason many men do—they need the money for their families. In fact, recent reports indicate that in nearly half of American households women are contributing almost half of the economic support. Requiring both marriage partners to be equals in the marketplace in order to be treated by the courts as equals at home is a form of market slavery that puts arbitrary constraints on the way a marital partnership may divide up the caretaking and breadwinning labor. Given that the marketplace doesn't offer an infinite range of job choices, equal division of all roles is a practical impossibility for many parents.

The opportunity cost of being the more flexible caretaker in a marriage is usually the major cost of childrearing that dwarfs all others (see Chapter 5). Family caretaking, however, isn't a very safe investment of anyone's time if it:

Results in unbalanced power and status within the marriage partnership.
Penalizes caretakers unequally when a family partnership breaks up.
Penalizes the parents of caretakers who are dependent on their children.

Taking the last problem first, if marriage is, among other things, a contract to take care of family dependents and if the primary economic ties between generations are to be retained within the family, provision for the parents of caretakers as well as the parents of breadwinners is a necessary clause in the marriage contract. Since there is considerable evidence that people tend to choose mates with characteristics similar to themselves (social scientists call it "assortative mating"), a family breadwinner is likely to have married someone whose parents made similar investments in their child.

Analytical studies have repeatedly shown high correlations between mothers' education levels and the achievements of their children. Parents who produce a family caretaker contribute as much to the next generation's reproductive success as do parents who produce a family breadwinner. It makes sense, then, that if Social Security were converted to a parental dividend, taxes should be based on a couple's joint return and the dividends distributed equally between the parents of husband and wife.

Basing contributions to retirement accounts on a couple's joint return isn't a totally novel idea. Splitting Social Security taxes paid by a couple equally between "Personal Security Accounts" for husband and wife has already been suggested in more conventional proposals for Social Security reform as a matter of simple fairness and as an alternative to the distortions that spousal benefits currently cause in the Social Security system. Splitting parental dividend accounts between the parents of husband and wife would be an application of the same principles.

As long as people stay married and continue to cooperate in taking care of each other and their dependents, basing parental dividends on a marital joint return would contribute considerably to making the family safer for caretakers. More intractable problems arise when one of the marital partners jumps ship and leaves the other partner with responsibility for dependents disproportionate to the means of support.

Given the fifty-fifty odds of divorce and the prevalence of no-fault property settlements and hard-to-collect child support, the likelihood of a caretaker's being left behind with few marketable skills together with responsibility for dependent children already makes any degree of specialization in family caretaking a rather risky undertaking. Requiring children to be directly responsible for financial support of their parents would make the caretaker's risk even greater. Is the only remedy for the economically devastating effects of marital breakdown on family caretakers to socialize the care of dependents and let our economic system penalize the family caretaking role into extinction?

ECONOMIC BALLAST FOR THE MARITAL BOAT

MARITAL PROPERTY

Given that the major form of property in modern economies is the capacity to earn income, the caretaking partner who sacrifices tenure and upward mobility in the job market is at a disadvantage within the partnership because of unequal ability to leave the partnership. If marriage is to be the fair and balanced relationship that both social theorists and family therapists suggest is required for effective cooperation, spouses need to have equal bargaining power within the partnership. In business terms, both partners need to own equal shares in the assets of the partnership regardless of who does what. As discussed earlier, the problem comes in defining the assets of a marital partnership. If one partner contributes more money while the other partner contributes more time and flexibility, the "time" partner will in most cases have also sacrificed opportunities to develop personal capital in the form of marketable skills. The trick in making divorce fairer to children and caretakers is broadening the definition of marital property to include human capital as well as financial capital.

Several proposals for divorce reform have suggested that post-divorce income should be shared equally among family members for a significant period of time based on the length of the marriage and the needs of dependents. Some might say this has a "retro" 1950s sound to it, conjuring up images from the stand-up comedy routines of that era—the predatory female who lures the helpless man into marriage, conceives a child, abandons the father for no good reason, claims substantial child suppport and spouse support (alimony) for an extended period of time, then spends most of the support on herself rather than the children. But how does that "take my wife . . . *please*" cliche measure up against the legions of men who have lured women into marriage and caretaking on the promise of "until death do us part," and "with all my worldly goods I thee endow," only to sire children, then abandon both mother and children to very reduced circumstances? Equal claims on post-divorce income by all dependents for a significant period of time would tend to equalize the economic threats of predatory behavior and presumably make both sexes think more seriously about the commitments of marriage. Perhaps just as usefully, such claims would reduce the attractiveness of "home wrecking" by predatory parties outside the marriage.

PARENTAL DIVIDENDS

Giving the more economically disadvantaged spouse greater claim on post-divorce income of the primary breadwinner would tend to equalize the terms on which both parties could leave the marriage, thereby making marriage a somewhat safer proposition for caretakers. Leaving marriage isn't, however, what most people concerned about the effects of divorce on children particularly want to encourage. Children don't need just economic support—they need the love, care, and guidance of both mothers *and* fathers. Another argument for effectively making parents shareholders in the family through their children, therefore, is that it would exert a centripetal force on both parents to stay together when staying together is in the best interests of their children.

Restoring $21-plus trillion worth of economic value to the marital partnership in the form of parental dividends would contribute to stabilizing the marital boat in several ways:

1. Given that opportunity cost of parental time is the major parental resource invested in children, putting a value on parental investment would provide more explicit recognition of the caretaking partner's contribution to the family enterprise which, according to Sen's theory of partnership power, would tend to give the caretaker more equal status within the partnership.

2. Returning $21-plus trillion worth of parental equity to the family enterprise would give both partners something very tangible to lose by behaving irresponsibly or uncooperatively in ways that threaten family stability. It would put a substantial premium on smoothing out differences and working together to achieve the best environment for growing children. In problem situations in which it is judged that staying together is better for the children, both parents would be rewarded for putting the children's welfare first.

3. Divorce would be further penalized by the necessity of splitting a child's parental dividend between two households. Given that parental dividends would provide a very explicit message about where old-age support actually comes from, couples would be made more aware of the costs involved in splitting up households and dividing up family resources.

4. If divorce is inevitable, noncustodial parents, who all too often drop out of children's lives both personally and financially, would have tangible incentives for continuing to make positive contributions to their children's welfare by supporting and cooperating with the custodial spouse. A state that grants a divorce can't revoke the divorce

when people don't honor the terms of the divorce decree, nor can the state even do much by way of enforcement if one party has left the state. The IRS or the Social Security Administration, however, could reduce or completely revoke claims on a parental-dividend account when people don't meet their post-divorce responsibilities to their children and to their children's caretaker.

There aren't, it seems, any perfect answers to balancing the claims of equity and fairness in marriage breakups. Given that our legal system already has such a poor track record of enforcing the claims for the child support it currently adjudicates, adjudicating additional claims on post-divorce income might have very little practical effect if noncustodial parents see nothing in it for them. As a reviewer of an academic study of child support notes, there is a practical limit on what can be collected from workers' incomes without driving workers out of the labor market or into the underground economy. If paying child support and spousal support were a condition for maintaining a parental claim on retirement support from children, however, the incentives to comply would be more positive.

Our tax system does collect Social Security taxes quite effectively. Social Security taxes could continue to be collected and deposited in parental accounts on the basis of a couple's joint earnings after divorce unless and until the lesser-earning partner remarries. Continuing joint post-divorce contributions to parental trust funds would relieve the disproportionate effects of divorce on the parents of caretakers. It would also remove any temptation for in-laws to interfere in a marriage in the hope of enhancing their own parental dividends.

TAXES AND WELFARE

It is hard to believe that a society that pays so much lip service to family values has allowed its tax and welfare systems to penalize marriage so severely—in some cases to the point of absurdity. Such policies have surely contributed to destabilizing the institution of marriage. Our system levies substantial penalties on marriage in at least three ways:

1. The federal income tax levies a substantial "marriage tax" on many two-income couples.
2. The Social Security system, which collects more taxes from 70 percent of taxpayers than the IRS does, makes no allowance for family dependents.
3. The welfare system cuts off many benefits to mothers and children if the mother marries a husband who has a job.

The findings of economists Daniel R. Feenberg of the National Bureau of Economic Research and Harvey S. Rosen of Princeton University were summarized in a *Washington Post* article as follows:

> The size of the marriage tax is now quite extraordinary. The hit on some lower-income couples this year will be as high as 18 percent of their income. Due to the combined effects of progressive tax brackets and the earned income tax credit, a married couple with two children and each adult earning $10,000 pays $3,717 a year more in taxes than they would if the same people were single and filed as heads of households.

Since the $3,717 tax loss is spendable dollars, the same couple would have to earn about $5,000 more in pretax income just to compensate for being married. A $5,000 income penalty for a couple with a $20,000 income and two children to support is an enormous price to pay for being married.

The Social Security system began in 1937 with a payroll tax rate of 2 percent on income up to $3,000 (a maximum payment of $60, equivalent to about $650 at 1997 prices). Over the years, the payroll tax has ratcheted up to a tax rate of 15.3 percent on income up to $68,400 in 1998 (a maximum payment of $10,465.20) and now takes a bigger bite out of most family incomes than the federal income tax. Unlike the income tax, however, Social Security taxes allow no deductions for spouses or other dependents. Allowing for inflation, even the income-tax deduction for dependents has shrunk approximately 30% in real terms (from $600 per dependent in 1948, equivalent to about $4,007 in 1997 prices, to $2,650 in 1997—a 33.8% reduction!). The tax system as a whole has thus become both increasingly regressive and increasingly unsupportive of family formation.

From all of the public rhetoric about family values, one would expect that Congress would be legislating marriage bonuses rather than marriage penalties (one-earner couples do in fact get a break, but two-earner couples with similar incomes are systematically penalized) and would be adjusting dependent deductions to at least keep up with inflation. Eliminating marriage taxes, adjusting dependent deductions for inflation, and converting Social Security to a parental-support tax would make substantial contributions to removing the anti-family biases that have crept into the tax codes in recent decades.

Perhaps the height of irony in what public policy has done to families is the extent to which the welfare system penalizes marriage. The welfare system literally says to very poor women that if they want food stamps, subsidized housing, access to Medicaid, and AFDC they should have children but not get married to fathers who hold jobs. Poor, working fathers have literally been made financial liabilities to their families. Pointing out the problems of current welfare programs, however, is not to propose how they could be changed for the better. Connections between welfare reform and the proposal of this analysis to treat the family as an investment institution are the subject of Chapter 10.

FUSION WITH INTEGRITY

Love is the only sane and satisfactory answer to the problems of human existence.

Love is the child of freedom, never of domination.
—Erich Fromm, in *The Art of Loving*

Love is the answer to our unrelenting, uniquely human, existential separateness and loneliness. Social psychologist Erich Fromm argued that while love has several manifestations (romantic love, parental love, neighborly love, love of God), love is always a form of fusion with integrity; that is, a fusion that allows all parties to retain their autonomy as individuals while giving freely of themselves. Coercion and domination subvert the integrity of love by creating power relationships that are its antithesis.

As noted by the work of Scarf and others, coercion and domination aren't very good for partnership efficiency either, inasmuch as they undermine the incentives of individuals to cooperate for the common good of the partnership. Since freedom, fairness, and efficiency are basic objectives of our democratic and capitalistic systems, power relationships within families where individuals spend much of their time and do much of their work deserve at least as much concern as the rest of our social relationships. The marriage contract that society has an interest in enforcing is one that promotes marital cooperation by protecting the investments of both partners in the relationship.

Divorce law defines what the marriage contract means in the eyes of the state by defining the terms on which the parties can leave. As various economic and political theorists have noted, the key to protecting both parties in a cooperative relationship is balancing the terms on which they can exit. Barring the exits from marriage indiscriminately, as rescinding discrimination laws and rescinding no-fault divorce would do, isn't the answer to marriage instability. Making it harder for caretakers to work outside the home or requiring an arduous divorce process that would hinder victims of abuse trying to escape their abusers are moves in the wrong direction. They would exacerbate the problems of unbalanced power that threaten any cooperative relationship.

In the context of arguing that women should abandon their quest for economic equality, Irving Kristol, co-editor of *The Public Interest* and prominent conservative thinker, has suggested that women should be allowed to leave marriage on a no-fault basis while men should be held to a fault standard in divorce proceedings. Kristol's first proposition—that women should forgo equality—was greeted with several well-aimed retorts on *The Wall Street Journal*'s Op-Ed page. His latter suggestion, however, is a laudable recognition of the frequently unequal exit positions within marriage; but implementing the concept is easier said than done. It is the economically dependent or semidependent spouse who needs special protection in divorce, which isn't always the wife. In a significant number of marriages, it may be the husband. In any event, giving caretaking spouses the legal right to leave a marriage without giving them the economic means to support themselves and their children doesn't solve the problem.

Since the most conspicuous cause of unbalanced power in marriage is a weaker economic position outside the marriage, that is the point that needs to be addressed directly. The state can't control people's affections or their living arrangements, but it does have considerable control over property and income. If marriage is viewed as a contract to take care of dependents, there would seem to be no apparent need for courts to return to the fault system of divorce in order to hold both parties equally responsible for supporting family members who have become dependent on the marriage, including spouses, children, and aging parents. Balancing the exit positions with respect to dependent care would require:

1. Recognizing the contributions of the more flexible partner (defined as the partner who has earned less income) as having value equal to the leading breadwinner's contributions. As Okin notes, if we really mean what we say about family values, this can hardly be controversial.
2. Including earning capacity (which represents approximately 70 percent of our economy's total assets) in marital property. For any concept of marital property to be relevant to all but the upper classes, earning capacity has to be included in family wealth.
3. Granting custody to the parent who has the greatest involvement with the children and not allowing custody demands to be used as leverage to get the less-affluent parent to forgo child or spousal support.

4. Extending obligations of the parties (including support of children, their caretaker, and the couple's dependent parents) sufficiently beyond divorce so that both parties are burdened by the consequences of divorce as equally as possible.

BEING REALISTIC

There isn't any way to make marriage completely safe or even to make the risks comparable to risks that investors take in other areas of the economy. The downside risks of marriage are extraordinarily large and uniquely personal. Marriage can turn into a living hell when one partner becomes a terrorist. Even in states with model statutes pertaining to domestic violence, court restraining orders don't stop bullets or baseball bats when one partner wants to kill or injure another. Family lawyers report that it is not uncommon for spouses to stay in marriages because they are convinced they will be killed if they try to leave. The courts haven't been very good at economic protection either. The hypothetical story of Jim and Janet related in Chapter 7 happens all too often—the family caretaker is stranded with all of the responsibilities and few of the resources. The major marital asset is earning capacity, and the courts have been reluctant to treat earning capacity as marital property. In any event, earning capacity is hard to capture when the person who owns it doesn't feel like working to support a broken family.

TYING THE KNOT: A MARRIAGE CONTRACT FOR THE MODERN FAMILY

The challenge is to make the modern family as safe and fair a place as possible for its participants while allowing couples to define themselves and their roles in the ways that best fit their diverse needs, talents, and circumstances. Families often face enormous challenges—caring for a very elderly parent, caring for a handicapped child, coping with rebellious teenagers—while trying to keep their heads above water economically. Modern couples are, however, finding many creative ways of working out their lives. The last thing families need at this point is a legal straitjacket that says they have to divide up family work in an arbitrary way if they want to have an equal claim on partnership assets in the eyes of the law. That is like saying that everyone in a business partnership has to do everything (accounting, marketing, production, research) in equal proportions in order to own equal shares in the business.

The marriage contract is currently the most ambiguous of contracts. If nothing else, it would seem that marital partners need the kind of predictability that contract law generally provides to other investors in long-term relationships. There is no point in wringing our hands about unwed mothers if we don't know what being wed means or if our legal system effectively says it doesn't mean very much. The ambiguity of the marriage contract could be reduced substantially by defining the terms of the economic partnership as specifically as possible, such as:

◆ Putting six Social Security numbers (the numbers of the couple and their parents) on the marriage certificate as marital dependents for whom the couple vow to share their combined financial assets, including parental dividend accounts, during marriage and for an extended period of time after divorce, perhaps equal to the length of the marriage or until the remarriage of the less advantaged partner.

◆ Adding the Social Security numbers of all children of the marriage at birth to the marriage certificate as dependents for whom the couple's resources are to be pooled and held jointly responsible for life.

◆ Giving strict legal precedence to the claim of legitimate dependents of the marriage to share in the joint assets of the marriage over any subsequent relationships or obligations either spouse may wish to undertake.

◆ Putting the full force of the courts and the collection powers of the IRS and the Social Security Administration behind the terms of the contract.

◆ Adjusting tax laws to reward or at least not punish people who unequivocally accept responsibility for taking care of their legal dependents by signing a marriage contract.

◆ Allowing parental dividends (as defined in Chapter 7) to reward those who honor the obligations of marriage and family.

The days when tribes could raid their neighbors for wives are over in most parts of the world. The days when men and women were forced to assume traditional gender roles in order to survive are also over in economically advanced countries, dating approximately from the late 1960s. Having just recently evolved from a gender caste system that assigned family roles at birth but provided extensive legal and social protections for those roles, we have reverted to an almost barbaric system of "anything goes" when it comes to protecting children and caretakers. Marriage currently means whatever the laws in 50 states and judges' varying interpretations say it means after the fact; and most of them say it means relatively little in terms of protecting a spouse who has disproportionately invested time in a marriage. *In order to remain a viable choice in a modern economy, invest-ment in marriage and family caretaking needs more protection by the state, not less, precisely because people are now much freer to avoid making family commitments.*

THE TIES THAT BIND

Repairing the family fabric in modern societies is going to require writing a social contract that:

1. Restores a degree of traditional economic agency between parents and children in order to retain the economic ties between genera-tions that are necessary to provide for meeting the dependency needs of both the young and the elderly.
2. Creates a new kind of economic agency between husbands and wives that enables both partners to retain their personal autonomy while merging their economic interests for the sake of achieving family goals.
3. Weaves the intergenerational- and intragenerational-family threads together in a cohesive and mutually supportive way.

The central remaining thread that can tie modern families together economically is the project of reproduction. While production of most goods and services has moved out of the household and into the market-place for technical reasons, reproduction still requires extensive coopera-tion between generations and between male and female. Reendowing the marriage contract with a portion of the wealth that reproduction generates is the most direct way to restore the family's economic center of gravity and to provide economic ballast for the marital boat.

Divorce reformers have been generally pessimistic about the likelihood of being able to capture more postmarital income for spousal support by defining income as marital property and subjecting it to additional income taxes. Parental dividends could change the postdivorce dynamics by put-ting a premium on financial accountability and on spousal cooperation for the good of the children. Social Security taxes, which are relatively easy to collect, could continue to be deposited in trust funds for the parents des-ignated on the marriage certificate for an extended period of time after divorce. Such provisions would go a considerable way toward protecting caretakers and thereby enhancing the value of caretaking in our society.

WAITING TO EXHALE: THE BATTLE OF THE SEXES

While many men have come to appreciate a more egalitarian definition of gender roles, the battle of the sexes continues; and the media frequently mirror the debates in dramatic ways. *Waiting to Exhale,* a movie based on Terry McMillan's book about the romantic misadventures of four successful black women, drew large crowds (mostly women) at the box office. Critics wondered why the entanglements of such accomplished women with a series of jerks and losers could have so much audience appeal. Feminists understandably protested the story's message of desperation about a woman's need to find a man. Nevertheless, McMillan's story obviously resonated with many women.

Allowing for the exaggerations of an entertainment medium, what resonated may have been the fact that, while economic independence can alleviate the gender-balance-of-power problem, for many women independence isn't enough. In the words of Whitney Houston's Savannah character, women also want love and homes and families. What was surely "right on" in McMillan's story is how problematic gender relations have become in modern societies and how hard it can be to combine the independence of careers with the demands of marriage and family.

One young woman recently wrote in the "My Turn" column of *Newsweek* that she was ridiculed by her friends for marrying before becoming established in a career. Meanwhile, sociologists quote statistics suggesting that women who establish careers first have relatively small probabilities of getting married. The problems career women have in finding mates are hardly a figment of McMillan's imagination—the stresses and trade-offs are very real. It is the inability to find mates that many "Murphy Browns" cite as their reason for deliberately conceiving children out of wedlock.

In another popular book/movie, *The Bridges of Madison County,* a middle-aged woman in rural Iowa meets the lover of her dreams but after a brief fling renounces passion for the sake of her quotidian responsibilities to a husband and children who don't deserve to be hurt. Many readers apparently identified with the plight of Francesca Johnson in being forced to choose between freedom and passion versus family duty and responsibility—it is the kind of choice many spouses and parents have undoubtedly made.

We can't always wait until everything is perfect to make the big decisions in life. We can't wait forever to find perfect mates, or for employers to organize the workplace in a totally comfortable way, or for men and women to reach a consensus on every aspect of what gender means in modern societies before making the kinds of commitments that families require. If we do, there won't be many families. There will always be risks and compromises, and marriage will always require a large component of trust. It does seem, however, that we could do better in terms of writing a social contract that is fairer to the people who take the risks of making the family investments on which our society depends. Addressing the enormous ambiguity that currently exists in society's interpretation of the marriage contract would be a good place to start.

IRRECONCILABLE DIFFERENCES: SOME CONTROVERSIAL ISSUES

Disagreement is not an easy thing to reach.
> —John Courtney Murray, Catholic theologian

UNCONVENTIONAL MARRIAGES

Although marriage has lost much of its traditional appeal for the younger generations, various nontraditional groups, notably gays and lesbians, are petitioning for official recognition of their domestic relationships. Since the major costs of traditional marriage are the economic burdens and dependencies associated with procreation and caretaking, it isn't illogical that nonreproductive unions would be attractive to people so inclined at the same time that reproductive unions are losing their appeal.

Politicians have perceived little gain in granting petitions for something that offends the sensibilities of a significant number of the heterosexual majority. If, however, the state paid more attention to the business dimensions of marriage and less to the personal and erotic dimensions over which, in reality, the state has little control, society might well see recognizing and privileging some nontraditional forms of "domestic partnership" as a good social bargain. The term "marriage" could still be reserved for heterosexual couples and the sexual polarity that the union of male and female represents—we don't have to say that heterosexual unions and homosexual unions are the same thing to recognize and formalize other kinds of commitments.

Given that converting Social Security to a parental dividend would eliminate much of the free ride that nonreproductive individuals currently get from the investments of "natural families," if two people want to pledge:

1. their fidelity to each other and
2. commitment to shared responsibility for themselves and their dependents even in the event of divorce, thereby making each other and their parents less likely to become burdens on society,

it's an offer that even the most committed opponents to nontraditional relationships might wish to consider.

Two people who are willing to put six Social Security numbers (their own and those of their parents) on their domestic-partnership license, designating people for whom they are willing to share financial responsibility unequivocally, would be making a substantial contribution to shouldering society's caretaking burdens. Given that sexual promiscuity of all forms is a community health risk and given that care of the aging is going to be an enormous economic problem in coming decades, domestic partnerships that commit to sexual fidelity and to carrying their share of the caretaking load would seem to have something valuable to offer society.

ABORTION

Harvard law professor Laurence Tribe points out that from a legal perspective abortion has never been treated as murder anywhere in the world at any time. No government has ever made abortion a capital crime or executed either a pregnant woman or an abortionist for murder. No society has ever categorically required parents to be good Samaritans to the extent of donating the use of their bodies to saving the lives of their children—no father has ever been forced to donate a kidney or a bone-marrow transplant or a blood transfusion to his offspring even if denial meant death for the child, nor is anyone currently proposing such draconian requirements other than for pregnant women. While many people believe sincerely that abortion is equivalent to murder, the practical issue seems to be the control of sexuality and reproduction. As a practical issue, how much control can a nontotalitarian state really exercise over such matters? Where is the center of such control actually located?

When a 15-year-old girl gets pregnant, society has to ask where her parents were and where the parents of her boyfriend were. Values don't just materialize out of the air. Of course there are influential factors in children's lives that are beyond parental control, but who has more control? Who has a better chance of conveying to young people a sense of self-respect and social responsibility sufficient to offset the messages of a culture run amok? Inasmuch as instilling values is a lot of work for parents, strengthening marital ties means, among other things, supporting and reinforcing the parents who have the primary responsibility for teaching and demonstrating to children the value of commitments to marriage and family.

If parents don't succeed in instilling the necessary values in their children, how much control can a legal system actually exercise? What kind of controls would it take to keep all potentially pregnant women from doing anything harmful to a fetus? What would it take to make every parent give their children all of the basic requirements for survival, growth, and development? Giving parents a tangible stake in their children's jobs and marriages may not restore the "cult of virginity," but it would put an economic base under the institution that has the best chance of teaching the young to take marriage seriously.

In Jane Austen's time, chaperoning behavior and counseling children in the art of choosing a trustworthy mate was considered a major responsibility of parents because family honor and fortune depended on it. It still does in Japan, the industrial nation with the lowest out-of-wedlock birth rate (1.1 percent in 1994 compared with 30.1 percent in the United States). As one Japanese teenager puts it, "Single mothers are not permitted in Japanese society." In the words of another Japanese teenager, "If my parents even knew that I have a boyfriend, they wouldn't let me out of the house."

Restoring incentives for parents to teach their children the value of marriage and to do things such as set curfews and stay up nights until their teenagers are home has a better chance of accomplishing the goal of influencing sexual behavior than any difficult-to-enforce, after-the-fact abortion law. Putting society's money where its mouth is with respect to investment in marriage and family could send a louder message to the young via their parents than any amount of public exhortation about family values.

THE CHALLENGE OF DEMOCRACY

However crass and commercial putting money behind our family values may seem, it is a nonviolent way of depolarizing some of our most divisive cultural wars. Finding nonviolent ways of settling differences between diverse groups of interests is the essence of democracy. As Jean Bethke Elshtain writes in *Democracy on Trial*:

> For practical politics to thrive, there must be a way for people who differ in important respects to come together.

> The democratic ideal . . . embeds at its heart the ideal of compromise. In a democracy, compromise is not a terrible thing. It is necessary, it

lies at the heart of things because you have to accept that people are going to have different views, especially on the most volatile matters and the most important issues.

When decisions are made in the political arena, it is a fight to the death—somebody wins the election and somebody loses. When decisions are made in the economic arena, however, individuals can give up some things they want less for things they want more. Some people want to work 80 hours a week while others prefer more leisure enough to sacrifice income for it. Some people want large, luxury cars while others prefer to drive small, efficient cars and spend the extra money on something else. Some people want an urban lifestyle while others prefer the country. Some people want the responsibilities of marriage and family and some don't.

Not everybody can have everything they want, but we have a reasonably efficient system for working out disagreements about economic priorities without going to war with each other. In contrast to the increasingly acrimonious debates about sensitive issues in the political arena, we settle most of our arguments about who does what and who gets what by requiring people to pay the costs and accept the consequences of their choices in the marketplace.

Of course there are important moral and philosophical questions that don't have economic answers. There are, to be sure, critical family issues (such as violence and abuse) that can't be left to the marketplace. The family has, however, always been held together by very strong economic ties that were reinforced outside the cash economy by tradition and technological necessity.

Given that both tradition and technology have changed fundamentally, we either have to design new ways to support the family economically or try to settle all of our differences about family issues in the political arena. The latter approach appears to be putting more weight on our political system than the system is able to bear. Given the stress that family issues are causing in our democratic system, letting our economic system carry part of the load of mediating some of our irreconcilable differences is an option that needs to be seriously considered.

9 SCHOOL REFORM AND THE FAMILY

THE CULTURE WARS, CONTINUED

Nowhere is it more apparent that we need to find a viable way of agreeing to disagree with each other than in our schools. Evidence of our society's inability to reach any consensus on public education appears in headlines almost daily:

"CRUSADER VOWS TO PUT GOD BACK INTO SCHOOLS USING LOCAL ELECTIONS"
The Wall Street Journal, July 15, 1992

"OUTFOXING THE RIGHT: MODERATES RECAPTURE A HANDFUL OF SCHOOL BOARDS"
Time, July 10, 1995

"DISTRICT'S 'LIFESTYLE' POLICY LEAVES TEACHERS SPEECHLESS"
AP, Merrimack, N.H., March 4, 1996

"SCHOOL-CLUB ACCESS LAW COMES BACK TO HAUNT: A UTAH SCHOOL DISTRICT FINDS THAT IF IT DOESN'T WANT A CLUB FOR GAY STUDENTS, IT CAN'T HAVE ANY NONACADEMIC ORGANIZATIONS"
The Philadelphia Inquirer, February 24, 1996

"SCHOOL BUREAUCRACY WANTED TO IGNORE REPORT OF MOLESTATION"
The New York Times, May, 23, 1995

145

**"IS A BACKPACK AN INALIENABLE RIGHT? A STUDENT
AND HER SCHOOL TANGLE IN COURT"**
The New York Times, March 13, 1996

**"PRIVATE BUSINESS, PUBLIC SCHOOLS: WHY HARTFORD
EXPERIMENT FAILED"**
The New York Times, March 11, 1996

**"LESSONS IN HYPOCRISY: TEACHERS SEND THEIR
CHILDREN TO PRIVATE SCHOOLS"**
The Wall Street Journal, June 13, 1995

"COURT LETS PUBLIC SCHOOL REQUIRE UNIFORMS"
The Wall Street Journal, December 5, 1995

**"HOLIDAY CHEER ABATES AS CHRISTMAS CLASHES
WITH DIVERSITY: FORGET ABOUT PEACE AND JOY.
THIS IS A SEASON OF CHAOS AND CONFLICT AS PUBLIC
SCHOOL SYSTEMS, PARENTS, AND CHILDREN THRASH OUT
AN INTENSIFYING ANNUAL DEBATE . . . "**
The New York Times, December 21, 1995

**"IN THE BEGINNING: IF YOU THOUGHT THE BATTLE OVER
THE TEACHING OF EVOLUTION IN AMERICA'S SCHOOLS
WAS SETTLED 70 YEARS AGO . . ."**
PBS, May 30, 1995

**"WILL SCHOOLS EVER GET BETTER?
PUBLIC SCHOOLS HAVE FRITTERED AWAY VAST
SUMS WITHOUT MUCH VISIBLE IMPROVEMENT . . ."**
Business Week cover story, April 17, 1995

WHO'S IN CHARGE HERE?

School uniforms, Halloween decorations, Christmas music, length of hair, creationism, metal detectors, sex education, prayer, condom distribution, locker searches, the pledge of allegiance, banned books, backpacks, lifestyle education—an infinite number of issues can make the public schools a political football, disrupt any discussion of education, and frequently land the contending parties in court. People care passionately about issues relating to their children; and the only venues for settling differences are expensive, adversarial, and exhausting for all concerned.

What is worse, big issues never stay settled. As in any highly politicized process, losing sides can always come back in the next school-board election, the next bond-issue referendum, the next administrative hearing, or the next legislature and start the argument all over again—witness the issue of teaching evolution, which, 70 years after the famous Scopes "monkey trial" in Tennessee, appears more contentious each year.

Who is in charge of this situation? The answer is, everybody is in charge and nobody is. Virtually every power group in our society has a finger in the education pie:

Taxpayers? They pay for it.

Legislators? They allocate it.

Courts? They adjudicate it.

Colleges of education? They certify it.

Federal, state, and local bureaucracies? They make rules.

Pressure groups, boosters groups, PTOs? They make demands.

Unions? They tell everyone what they can't do.

Superintendents and principals? They answer to all of the above.

Teachers? They have considerable freedom behind the classroom door but little control over any decisions outside the classroom (frequently, not even textbooks).

Parents? They have the most resposibility for the welfare of their children and the most detailed knowledge of the needs and interests of individual students but have the least say in school business, even though as taxpayers they are forced to pay for most of it.

While there are many notable exceptions, it is fair to say that our system of public education is generally a mess. The schools have become a place where power is so diffuse that nobody can be held responsible for what happens to our children. That the system works as well as it does is surely a tribute to the faith and good will of many committed individuals, but the system needs more than faith and good will. *The question has to be asked: how much longer can we entrust the enormous parental investments that children represent (see Chapters 4 and 5) to an educational system that has so little accountability?*

PROPOSALS FOR SCHOOL REFORM

Privatization, vouchers, parent-teacher advisory committees, computerization, magnet schools: there is no shortage of suggestions and panaceas for trying to make our schools work better. Several dimensions of reality, however, are generally omitted from most discussions of education reform.

SCHOOLS ARE AN EXTENSION
OF THE FAMILY

After all is said and done by legislators, school boards, bureaucrats, judges, teachers' unions, and administrators, most observers agree that a student's family situation is the primary determinant of his or her success in school. There is no individual in the whole educational process, other than a parent, who can be held responsible when a particular child doesn't achieve up to his or her potential. School, then, is essentially an extension of a family's responsibilities. Students don't come from taxpayers per se or from legislatures or from courts or from bureaucracies or from any of the other power centers in education—they come from families. Education is part of the developmental process in which families are engaged from the date of conception of a child. It follows, then, that families are the biggest stakeholders in the education process.

SCHOOLS NO LONGER HAVE A
CAPTIVE LABOR FORCE

Women have traditionally seen teaching as an extension of their family roles. Prior to the 1960s, most educated women went into teaching while waiting for marriage or remained in teaching while relying on husbands for their chief means of support. Women had little choice in the matter because society's assumptions excluded them from most other professions and occupations; but our schools are no longer subsidized by bright, well educated women who automatically go into teaching. Analysts who attempt to correlate such things as per-pupil expenditures and class sizes with measures of outcomes such as test scores can't explain why we are spending so much more and getting so much less. Among other things, no one has addressed the fact that there has been an enormous withdrawal of intellectual resources from the schools by women who are now going into other professions and occupations.

In many cases, teachers who graduated Phi Beta Kappa from the likes of Wellesley have been replaced by people at the bottom of their college classes at the least competitive colleges and universities. Of course, some very talented and dedicated people still go into teaching; but the fact remains that schools no longer have a monopoly on the best and brightest female talent. Schools are faced with a new situation in which they must compete for the kind of talent our mothers and grandmothers routinely supplied. Unfortunately, the system isn't set up to function competitively.

WE ARE NO LONGER AN UNLETTERED AND UNWASHED NATION

In contrast with the schoolmarms and schoolmasters of earlier years, teachers aren't the only educated persons in most communities. The basic education level of the general population has risen dramatically in recent decades. Given that many parents now have as much or more education as the average teacher, the assumption that parents need teachers or educational bureaucrats to determine their children's educational needs has become obsolete, if not somewhat insulting.

We still have very disadvantaged populations whose children must look to the schools to learn basic skills and culture, beginning in some cases at the level of Head Start; but that is no longer the situation of the majority of students. A school system based on the model that served our poor rural and/or immigrant forebears well is out of touch with current reality.

ONE SIZE NO LONGER FITS ALL

We have become a very diverse nation—diverse in our value systems, diverse in our education requirements, and diverse in what families want and need from schools. It is not unreasonable for families to want their children's schools to reinforce values compatible with what parents are trying to teach at home. Teaching values to the young is always a tough job, and the ultimate responsibility falls on parents.

Whether it is a religious value system or a humanist value system or some combination thereof, parents can only teach effectively what they really believe. In our multicultural society, there is no one set of values a public school that everyone is required to attend can teach without offending major constituencies. The alternatives are to battle continually over what schools should teach and how they should teach it or to let parents exercise far more choice in determining where their children go to school.

Values aren't the only way in which we have become increasingly diverse. While some students have a full-time parent at home, many parents are now dividing up the breadwinning and caretaking labor in alternative ways. One spouse may work days while the other works nights in order to keep the home front covered. Some parents work mornings while others work evenings. Some commute long distances while others work close to home. Some parents need longer school hours and year-round schedules while others want to be with their children after school and to take family outings in the summers. Some parents would prefer to have their children going to school in the "daytime neighborhood" where they work rather than in the "evening neighborhood" where they live, which is more flexibility than most school bureaucracies can handle. Today's parents, who are often very stressed from earning a living and caring for families, need support and accommodation, not bureaucratic rigidity, from the dominant public institution in their children's lives.

Some students come from homes with a solid structure and parental support while other students are deprived. Some students begin kindergarten with a vocabulary of 4,000 words while others begin with 40,000. Some students need a "holistic" kind of school that attempts to compensate for parenting deficits while other students come from families that are fiercely committed to doing their own parenting. Some students thrive in a strict, highly disciplined environment while others do better in an educational setting that encourages flexibility and creativity. Some students are on a fast growth curve while others mature too slowly or too unevenly to fit into the lockstep that public school typically requires. In short, there are no generic students and no generic families. In a post–industrial information economy, the differences become more pronounced and more divisive as the length and necessity of schooling increase.

WHO SHOULD BE IN THE DRIVER'S SEAT?

Somebody needs to be installed in the driver's seat if the school bus is to stop going in circles. Many kinds of public goods and services are financed by taxes, but we don't have six different constituencies telling the highway contractor how to run the road grader or how to mix the concrete. If we did, nobody could be held responsible when something is done wrong. The contractor is the agent in charge—the person who has both responsibility and control. The contractor may subcontract out much of the work, but the contractor is where the buck stops in terms of responsibility.

What the public schools lack is agency. Agency combines risks, rewards, responsibility, and control in the same place. Given that:

1. Someone needs to take responsibility for a child's overall development;
2. Education is a major component in a child's growth and development;
3. Parents have the biggest stake and the most immediate interest in the total development of a particular child, even more so if we are to hold parents responsible for their own retirement through their children; parents are the logical agents to be in charge of their children's education.

HOW MUCH AGENCY DO PARENTS HAVE IN PUBLIC SCHOOLS?

What kind of agency do parents have who can't afford to pay both public-school taxes and private-school tuition? Urban middle-class parents have a choice of living in the city or in the suburbs. Stay-at-home parents have the option of home schooling or volunteering in their children's class-rooms. The latter option, which essentially involves going to school with the student, may gain special access to a teacher's ear and put a parent in a position to lobby for a child's assignment to the best programs and the best teachers in the public school. Parents can be active politically in PTOs and school board elections, make political contributions and go door to door soliciting votes, thereby gaining some voice in school policies and perhaps special favors from school bureaucracies.

But that's about it in terms of parental choices—sell your house and move to a different school district, let one parent stay home full time to teach at home or to go to school with the student, or become very active politically. The first two choices can be prohibitively expensive; and as any-one who tries to change anything through public-school politics quickly learns, such action is an enormously frustrating, time-consuming, and somewhat risky process. When your child is literally a hostage of a particu-lar school system, you have to be rather naive to think you can criticize a teacher or an administrator or a school-board policy without risking nega-tive repercussions for your child.

An illustration of how powerless parents feel was provided by the case of Paul Solomon, a teacher in Greenburgh, New York, who admitted in court to having an adulterous affair that was linked to the murder of his wife allegedly by his lover. The community was in an uproar over whether the teacher should continue to work with children, but many parents were reluc-tant to express an opinion openly. According to a statement made anony-mously by one parent:

> Everybody is afraid for their children. You don't want him to be angry with your children. I am not saying that he would retaliate, but I don't want anything to jeopardize my children's education, and they may well have him as a teacher in the future.

If parents feel intimidated about voicing opinions in such an extreme case, how can parents hope to exercise control over what their children are exposed to in everyday situations where facts are much harder to establish?

In most situations, parents are virtually helpless to change anything within the classroom or to get a child assigned to another teacher. Teachers are insulated from parents by all of the other power groups in education. Parents who are politically and bureaucratically savvy may be able to talk to someone who knows someone who can get something changed, but such efforts are frustrating and time-consuming and very unfair to those who don't have similar access. The alternative is to sue the school, which parents regularly do over matters of questionable significance.

EDUCATION FROM THE SUPPLY SIDE

Schools are now forced to operate in a very different world on the supply side of their operation because they have to compete with many other occupations for the kind of talent our mothers and grandmothers historically provided. It is difficult to estimate the amount of employee subsidy that women have effectively withdrawn from the schools, but it literally amounts to billions of dollars per year. With all due respect to the talented and dedicated individuals still out there, schools that pay teachers $35,000 a year are now very often getting an employee whose salary reflects what the same employee could get elsewhere in the economy—not a woman whose talents and education are equivalent to a $50,000 manager or accountant, a $75,000 scientist or engineer, a $100,000 lawyer or doctor, and so on. Schools are now much more likely to be getting the talent they pay for than has historically been the case.

The education system has responded to its diminished ability to recruit the best female college graduates by allowing colleges of education to certify the sometimes barely literate as competent to teach, by installing administrators who promise to "crack the whip" over teachers, and by buying teaching materials designed to be "teacher-proof." As various observers have noted, "Public schools have been run on an industrial model, with teachers treated as passive, not-too-bright widget turners." "Teachers were told what to do and how to do it, like assembly-line workers." In the voice of one teacher:

> In four years of teaching in New York City I have never been asked my opinion on any matter of policy. I have only been spoken for in articles and newspapers as if I were some amorphous "teacher" who "wants" or "says" or "thinks" according to some poll or expert.
>
> Well, I'd like to speak for myself and I'd like to say that I can't teach. . . . If I were Socrates come back to life, I could not teach in the New York City school system.

Just look at my average day. I arrive at school 40 minutes early to take care of necessary business, as there is little time during regular school hours. This early business involves picking up attendance books, forms and reproducing lesson materials. . . . The bells start ringing. My students and my days are ruled by bells which ring loudly every 41 minutes with Pavlovian intensity. . . .

Paperwork includes recommendations for students, reports to the administration, cards for everything from misbehaving students to broken window shades, book receipts and subway passes. I must record and balance latenesses, absences and presences in a little red book containing attendance cards. I must read the daily announcements. . . .

I must collect, distribute and store books. I must make sure that the windows are not open more than six inches from the bottom . . . I must keep an eye out for signs of neglect, abuse, drug use and poor attendance. I must follow up problem students with the deans or the guidance counselors. I must correct essays, exams, homework and prepare students for state exams. I must keep records that prove I do all this.

In addition to noncompetitive salaries, the way teachers are often treated as glorified clerks, social workers, and babysitters is a further hurdle for talented people who still want to teach.

What would it take in today's economy to get National Merit Scholars to consider teaching as a viable profession in significant numbers? Competitive salaries? Less bureaucracy? More professional respect? Probably, all of the above; but it mostly comes down to money. When people are paid like professionals, they tend to command the respect of professionals.

Paying competitive salaries means paying teachers on a par with other professions open to talented college graduates. As was argued in Chapter 3, society has always paid the implicit opportunity costs of having very talented women in the classrooms, even though the amounts on the paychecks may have been small. What has changed is simply that the costs are now more explicit. If we want top college graduates in the schools rather than assembly-line workers, we are going to have to pay top dollars explicitly rather than implicitly.

Paying teachers the salaries necessary to attract the top of a college class is currently almost unthinkable because society still views teaching as a "women's profession" and has a hard time conceptualizing teachers as competitive professionals. An even more intractable problem is that neither taxpayers nor parents are about to give large sums of money to an institution that can't be held accountable for results. If schools are to function effectively in the economy of the next century, we have to understand how much the feminine economy has changed and what that implies for education. Schools have to learn to operate as a competitive institution rather than as a monopolist on the supply side of their talent market.

Market controls also have to be created on the demand side of the market—the customer has to be able to say no for the schools to function as a competitive institution. We have to decide who the primary customer is and put that customer in the driver's seat. Somebody needs to have "agency" with respect to the project of education. Considering the enormous investment that parents typically make in children and considering the social necessity of holding families responsible for producing the next generation of children, the logical agent to be in charge of a particular child's education is the child's parents. Whoever is in charge needs to have effective control over the demand side of education.

THE DEMAND SIDE OF EDUCATION

It is surely frustrating for many parents who can select the kind of vehicle they want to drive; live in the type of house, condominium, or apartment they prefer; purchase the clothes, food, and recreation they desire; but be so helpless with respect to the thing that many parents care most about as consumers—their children's education. What would it take to put parents in the driver's seat?

PARENT MANAGEMENT COUNCILS?

What doesn't work is bringing parents into school management collectively. Running schools by committee turns out to be at least as chaotic (if not more so) as running schools by bureaucracy. Either the parent councils are just window dressing with no real power, or they are an invitation for "Family Feud." One account from the *Chicago Tribune* tells the tale:

> The cafeteria at Chicago's Morgan Park High School was jammed, and tempers were rising. Only a week earlier, the school's new eleven-member, parent-led governing council had voted not to renew principal Walter Pilditch's contract. The move had sparked violent protests among students, parents and teachers, resulting in seven injuries and ten arrests.

Asking parents to be directly involved in managing schools is like saying consumers should collectively manage an automobile factory. Consumer A wants something different from consumer B. *Whose* car gets produced? *How* do consumers find time to manage a factory intelligently on a volunteer basis in addition to their regular jobs while fighting with each other and with a full-time management that has everything to lose? It isn't a winning concept.

MAGNET SCHOOLS AND PARENTAL CHOICE

Another nearly empty gesture toward putting parents in the driver's seat of education is to give parents some choices within the existing school system. Parents who can negotiate the school bureaucracy and can afford to transport their children to different schools may derive some benefit, but such policies do relatively little to provide parents relief from a monopolistic system. The same teachers and the same administrators are shuffled around the system and thus the same bureaucracy controls the whole show.

To the extent that magnet schools and parental-choice plans actually offer some better alternatives, parents then have to fight over who gets to take advantage of them. A parent in New York describes what parental choice is really like:

> When Donna Sands first sought her daughter Laura's admission to Public School 87 on Manhattan's Upper West Side, Ms. Sands wrote two letters of application. Then she got letters of recommendation from two college professors, four parents of children at the school, the directors of two pre-kindergartens that Laura had attended, Laura's teacher, Laura's speech therapist and "anybody I could think of who either knows me or had met Laura."
>
> After that, Ms. Sands called the director of admissions at P.S. 87 once a week and explained that she was not trying to be a pest but just wanted to know the status of Laura's application. She also volunteered to work in the school library and made it clear that she planned to be an involved parent.

This is parental choice?

CHARTER SCHOOLS

An increasing number of states (25 at last count) are allowing parents, teachers, and students to opt out of some of the rules and constraints on existing school systems by taking their per-student tax subsidy with them to a newly chartered school run by a private group. How much freedom a semi-autonomous charter school actually permits depends on the details of each state law and how many entrepreneurial groups emerge to start new schools. There could be a large number of charter schools in a particular area providing a wide range of educational choices, or there could be very few new schools operating under most of the same rules as the existing system.

One choice charter schools don't provide is the option of a "ticket upgrade"; that is, an option for parents to supplement tax funds with private resources (whether tuition payments made by parents or scholarships made available to poor students) and thereby expand their education options beyond the public system. Another choice that semipublic schools can't offer is the opportunity for a religiously oriented education. Since religious and ideological issues are responsible for much of the conflict currently tearing schools apart, many of the battles over public education will continue regardless of the extent of charter schools. In any event, if individual parents have to fight with both an old school bureaucracy that is to some degree still in charge of things and a new administrative variation, charter schools could simply compound the problems of concerned parents.

Charter schools essentially challenge parents and teachers who are dissatisfied with existing schools to "see if you can do it better within the parameters we lay down." That is like telling consumers that if they want a reliable car they have to build a new factory and manage the factory themselves, subject to various controls by the management of the existing factory (charters typically have to be approved by local school boards). Even if parents and teachers roll up their sleeves and build a school that succeeds in being a shining example of what parent-teacher cooperation can achieve, some politician, bureaucrat, or advocacy group is likely to say it is unfair to children in less successful schools. That was the charge made against the Bronx New School by a district superintendent, even though students in the school were selected by lottery.

One considerable advantage of charter schools is that whereas vouchers tend to go first to students who are already in private schools, charter schools pull students and money out of existing public schools proportionately. Charter schools thus have the advantage of getting over a transition effect that is difficult for any voucher proposal to overcome.

VOUCHERS: EFFECTIVE PERESTROIKA

"The Soviet economy is like a car that is in such bad shape an overhaul of the engine is not enough. It needs to be built from the chassis up." The report's conclusions support calls by radical reformers in the Soviet Union for Gorbachev to accelerate economic reforms, something he has been unwilling to do because the initial transition means worse economic problems in the short term.

*The system is in such desperate need of overhaul that even massive financial
assistance from the West "would be of little or no lasting value" without radical free-market reforms, concluded the study by the International Monetary
Fund, the World Bank and two other economic institutions.*

Many critics of public education argue that our schools also require a
version of *perestroika*, that before we can put more resources into the system the system must be substantially restructured, which is what advocates of vouchers have in mind. Education vouchers were first proposed by
Milton Friedman, a conservative, Nobel–Prize-winning economist, as a
way of retaining public finance of education while breaking the government's monopoly on the administration of education. Friedman's proposal was made in 1955, before dramatic changes within the family
economy and their effects on the schools made the problems of the public
schools considerably more urgent than they were in the 1950s.

Freely transferable education vouchers could create a competitive market on the demand side of education by enabling parents to make choices
with respect to their children's education with the same freedom they
have to choose other goods and services. Parents would be able to consider
scheduling, location, curriculum, their own children's needs and interests,
teacher rapport and effectiveness, a school's philosophy on social issues—
whatever factors have the highest priority for a particular family. The most
significant liberating effect would be that we wouldn't all have to agree on,
and therefore wouldn't have to fight over, every dimension of education
for every child any more than we all have to agree on what kind of car we
drive. The second liberating effect would be that education would be
made accountable to its most important customers; and once the system
is made accountable in a realistic way, it would become a more viable and
credible vehicle for the resources that schools need to compete in today's
environment.

Would parents sometimes make mistakes in judging which school is
best for their children? Undoubtedly, but who can do it better? Would
some parents choose schools with the fanciest athletic facilities or the
most frivolous courses and waste taxpayers' money? Probably, but it would
be difficult to exceed the current distortions of school budgets in favor of
athletics and frivolous courses that many schools already have. Would
some parents not care enough to try to find the right school for their children? Unfortunately, but those families need more help than any school
can give them.

SEPARATION OF CHURCH AND STATE

Allowing tax vouchers to be used at religious schools is a very troublesome constitutional issue. Clearly, however, we are never going to settle our religious differences with respect to education through the political process. It is precisely the desire of various groups to escape what they perceive as forced religious (actually secular) indoctrination of their children with their own tax dollars that is causing much of the turmoil. Given that everyone is forced by the state to pay school taxes, allowing people to use taxes to send children to schools consistent with their values is, quite arguably, a separation of church and state rather than a violation of it.

THE CHANGING POLITICS OF PUBLIC EDUCATION

Although school vouchers have been favored primarily by the conservative side of our political spectrum, the politics of vouchers are likely to change dramatically when conservative fundamentalists succeed in winning school-board elections or in passing parental-rights laws. Then it will be liberal parents who become concerned about educational policies that violate their values. Given the level of political organization and determination by the right to fight for its values, the left will have to devote equal time and resources to politicking in order to protect liberal values in their children's education. When all sides become exhausted from the trench warfare, letting families make their own choices about their children's education is likely to look good to both sides of the political spectrum.

LOGISTICS OF TRANSITION: GETTING THERE FROM HERE

Unfortunately, reforming the structure of public education by creating a competitive market for education encounters the same kind of transition problems as reforming Social Security or restructuring the Russian economy. It's hard to think of a way to do it without hurting people in the process. There is a threshold effect that is difficult to surmount. The first effect of vouchers as they are typically proposed (for example, California's Proposition 174 in 1993) would be to take money from public-school budgets and give it to students already in private schools. Since there wouldn't initially be very many slots open in private schools to which public-school students could transfer, the 90 percent of students currently in public schools would be stuck where they are with approximately 10 percent less financial support until more private schools are opened to accommodate them.

As with Social Security, there needs to be some kind of initial buyout to get over the threshold of reform. The buyout essentially would consist of compensating the people who currently pay twice for their education by paying both public-school taxes and private-school tuition. Raising taxes or decreasing public-school budgets by any amount to compensate the most affluent students for their educational choices is obviously not a politically attractive option. It might, however, be money well spent. The alternative is to let the schools decline to the point where there is no support for public-financed education by the people who pay most of the taxes. Then, the most disadvantaged will truly be left behind.

THE ISSUE OF EQUALITY

The most troubling argument against transferable vouchers is the fear that the poor will be left behind—that the middle class will take their public vouchers, augment them with private subsidies, and go to better schools. This argument goes to the heart of our democratic ideal that every child should have an equal chance in life and that public school is the best way to provide it. There is already a very wide gap, however, between the ideal and the reality because our education system is in fact highly segregated by economic class. The rich send their children to private schools and the middle classes move to the suburbs.

Even in comprehensive school districts with significant economic diversity, economic integration is frequently an illusion. In such school districts, it is middle-class parents who can afford the time to volunteer in the schools and get teachers' and administrators' attention, dominate the PTO boards and boosters groups, and know how to manipulate the bureaucracy. It is middle-class parents who hire tutors, send their children to summer or after-school enrichment classes, and spend hours helping with homework in what amounts to home schooling.

Middle-class parents have many ways of privatizing education for their own children within the public-school framework that can make it difficult for poor children to compete on an equal basis. Middle-class children thus tend to fill the honors and advanced-placement classes while poor children take the general and remedial classes. Pushing students through the same schoolhouse doors doesn't mean they get the same education.

THE PROXIMITY THEORY

The proximity theory of equal education hopes that activist, educated, and informed parents will make the schools work for children of the passive, uneducated, and uninformed. The argument against vouchers—that it would leave the poor behind—assumes that the poor aren't already being left behind and that middle-class parents effectively represent the interests of poor children within the educational bureaucracy. It is true that middle-class parents sitting on PTO boards or parental advisory committees can demand repairs of physical facilities and bring up parental concerns about bus schedules, vacations, starting times and various other administrative details. It is also true that middle-class parents volunteer considerable time in numerous extracurricular boosters groups (athletics, band, chorus, drama, etc.) and raise large amounts of money that are shared by all participants. Where students share common activities and facilities, the more advantaged and activist parents can look after the interests of all.

Where the advantaged can't take care of the disadvantaged is the venue where it matters most—in the classroom. Middle-class parents typically have the most information and the most concern about what is happening in the accelerated and college-prep classes where their own children are. Their children tell them which honors English teacher is having a nervous breakdown and losing control of the class, which teacher of advanced biology doesn't know how to use a microscope or how to dissect anything, or which guidance counselor is giving out-of-date advice about college admissions. The same parents, who may honestly have the welfare of the whole school at heart, look at each other blankly when the subject of general and remedial classes comes up (if it ever does) because they have no knowledge of what is happening in areas in which their own children aren't involved.

Given the typical level of parental frustration in trying to deal with problems with which they *are* familiar and have a direct interest, it is difficult to imagine how busy middle-class parents can take on problems about which they have little insight and little access to factual information. Even when middle-class parents are made aware of the concerns of poorer students, it can be very naive to assume their interests will coincide, as a conflict at Chicago's South Loop Elementary School illustrates:

War Between the Classes: The Prize Is a School

It is frustrating for educators when the poor and affluent share the same school. The problem isn't the children. It's their parents. One night last week Richard Stephenson, district superintendent for Chicago's new South Loop Elementary School, was trying to calm yet another raging quarrel over parent-council elections. One angry faction was from the integrated, middle-class Dearborn Park neighborhood, the other from a public-housing project nearby, Hilliard Homes.

> The condo-and-townhouse crowd fears South Loop will become a remedial school for the ghetto; the project parents worry it will turn into an exclusive academy for the well off. "It's chaos," Stephenson says. "These people have vastly different expectations about who this school is for."

Equality of opportunity is a very noble and moral goal, and any responsible democracy must do everything reasonable to provide it. The only thing worse than inequality, however, is a facade of equality with nothing behind it. Phantom equality creates enormous frustration by confusing issues and by casting blame on people for not taking advantage of something that doesn't really exist. Children who don't have parents serving as their advocates in the school system and augmenting their education with parental time and private resources aren't in the same game as children who have that kind of support.

A newspaper report on the attempts of the Montclair, New Jersey, school system to integrate its schools economically and racially illustrates some of the problems:

> If ever a town labored for integration, it is Montclair. Since a 1968 court desegregation order, this suburban enclave has struggled mightily for racial balance in its schools and to keep its neighborhoods stable . . .

> "What seems to have happened is that desegration in Montclair stopped at the schoolhouse door," said David Herron of the district's Human Relations Council.

> Montclair is not alone. Across the country, parents and civil rights groups have unearthed varying degrees of segregation within integrated districts.

While politicians, school officials, and parent councils were wringing their hands, individual parents provided a worm's eye view of the situation as they saw it:

> Some parents say the problem has less to do with race, and more to do with socioeconomic status. In a district in which parent requests for courses, houses, and even teachers are given serious weight, some say the real dividing line is between those who know how to use the system to their advantage and those who do not.

> Many say privately that for whatever reason, too many black parents fail to work the system.

> Joanne McGhee said her daughter has always struggled in school. But Ms. McGhee said once teachers stopped seeing her as a black single parent and began seeing her as someone who would closely monitor her child's progress, things improved somewhat.

"There are some racial problems, but I know white parents who are dissatisfied," she said. "You have to be a very educated consumer to deal with the Montclair school system. If you don't know the system, your kids are not going to make it through."

While "protecting the poor" is the argument most often given for resisting structural reform of public schools by teachers' unions and education bureaucracies, it is students from poor families who are most conspicuously underserved by the present system; and it is private, parochial schools in inner cities that have had some of the most notable successes at educating poor students. One writer, John Miller of the Manhattan Institute, cites a 1992 survey taken in Los Angeles that indicates that support for school vouchers increases the lower a family is on the economic ladder. One interpretation of such surveys is that poor parents are simply naive and don't understand what is best for their children, but that is a presumptuous interpretation.

The argument for rejecting a voucher system for the sake of protecting the poor rests on the assumption that public schools are an effective mechanism for transferring educational resources from the middle class to the poor. That is a very questionable assumption considering the energy and savvy that many middle-class parents devote to skimming the system of the best teachers and programs for their own children. Poor children actually may be subsidizing the middle class in terms of effective per-pupil expenditures in schools that they mutually attend.

In any event, resource transfers could be achieved more efficiently by scaling school vouchers inversely to income; that is, giving poorer students larger vouchers. (Some handicapped children would obviously need larger vouchers to meet their special needs.) An additional way of ameliorating inequalities would be the formation of schools that provide opportunities for students and/or parents to work for part of the tuition—a possibility that would surely occur to entrepreneurial schools in poor neighborhoods if they had the flexibility to implement it.

Why shouldn't poor parents want the chance to try to find a better education deal for their children than many of them currently have? What do children who are in schools riddled with drugs, guns, gangs, and inertia have to fear from "being left behind?" What do students in schools where less than 40 percent of ninth-graders graduate from high school and less than 1 in 10 graduate with reading ability above the national average (to cite some of the worst-case statistics) have to lose from a voucher system? There are substantial reasons for believing that the kinds of educational choices represented by vouchers would help the poor most of all.

WORKING THE SYSTEM: THE PRIVATE COSTS OF PUBLIC EDUCATION

"Working the system" is the hidden cost of public education. What parents can't buy directly with money they try to buy indirectly with time and manipulation. Parents of children in public school are like the people who had to stand in long lines for bread and toilet paper in the old communist system. Official prices were low, but you had to pay with time or bribes to actually acquire anything.

There is now a kind of black market in education in which parents try to get through the back door of the public school what isn't available through the front door. It's called "guerrilla parenting" and embodies everything from organizing school boycotts, to sitting in the principal's office demanding attention to a problem, to giving expensive gifts to teachers at Christmas, to setting up a blackboard at home and compensating for what doesn't get taught at school.

Even the very ordinary activities of family involvement in children's education and activities can absorb large amounts of parental time and resources. A week in the life of a student's parents can be unbelievably hectic:

> You say *you're* busy?
>
> You can't begin to know what busy is until you take a peek at the entries for the next two weeks in Vera Darby's date book.
>
> End-of school parties, awards banquets, recitals, teacher- and volunteer-appreciation days, T-ball games, Girl Scout and Cub Scout get-togethers, and field trips leave Darby and other parents little time to catch their breath. . . .
>
> It would be one thing if all parents had to do was show up at the engagements on their calendars and wait to be entertained.
>
> But a date book can't show the number of carrots they have to peel for veggie trays, the number of watermelon balls they throw into the fruit bowl, or the liters of ginger ale they pour into the punch.
>
> "It really tests your organizational skills," said Darby, whose involvement with the activities of her three children, ages 15, 9, and 8, keep her on the go. "I have to keep a running list daily of what has to be done, tick them off, and go on to the next."

Beyond routine parental-support activities, parents are buying "ticket upgrades" for their children's public-school educations in various ways. Parents are cleaning, shoveling, and even teaching to aid schools. According to *The Wall Street Journal*:

> Many parents are learning that their children's free public education carries a hidden cost: Doing it yourself or doing without.

Today's school volunteers have moved miles beyond bake sales. Susan Natale, New York City mother of two, spearheaded construction of a playground at Public School 9 on the Upper West Side of Manhattan. Appalled by rusty, jagged equipment, she proposed replacing it in 1987. Monitoring the project daily, she dickered with city agencies and contractors throughout its construction. "It took six years—I almost died," she says, waving her phone bills from that period. In the worst month, 658 calls were made from her apartment, most of them on school business.

Increasingly, threadbare public-school systems are turning to parents for goods and services that taxpayers have stopped providing. Walk the halls of an urban school these days, and it's common to see parent-volunteers patching, scrubbing, cooking, teaching and otherwise filling gaps in budgets that no longer cover the basics, much less the frills . . .

Jacquie Boslet, president of the parent-teacher association council in Irvine, [California] recently reported to the school board that parents had donated 280,624 hours of service this school year . . . Calculated at $8 an hour—which the PTA estimates schools would have had to pay outsiders—that amounts to $2.2 million in sweat equity.

Some busy parents hire "volunteers" to work for them in their children's classrooms. In lieu of or in addition to sweat equity, parents supply significant amounts of financial equity to their children's schools. Parents raise or contribute money to buy computers, pay instructors, and build facilities, all of which increase the real costs of public education and raise serious questions about the actual equality of opportunity that public schools are supposed to provide. Critics of such parental activities argue that activist parents should be devoting their energies to lobbying legislatures to fund all schools adequately. From a parent's standpoint, however, putting one's time, energy, and money into a local school or into a particular classroom where the results are visible, relatively controllable, and directly relevant to one's own children is a very different project than getting involved in legislative politics.

THE STUDENTS WHO WILL BE LEFT BEHIND

Perhaps the most shocking news about schools in recent years is the number of students and teachers who feel physically threatened at school and the extent to which some schools are becoming armed camps. Every day, 135,000 children reportedly take guns to school. "Kids and Guns: A Report from America's Classroom Killing Grounds," was a *Newsweek* cover story. The problem of weapons and violence in schools isn't restricted to New York City, said *Newsweek*, but extends throughout the country. Even ele-

Stand by Me

mentary students in fourth and fifth grades have guns. In what is turning into a modern version of the "Wild West," a Florida Senate committee approved a bill that would allow all teachers to carry stun guns to class for self-defense. Even Joe Clark, the charismatic and physically imposing principal of *Stand and Deliver*, patrolled the halls with a baseball bat. Students prone to violence are what everyone, rich and poor, wants to escape. They will be the students that no conventional school will accept or retain if it has a choice.

In areas where a significant number of students come from homes in which family discipline has broken down, teachers have no choice but to take measures to protect themselves. Teaching in an environment in which one has to worry about physical safety, however, requires special facilities and special teachers with special training. Parents who are still in control of their children (which includes most poor parents) are going to be increasingly desperate to get out of situations in which their students' very lives, not to mention their educations, are at risk or where controlling the risk means running a school like a military operation.

TOUGH KIDS NEED TOUGH TEACHERS

Realistically, some schools need to be designed for students who require the discipline of a boot camp. Parents or guardians who for whatever reasons are unable to cope would, in many cases, probably welcome a school that could provide safety, order, and strict discipline for their children *before* children drop out or are expelled and get into so much trouble they wind up in reform school or in prison. Many families in the recent past have relied on the military to provide the discipline and maturing experiences that neither home nor public school could offer.

Before the end of the Cold War and its accompanying military cutbacks, kids could drop out of high school or barely scrape through school, join the army, grow up under the direction of a drill sergeant, get a GED and/or learn a trade skill, and go on to make something of themselves. The military has served as an education option that provided structure, discipline, a reference in the form of an honorable discharge, and vocational training. With the post-Cold War downsizing of the military, however, an important educational and developmental option has been foreclosed for many families, especially the less affluent. What will take its place?

One option might be variations on the kinds of private military schools that more affluent parents who can afford it already utilize. The kind of flexibility that a fully transferable voucher system could provide would permit parents to opt for a wide variety of educational choices.

SHOULD EDUCATION STILL BE TAX FINANCED?

In response to a proposal to convert Social Security to a parental dividend, childless individuals may well ask why they should be taxed to pay for children's education at all. It's a fair question, but several points need to be considered.

First, we had public education before we had Social Security. Public finance of education isn't something invented by the Great Society of the 1960s or by the New Deal of the 1930s. Whereas Social Security began in 1935 and was expanded to the system we have now in the 1960s and 1970s, compulsory education was adopted by the state of Massachusetts in 1852 and extended to all states by 1918. At a time when children were still caring for their own parents in old age, voters decided that publicly financed education was a good investment for society as a whole. We didn't try to educate people for as long then as we do now; but our economy is now considerably more complex, knowledge driven, and affluent than it was in 1918; and education has become considerably more important for society as well as for individuals.

Given that there will always be a need for some kind of safety net for the elderly who have neither children nor other resources to support themselves and given that the next generation of children will have to finance all of society's safety nets, children's education would still represent an investment in society's collective old age, albeit a considerably reduced one. But the ability to pay for safety nets is just one of the social effects of having an educated population. Other benefits include living in a society that is generally more literate and more productive and has lower crime rates and better informed voters, factors that are surely even more compelling now than they were in 1918. Democracy requires an educated citizenry.

Second, there are several unique factors that argue for public financing of education. For obvious reasons, the capital markets don't work for financing investment in human capital as they do for tangible capital, a fact that tends to skew investment in inefficient ways. Like most investors, parents have an acute liquidity problem—their financial needs tend to be greatest in years when cash flow from the investment is non-existent. Unlike other kinds of investors, however, parents don't have access to the capital markets to finance their investments—most parental expenditures have to come out-of-pocket.

Even though education has a long-run economic payoff similar to or greater than the payoff of business investment, banks don't finance education until the college level and even then only with government guarantees.

The only educational investment most banks are willing to make without government subsidies or guarantees is for medical students. Without tax finance, much economically productive investment in education would be impossible.

These were the kinds of arguments that led Milton Friedman, one of the most conservative of economists, to conclude that financing of education up to some basic level is a legitimate and necessary government function. As Friedman noted:

> Investments in human beings cannot be financed on the same terms or with the same ease as investment in physical capital. It is easy to see why. If a money loan is made to finance investment in physical capital, the lender can get some security for the loan in the form of a mortgage or residual claim to the physical asset itself and he can count on realizing at least part of his investment in case of default by selling the physical asset. If he makes a comparable loan to increase the earning potential of a human being, he clearly cannot get any comparable security. In a non-slave state the individual embodying the investment cannot be sold.

EDUCATION AND THE AMERICAN DREAM

Education has always been a major component of the American dream since the founding of the Puritan colonies, a dream that a recent book calls "almost a secular religion." The dream of building a democratic society in which every person no matter how lowly born could get an education and could go as far as talent and ambition could take him or her has been an inspiration to generations of Americans. It's not a dream to be tampered with lightly because the dream has been a reality for many of our forebears. It is difficult to understand or to explain why a system that has seemed to work so well for so many for so long now has so many apparent problems.

Despite the primary focus of this book on family issues, it would be an overstatement to attribute all of the negative changes in education to the breakup of the traditional family. There are other forces at work as well. One factor that transcends family issues is the reality that economic development and technological advances now require much more from our education system in terms of both length of education and inclusion of all children across the economic spectrum.

Another variable that has changed is the size per se of public-school systems associated with urbanization. In small communities in which everybody knows everybody, including teachers, school-board members, and janitors, parents have more information about what goes on in their schools and more direct control over school policies. There are fewer layers of bureaucracy, and the political process is more manageable. A small community creates a sort of "natural-monopoly" situation when there aren't enough students for more than one school to operate effectively, and that is the model on which we have built our whole system. But what works on a small scale can be a disaster on a large scale.

Another significant factor is simply the passage of time since 1918. As school systems increase in size and as management becomes distanced from parental oversight, school budgets become increasingly attractive targets for seekers of favors, patronage, and graft. It takes time for predators to learn how to infiltrate a system, but they eventually learn. Over time there is an almost inexorable tendency for large public-school budgets to become, in the words of one review commission, "a trough of patronage."

Like all institutions that exist over time and are big enough to be lucrative targets, public education has been subjected to the subtle but almost inevitable process of institutional sclerosis that economist Mancur Olson describes in *The Rise and Decline of Nations* as "the rich nation's disease." Wherever power and resources are concentrated, people gradually organize themselves for purposes of increasing their shares of the pie or for defending their shares of the pie. Organizational costs and conflicts tend to increase and consume institutional resources until there is nothing left worth the cost of fighting for it.

Diseconomies of scale, institutional sclerosis, and many other changes in our economy and in our society have affected our schools; but surely the most relevant factor is the enormous changes that have occurred in the feminine economy. Before there can be schools, there have to be teachers. Before there can be teachers, there have to be pupils; and before there can be pupils, there have to be parents and families.

Where did we get the idea that we can make schools parent-proof and teacher-proof? Given that parents and teachers are the essential elements of the process, how did we get to a situation in which the basic strategy for educating our children is a system in which teachers have little control and parents have virtually none except through incessant political fighting, back-door manipulation, and guerilla action? However we got there, it is increasingly obvious that it's a dead-end street and that turning the school bus around is necessary, though it won't be painless, easy, or cheap.

Putting individual parents in control of their children's education can't cure all of the problems; but it could kill three birds with one stone. It could:

1. Reduce the pressures on today's parents who are already enormously stressed trying to cover the bases at home and at work without also having to manage their children's education under very frustrating conditions.
2. Convert the basic structure of our school system from monopoly to competition, thereby enabling the system to function in the competitive environment with which it now has to deal.
3. Break up the concentrations of power that cause the diseconomies of scale and serve as targets for the conflicts that contribute to institutional sclerosis.

IT IS PARENTS

Students come from the same place babies come from; that is, from parents, even the relatively poor of whom typically make large investments in their children (see Chapter 5). Parents are their children's first teachers. It is parents who have to produce healthy, motivated children before the education process can begin. It is parents who have to watch out for the interests of each child as he or she moves through the long developmental process of becoming an adult. It is parents who have the ultimate responsibility for making the education process work for their children.

Effects of handicaps such as poverty and discrimination on a child's chances in life aren't to be underestimated; but the one thing that all children have to have is a family to guide them, support them, inspire them, and run interference for them. It is true that some families can't or don't do their jobs and that some schools must be designed for unparented children, but parents who are making enormous parental investments in their children can hardly be comfortable with schools designed for the unparented. Most schools need to operate on the assumption that parents are doing their job.

Columnist William Raspberry notes that, while it is a media myth that more black men of college age are in prison than in college, it appears that something significant has happened to the drive of young people to overcome the obstacles and temptations that stand in the way of getting an education. While acknowledging that bad schools, limited opportunity, poverty, and discrimination all play a role, Raspberry asserts that possessing cocaine is a choice and that, "To a greater extent than we are willing to acknowledge, jail is a choice."

In contrast to the social dysfunction of many of today's disaffected youth, Raspberry recalls W.E.B. Du Bois's description of an extraordinary thirst for education by one of the most disadvantaged groups in all of history—America's newly freed slaves following emancipation. "These newly free men displayed what Du Bois called 'a frenzy for schools,'" Raspberry notes, and suggests: "Shouldn't we be asking ourselves what happened to that frenzy for education—and how we might begin to get it back?"

How do we get back the passion that poor immigrant children and newly freed slaves once had for education? Newly freed slaves obviously didn't get their passion for education *from* schools they had never attended—they must have taken it *to* school with them. If they took it with them, where did they get it? Where else could young people have gotten it but from their families?

Teenage drug possession is a choice, as is teenage pregnancy; but they are choices made by individuals hardly old enough to know what their other choices are unless someone has given them a sense of the possibilities of life and instilled sufficient character to resist early temptations. Since instilling the character and passion necessary for getting an education has to be done primarily at the family level, it doesn't make sense to have an educational system that takes most of the important decisions away from parents. If parents are to take responsibility for the rearing of their children, they have to be able to make the important decisions. The most effective way to bring parents into the education process and to reconnect the primary source of demand for education (families) with the primary source of supply (teachers) is to break the public-school monopoly and give parents a real voice in how their children are educated.

10 WELFARE REFORM AND THE FAMILY

SOME MATTERS OF PERSPECTIVE

This chapter suggests several aspects of the preceding arguments that can help frame the welfare issue:

FRAME 1: WELFARE IN REVERSE

Most of the support for welfare programs is based on the desire to help poor children who obviously are not responsible for their fate, while much of the opposition to welfare is based on the belief that public welfare programs encourage behavior that results in more poor children; but neither those who want more government support for poor families nor those who want less seem to be aware of how small are the numbers they argue about relative to other policies that adversely affect families.

As has been noted at various points in the preceding discussion, the family's caretaking functions have been squeezed by numerous legal, tax, and administrative trends in recent decades:

1. Income-tax deductions for family dependents have shrunk about 34 percent in real dollars since 1960.
2. Our tax system has shifted relentlessly toward taxes that allow no deductions for family dependents. Payroll taxes have grown from 2 percent of wages and salaries in 1937 to 15.3 percent and now exceed income taxes for 70 percent of American taxpayers.

3. The Social Security system has grown to the point that it is currently transferring over $360 billion per year out of the family and expects to transfer over $21 trillion (an amount that exceeds the total tangible wealth of the U.S. economy) during the lifetimes of people currently in the system.
4. A substantial tax on marriage has been introduced into our tax code for many couples.
5. Entitlements of family caretakers to spousal support in the event of marriage breakdown have been substantially reduced while the rate of divorce has risen to almost 50 percent, making the role of family caretaker a much riskier occupation.
6. Public-school systems have grown very large and bureaucratic. Parents have little control over the schools their children are required to attend except through politicking, going to school with the student, or suing, all of which add to the parental frustration, expense, and fatigue of trying to rear children.

Most of the deprivileging of families just outlined has differential effects according to income class, primarily to the disadvantage of the working poor:

1. Relative to income, any flat deduction for dependents is more important to the poor than to the rich.
2. Payroll taxes are levied only on wages and salaries—not profits, interest, dividends, or capital gains. Furthermore, there is a cap on the amount of income subject to payroll taxes ($68,400 in 1998). Only wage and salary earners with incomes under the cap pay the 15.3 percent payroll tax that makes no allowance for dependents.
3. Relative to net worth, lifetime transfers of wealth out of the family through the Social Security system are about twice as large for poor families as for rich families (a ratio of 7.6:1 as compared with approximately 3.8:1—see Table A.4 in the Appendix).
4. The biggest impact of the marriage tax relative to income falls on two-earner families with combined incomes of about $20,000, in which case couples may be subject to an 18 percent tax on their income for being married.
5. Community property laws can protect spouses in no-fault divorces when there is substantial property to distribute but are of no help when couples don't own property. Except for the relatively rich, no-fault divorce has eliminated much of the protection that the marriage contract has traditionally provided for the caretaking roles.

6. The rich can opt out of public schools, and middle-class parents have more ways of getting what they want from public-school bureaucracies than do poor parents—see Chapter 9. It is poor families who are usually stuck with the worst consequences of school monopoly and bureaucratization.

During a period when the job of childrearing has been getting longer and more complex, families in general and poor families in particular have been hit with one inadvertent effect of public policy after another. If we wanted to make the poor, working family extinct, it would be hard to come up with a more comprehensive plan of attack than the reverse welfare that has encroached on our retirement system, our school system, our tax code, and our divorce laws. This conclusion emerges without even getting into ways in which welfare programs may be discouraging marriage and encouraging family disintegration among the poor.

FRAME 2: THE FAMILY IS A WEALTH-PRODUCING INSTITUTION!

Another point to be remembered before getting into welfare specifics is that the family as an institution isn't a charity case. Somehow in public discussion, "family" often gets equated with "poor," and "poor" tends to be equated with "dysfunctional." The truth is that in a very real sense most families are neither poor nor economically dysfunctional.

Even in the bottom third of our income distribution, the average family invests a small fortune—$146,180 in cash outlays for the first child in 1997 dollars according to USDA statistics and another $283,500 worth of parental time according to the estimates in Table 5.3(a)—just to rear a child to age 18. College tuition, extraordinary medical expenses, and career compromises can easily cost much more. If a couple were to save all the extra money they could earn and accumulate in lieu of bearing and rearing two children, the same "poor" parents would, by the most conservative estimate, be likely to have a net worth over 1.3 million (in 1997 pre-tax dollars—see Table A.3 in the Appendix) at age 67. Comparable numbers for the middle and upper thirds of the income distribution are $2.0 million and $3.4 million, respectively.

These numbers are dependent on the details of a family's specific situation, but they aren't far-fetched. Parental costs are not small numbers, and parental investors are not small players in our economy. Business investors with net worths of $3.4 million or $2.0 million or even $1.3 million would never be considered charity cases, even when they are receiving substantial protections and subsidies at the expense of taxpayers and consumers.

Why, then, are businesses and families perceived and treated so differently? Why are various forms of business assistance considered economic investment while family assistance is thought of as public charity? Presumably, it is because businesses are perceived as active and affluent while families are perceived as passive and poor. Families *appear* to be poor because of their particular circumstances:

\ ■ Parents have no access to the capital~~children~~ markets for financing their investments. Whereas a business can do most of its investing with borrowed money, parents have to pay everything out of their own pockets. In terms of cash flow during the childrearing years, many families and most single parents really are poor.

2 ■ Unlike businesses, families have no contractual claim on the wealth they produce. In terms of having any recognized claim to a return on their investments of time and money, parents are in fact destitute.

The purpose of the analysis pursued in the preceding chapters has been to address the second problem; that is, the family's long-run contractual arrangements between parents and children and between mothers and fathers. No attempt will be made here to undertake an analysis of the short-run cash problems that are the focus of most welfare programs, except to note some connections between the two kinds of problems. Clearly, addressing one kind of problem doesn't solve the other. Parental dividends in the retirement years won't necessarily solve the family's cash-flow problems in the childrearing years, though they may help considerably by encouraging parents to work out their marriage problems for the sake of the children and by providing a substantial incentive for custodial parents to be cooperative and for noncustodial parents to be financially responsible. Given that single-parent families are a major factor in the poverty of children, this effect could prove quite helpful in reducing the numbers of children living in poverty.

Writing a social contract that restores the family's claim to a portion of whatever income-earning wealth it succeeds in producing could also serve to strengthen and reinforce family-assistance programs and social safety nets for families. Explicitly recognizing the investment role that families play in our economy would, for starters, change the category in which family assistance is generally perceived from "charity" to something akin to a small-business assistance program. More substantively, providing real incentives for families to do their jobs well could change the dynamics of family assistance.

It is understandable that taxpayers, who in many cases aren't too far away from poverty themselves, resist giving money to poor families when there are no visible incentives for using family resources well and no visible penalties for welfare families who waste taxpayers' money. Business charity isn't viewed the same way as family charity because, among other things, there are strong incentives in place for efficient use of whatever resources a business receives, regardless of the source. Whether revenue comes from government subsidies or from sales at the cash register, there are future profits to be made when resources are used responsibly and potential profits to be lost when revenues are misspent. Businesses are held accountable in a substantive way for what they do with resources. Providing a degree of economic accountability for families could serve to make public assistance to families both more effective and more politically viable.

FRAME 3: THE DEMAND SIDE OF POVERTY

William Julius Wilson, a Harvard University sociologist, has made an extensive and provocative argument that family poverty and family breakdown are largely due to trends on the demand side of the labor market, particularly in the inner cities. Wilson maintains that increases in joblessness and illegitimacy rates of the ghetto underclass are primarily due to structural changes in the labor market that have vastly reduced the demand for workers in the inner city. Good jobs have either left the country or moved to the suburbs, taking with them middle-class workers, middle-class role models, middle-class institutions such as churches and civic groups, and the services of most professionals. The major thrust of Wilson's analysis is that when jobs and community institutions disappear or move away from people babies tend to be born to single mothers for the simple reason that there is a shortage of fathers with the ability to support families.

Wilson's point, that poor families need accessible jobs and that creating jobs where people are is a crucial step in breaking cycles of poverty, is certainly well taken. There are, however, two ways for people to be poor. One way is to be qualified for jobs that aren't available. The other is to be unqualified for jobs that do exist. Disappearance of good jobs from the U.S. economy for people who are healthy and willing to work but lack a college education has received considerable attention in the media as a cause of the growing inequality of incomes in recent decades. There is apparently much truth in that part of the story.

The other side of the poverty story is the supply side of the labor market, which is the focus here. Creating good jobs won't do our economy any good in the future if no one produces good workers to fill them. Producing qualified workers is a project that gets progressively more difficult as economic development advances. Parents no longer just have to worry about keeping children alive or getting them through sixth grade or even through high school in order to find a place in our economy. While creating jobs on the demand side of the labor market has long been a major concern of the institutions that manage national economic policy, as it should be, what generally gets ignored is that the supply side of the labor market is *equally* important. The supply side of the labor market is primarily the family. A basic fact of economics is that supply and demand have to work together like two blades of a pair of scissors—one blade alone won't cut it.

FRAME 4: THE BLAME GAME

Much of the welfare argument is about whose fault it is when people are poor. Conservatives tend to blame individuals and liberals tend to blame society. Perhaps we should consider the possibility that a lot of poverty may be neither the individual's fault nor society's fault, at least not in any simple way. If parental responsibility and parental investment are as important to a child's chances in life as many people believe and as the argument developed here suggests (see especially Chapter 4), much of what happens to people in life is the luck of the draw with respect to who their parents are—and not just how rich their parents are, but also how effective and responsible they are.

Being born to irresponsible parents is obviously not any child's fault. It may not be the fault of the parents either—they may have grown up under very disadvantageous circumstances themselves and never had much of a chance in life either. Does that necessarily mean it's society's (that is to say everybody's) fault? It is only society's fault if there are things that a society can realistically do to eliminate the differential effects of responsible and irresponsible parenting. It's not clear in many cases that such remedies generally exist.

THE MURRAY HYPOTHESES

Some people argue that there is very little any society can do to help poor families because means-tested relief programs ultimately prove counterproductive by creating a culture of unemployment and illegitimacy. Any discussion of welfare reform has to deal with the argument Charles Murray makes in his book, *Losing Ground*, in which he contends that welfare programs are destroying the economic classes they are intended to help by rewarding behavior that is the opposite of what people need to do to avoid or to escape poverty. Most people concerned about the poor would surely wish for a better way to provide assistance than to tell very poor women, in effect, that if they want medical care, housing subsidies, food stamps, and living allowances, then what they need to do is have a baby at 15, don't get married, and don't get a job. To think that people don't respond to such perverse incentives is to assume that poor people are totally stupid, passive, and out of control of their lives.

In one of the odder twists in the public-policy dialogue, that latter assessment is pretty much what Murray argues in his subsequent book, *The Bell Curve*, co-authored with Richard Herrnstein. In *The Bell Curve*, Murray and Herrnstein attempt to prove that much of the behavior that causes poverty is genetically determined and therefore impervious to any social or educational programs that might be reasonably devised. Because certain ethnic groups are disproportionately poor, Murray and Herrnstein also have to argue that a bell curve of inherited talents exists among ethnic groups as well. According to Murray and Herrnstein, it isn't just individuals who are genetically doomed to poverty, but entire ethnic populations.

While in one book Murray argues that the poor are rational and entrepreneurial enough to take advantage of welfare programs in every sly way imaginable, in the other book he professes to prove that the behavior of poor people is so genetically determined that they lack even the most basic perception of cause and effect and therefore are beyond help. Clearly, the argument developed in the preceding chapters for treating families, including poor families, as potentially rational investors and providing positive economic incentives for responsible family behavior is aligned with Murray's first hypothesis and disavows the second.

If Murray's first hypothesis is correct, poor people do respond behaviorally to economic incentives in their personal lives as well as in the marketplace. This is not to deny that a bell curve of inherited talents exists among individuals. It is to deny that the kind of genetic talent distribution that exists among individuals is replicated among ethnic groups and that it determines the income distribution irrevocably in the way that Murray and Herrnstein describe.

Murray and Herrnstein overlooked significant aspects of America's ethnic history. In his book, *Ethnic America*, Thomas Sowell examines the IQ records of various ethnic groups that were at one time both poor and "stupid" as measured by army tests of draftees in World War I. Jewish, Italian, and Polish immigrants (ethnic groups that now have above-average IQ scores and above-average incomes) tested significantly below the average only a few generations ago. Since genetic evolution doesn't happen in that kind of time span, those ethnic groups must have learned how to make better use of a given genetic endowment, both in real life and in the taking of standardized tests. They didn't learn it overnight, but they learned it within a few generations.

A hard-line conservatism that defends the status quo by arguing that the poor are too genetically handicapped to change their behavior in positive ways but clever and adaptable enough to change their behavior in negative ways contradicts itself. A soft liberalism that assumes the poor will take advantage of every opportunity for positive changes in behavior while ignoring all incentives for negative behavior is equally contradictory. It isn't contradictory, however, to think it is possible to help poor people change their lives in positive ways with behavioral incentives that are consistently constructive at the level at which people live.

Considering the number and the magnitudes of adverse trends that have been pressing on families, particularly poor families, welfare programs can hardly be blamed for most of the family disintegration that has occurred in our late-twentieth-century society. If we *really* want to help poor families, we need to reverse the policies that are making it so much harder for the working family to be an economically viable institution (see Frame 1 above).

Ways to Help Families, Especially Poor Families

1. Reverse specific changes in the tax code that hit poor families especially hard (items 1 and 4).
2. Deposit payroll taxes in parental trust funds and convert Social Security to a parental dividend that would keep payroll taxes (item 2) within the family and return to families a portion of the wealth they produce (item 3).
3. Revise the divorce laws that serve as the prenuptial contract in our culture to increase protection for family caretakers and for the parents of family caretakers in ways that are consistent with the lives of modern families (item 5).
4. Provide transferable school vouchers that put control of children's education in the hands of the people who have the ultimate responsibility for the development of each child, thus making schools and parents allies rather than the adversaries they so frequently are (item 6).

None of these actions would address the short-run concerns of welfare programs directly, but they could have considerable indirect and long-run effects. Providing positive incentives for families to do their jobs well could decrease the numbers of neglected children, reduce the ranks of single-parent families that are a major cause of child poverty, and encourage the involvement of noncustodial parents. In the long run, putting an economic base under the family's caretaking functions should make welfare programs and safety nets less necessary by addressing a major determinant of everyone's chances in life—the level of parental investment in children's welfare.

11 A SUMMARY ARGUMENT

THE MOST VEXING QUESTION

When a group called the Voices of Florida (comprised of 6 newspapers, 11 television stations, and Florida Public Radio) conducted detailed interviews with the four leading Republican presidential candidates in the spring of 1996, all of the candidates said family values were very important, but none was willing to say anything about policies. Reporters covering the interviews noted the contrast between rhetorical emphasis on family values and the conspicuous absence of any specific proposals:

> The presidential candidates are mindful of this abiding concern, sprinkling their stump speeches with references to "family values" and positioning themselves as champions on the issue.
>
> There is a problem, however. There is little consensus among candidates and voters on what the term means.
>
> For a few, they include positions on such hot-button issues as abortion, gay rights, and school prayer. For others, such things are irrelevant.
>
> Perhaps most important, neither candidates nor voters readily propose specific policies that might answer the public's worries . . .
>
> The most vexing question for candidates and voters alike seemed to be what the next president could actually do to strengthen family values.

At least the Republicans have been willing to focus attention on the family as an important issue. In his recent book, *We're Right, They're Wrong,* political consultant James Carville scolds his fellow Democrats for timidity in acknowledging the social problems associated with family dysfunction. Carville argues that issues such as the effects of absent fathers on children's welfare shouldn't be left to the Republicans and that Democrats ignore such issues at their peril. The time has come for all of us, wherever we are on the political spectrum, to get serious about the value of family, which means revising some of the basic assumptions of our culture.

It's hard to argue with thinkers who have been dead for centuries, but some very influential ghosts continue to argue with us. The extent to which the caretaking half of our economy has been submerged by the dominant minds of Western culture is a major part of the reason why family issues now seem so perplexing. Recalling where we've come from intellectually and how recent the emergence of women from the home and from the cultural mystique surrounding women actually is provides considerable perspective on our current problems.

THOSE VULGAR PHILOSOPHERS

Contrary to popular impression, calling women's reproductive and caretaking labor "shit work" is not a vulgarism that originated with radical feminists in the twentieth century. Male philosophers have, in effect, been doing so since the beginning of intellectual history. Even those misogynistic Enlightenment philosophers of the seventeenth and eighteenth centuries, cited both respectfully and despairingly throughout this analysis, can't be held responsible for originating the intellectual devaluation of women's work. Such denigration goes all the way back to the Greeks and continues, with some notable detours, up to the intellectual present. Jean Bethke Elshtain's analysis of the philosophical treatment of women's private roles provides a useful summary.

Plato, the father of Western political philosophy, reduced human procreation to an activity that man shares with the beasts, with all "inferior subrational existence," and relegated women in general to the same class as slaves as far as having any right to a public voice was concerned. Plato would allow women into the elite Guardian class of his Republic, but only if they were willing to be disconnected from their children and from their sexual identities as females. Aristotle followed Plato with a rigid concept of women's inherent inferiority—they were to be viewed as an inferior life form, a kind of misbegotten man. Culture, according to these philosophers, was something separate from nature. Culture was where rational men were free to think and to act and to play public roles. Nature was where women were "unfree" and required to perform their private biological functions.

A major detour from the Greeks' misogyny was provided by early Christianity, which challenged the superiority of public roles over private life at a time when public life under the late Roman empire was conspicuously debased and corrupt. By insisting that "the last should be first," early Christianity and the writings of St. Augustine elevated everyday life and provided status and language for the caring and nurturing functions of women. In the medieval period, however, St. Thomas Aquinas resurrected the texts of Aristotle and returned the church to the Greek emphasis on the inherent superiority of masculine roles in public life and, by comparison, the inherent inferiority of feminine roles in private life.

In the Renaissance era, Martin Luther challenged Aristotelian church dogma concerning man's obligations to public religious authority. In the subsequent Enlightenment era, philosophers challenged men's obligations to monarchical authority. Men were to be free, rational, independent individuals in charge of their own destiny vis-a-vis their God and their state. Neither the Protestant Reformation nor the democratic revolution, however, effectively challenged the "natural" obligations of women to accept male authority. That challenge awaited the feminist movement of the twentieth century, which followed up the suffragettes' demand for political freedom with demands for economic freedom as well. It is the freedom of women to choose their economic roles (what they do with their bodies and their time) that now threatens the assumption, so fundamentally embedded in our culture, that the public, rational, competitive (i.e., masculine) economy can free ride on a private, irrational, altruistic (i.e., feminine) economy.

It is against this cultural backgound that our political system must cope with the consequences of the breakdown of the gender caste system. We literally have to invent some new ways of thinking about a society in which women are free to make the same kinds of choices as men and an economy in which family work must compete with the marketplace for everyone's time and energy. If we want the family's traditional caretaking work to continue to get done in the next century, it will have to be consciously transferred from the category of inferior, irrational "shit work" to which Plato and his many heirs have consigned it. The suggestion made here is that for purposes of understanding where reproduction fits into the economic scheme of things the appropriate category is investment.

RHETORIC AND REALITY

There is, of course, another rhetorical thread in Western culture concerning women's work and the family—the romantic thread that emphasizes the emotional dimensions of family life. The romantic thread, developed primarily through art and literature, idealizes family relationships. In its extreme form, the family is characterized as a lifelong love affair among saints with the maternal role exalted to something slightly below the angels. Needless to say, such idealizations ignore reality as much as the philosophical models that have viewed women's roles as inferior and subrational. Lifelong love affairs between husbands and wives and between parents and children do exist, but many families fall short of the romantic ideal. When families fall short, society has to cope with the practical consequences.

As an institution, the family never has operated on love alone, but has in fact been held together by very substantive economic ties. Increasing costs of family functions in modern economies make it even less likely that a model that relies solely on affective emotion will be viable in the future. No amount of romantic rhetoric can hide the costs of reproduction in our kind of economy. Somewhere between the patriarchal characterization of reproduction as a function on the level of the beasts and the romantic idealization of families as an association of saints we have to find a way of reducing the schizophrenia in the way we think about families.

AN INSTITUTION IN TRANSITION

There is a peculiar tension between an old idea system from which the energy is gone but which has the heaped-up force of custom, tradition, money, and institutions behind it, and an emerging cluster of ideas alive with energy but as yet swirling, decentralized, anarchic, constantly under attack, yet expressing itself powerfully through action.

Social institutions tend to become a subject of study only when they are perceived as beginning to deteriorate or change.

The first quote was written in 1986 by Adrienne Rich, a self-described radical feminist; but the second is from a scholarly commentary on an ancient treatise written by Xenophon in the fourth century B.C. Although separated by 24 centuries, both Rich and Xenophon were concerned with what they perceived as radical changes in family life. Xenophon, a student of Socrates and a contemporary of Plato and Aristotle, appears to have written his treatise, *Oeconomicus*, out of concern for the disruptions in Greek family life caused by the Peloponnesian War. Unlike most of the Greek writers who glorified men's roles in public life and scorned domestic work, Xenophon viewed the family as the basic unit of society and considered labor performed within the household to be the main source of community wealth and progress.

Xenophon appears to have had a rare (for his or any other time) understanding of the family as an economic system and of the threat to community welfare that disruptions of family life represented. Xenophon's unique perceptions and objectivity were undoubtedly stimulated both by a disastrous war and by his own status as an outcast, having been forced into exile from Athens for sympathizing with Sparta. Extraordinary events and extraordinary circumstances tend to produce new ways of looking at things.

If Xenophon were alive today to continue his analysis of the family as an economic system, he would surely say that the modern family is undergoing a similar period of extraordinary transformation. Like the Spartan households that were threatened by loss of control over their helots, the modern family is losing much of its hold on the share of our economy's resources that families have traditionally claimed. Both men and women are investing conspicuously smaller shares of their time and money in family functions than our grandparents did. Part of the resource reallocation out of the household makes economic and social sense given that a considerable amount of domestic work has been transferred into the marketplace for compelling technological reasons.

The family values lament heard so persistently in our culture suggests, however, that technology can't replace everything our grandparents did at home and that society feels enormously threatened by what is happening to the family's caretaking functions. One has to be struck by the amount of discord in public discussion of family issues. Large numbers of people are insisting that large numbers of other people should be doing something they're not doing or are perceived not to be doing very well. Society obviously wants something more from families than it is currently getting.

What is missing from the hand-wringing about family values is an understanding of the degree to which the economic rug has been pulled out from under the family. Part of the "rug-pulling" has been caused by structural changes in our economy that are more or less inexorable (the advance of technology and the changing roles of women) while other parts are due to unintended but no less powerful effects of government programs, laws, and policies that have been heedlessly implemented on the assumption that the family as an institution can be taken for granted. Putting an economic rug back under the family means paying unaccustomed attention to issues of family business.

TAKING CARE OF FAMILY BUSINESS

One answer to that vexing question of "what can we do?" is that we can stop treating the family as something it isn't—a passive, peripheral component of our economic system. We can stop assuming that women are going to volunteer for the caretaking jobs regardless of how our society treats caretakers. We can stop pretending that the family can operate on love alone (although love is not to be discounted as a powerful driving force). We can stop treating the family as a poor relation looking for a handout when in fact it is the rest of society that rides free of charge on families in terms of bearing society's reproductive costs. We can get real about the economic facts of life and about tending to family business.

Before we can deal with the family in any realistic way, though, we have to do some family bookkeeping. We need a realistic idea of the kinds of resources families require to do their job. Any realistic assessment of a family's resource needs quickly gets into very large numbers when the opportunity costs of parental time, parental risks, and parental constraints are estimated. The absence of any concept of family accounting has resulted in some very misguided ideas about social policies.

It is often said (for example, by the Concord Coalition) that the Social Security crisis is a conflict between generations, that we are unfairly robbing the young to support the elderly. Considering what children typically cost parents, however, it's hard to see how parents in general can be considered exploiters of children. The real social conflict is between those who pay the costs of investing in children and those who don't. Some basic concepts of family accounting can provide essential insights as to where the pressure points on our society actually are.

NEW FAMILY INFRASTRUCTURE

Investing one's time and energy in family caretaking has become an extraordinarily expensive and risky undertaking because there is very little social or legal infrastructure that supports family investment in any substantive way. As reformers in Eastern Europe have painfully discovered, market economies require a basic infrastructure of property rights, contracts, and reliable law enforcement in order to function. The family's traditional social contract that has provided extensive protection and support for the caretaking roles is rapidly becoming nonoperational in modern societies and leaving individuals to fend for themselves in family relationships. But given that parents can't negotiate with babies and given that it is difficult for lovers to mix romance with business, however, it isn't realistic to expect family members to write their own contracts the way the rest of the economy does.

In the wake of the demise of the family's traditional social contract, society needs to provide some new family infrastructure. As noted earlier, there are basically two kinds of infrastructures from which to choose:

Socializing more of the costs of family
Privatizing more of the benefits of family

Most of what has been proposed as "family policy" has been along the lines of socializing the family's costs in ways that would make "the whole village" collectively responsible for much of the family's traditional caretaking work.

IT TAKES A VILLAGE, BUT WHICH VILLAGE?

"It takes a village to rear a child," a wise African adage that originated in a tribal setting, is frequently cited in discussions of public policy with respect to the family. The problem with applying a tribal adage to the modern family, however, is that people now live in many different villages simultaneously. We live in the "village" of the immediate family where our most intimate relationships are formed. We also live in a village of neighbors, a village of extended family and friends, a school district, a town or city, a state, a region, a nation, and even a global village that literally encompasses the whole world via satellite communications. All of these villages have some impact on the development of children but, obviously, not all in the same way.

It is crucial to assign society's caretaking tasks to the right villages for two reasons:

So the work will get done.
So a village's credibility and authority won't be compromised by promising things it can't deliver.

The federal government is the wrong village for the primary job of taking care of the elderly because government can't rear the next generation of children required to produce the supply side of old-age security. The federal government can, however, provide an intergenerational infrastructure by writing a social contract that makes explicit what minimum support children owe their parents and by using the state's enforcement powers to collect the necessary payments.

A government monopoly is the wrong village for managing education because schools now have to compete on the supply side of eduction for the talented women who in earlier generations would automatically have been teachers. On the demand side of education, there is too much diversity among families as to what is wanted and needed from schools for any political process to resolve the differences, except in very small, homogeneous communities. There is still a need for government to use its taxing powers to provide financial infrastructure for schools because of the absence of private capital markets that finance investment in education.

Government *is* the village in which to write a prenuptial contract to provide a legal and economic infrastructure for marriage that is more consistent, predictable, and supportive of the caretaking roles than the divorce laws and judicial interpretations of most states currently are. For purposes of consistency and enforcement across state lines, divorce laws need to be substantially federalized by the national village and, ideally, extended across national boundaries with international treaties.

Given that old-age insurance in the form of Social Security and Medicare is the federal government's biggest domestic undertaking and that public schools are the biggest expenditure of state and local governments, the impending crisis in old-age entitlements and the unending problems of public schools threaten the credibility of government at every level. Restoring faith in government requires assigning tasks to the right village. What government villages do best is to provide legal infrastructure for private undertakings, a point that was made two centuries ago by Adam Smith, the father of classical economics.

Adam Smith and Eve Smith

Adam Smith was that very practical-minded Scottish philosopher who provided the first economic model that could serve as an alternative to the feudalistic caste system for organizing human time and energy. Smith applied his practical mind to understanding what was happening around him in the early stages of the Industrial Revolution. What he saw was a new form of human organization emerging amid the chaos of breakdown in the feudalistic order. Smith saw men emerging from the feudalistic ties of birth and caste into the marketplace of business contracts and competition and was able to show how the marketplace could be made the servant of humanity rather than the master.

Because of the obvious historical parallels with what is happening to the modern family, it is relevant to contemplate what that Scotsman (or better yet, his female counterpart) would say about the apparent social chaos caused by the breakdown of another kind of system. An Eve Smith surely would point out some of the important facts of life that Adam Smith overlooked, while agreeing with much of his general analysis:

◆ Eve Smith would note that Mr. Smith's greatest weakness, like most of the philosophers who preceded him, was in foolishly assuming that public man could be separated analytically from private woman and that his economic theories could ignore women's contributions as having no relevance to the public economy. Because Mr. Smith's theories were all about competition among healthy, rational, adult males and made virtually no mention of the dependency phases of life or their caretakers, he only told half of the economic story.

◆ Ms. Smith would be quick to remind Mr. Smith that women have always worked, even though economic statistics have omitted most female labor. Changing the social arrangements by which half the human race allocates its labor can hardly be a small project in any economic system.

◆ Eve Smith would concede Mr. Smith's greatest contribution to social theory—his understanding of the benefits of economic agency (that is, locating decision making where the most information and the strongest incentives are) and the importance of tying demand together with supply, as market systems tend to do.

◆ Concerning Mr. Smith's insights about the advantages of specialization and exchange within a system of contracts and property rights, Eve Smith would point out that division of labor isn't something to be forced on anyone in a free society. If cooperation and exchange are to continue to flourish in our most basic social unit, family members also need reliable contracts.

◆ Like any woman who has actually done it, Eve Smith would surely inform Mr. Smith that family caretaking is a lot of work and not something to be taken lightly. Although Eve Smith would undoubtedly note the risks and excesses of unfettered capitalism, she would also conclude along with almost everyone else at this point in time that Mr. Smith's system of markets and contracts is the most efficient system yet devised for getting most of society's work done. Given that conclusion, Eve Smith would surely try to figure out a way to make the market system serve the family in some of the ways that it serves the rest of the economy.

◆ It seems likely that an Eve Smith would conclude that an economic system that tells the truth about the value of family functions to the people doing the work has considerable potential for converting the marketplace into a servant of the family.

IS NOTHING SACRED?

Many people concerned about family stress and cultural decline would undoubtedly argue that Ms. Smith has it backwards in promoting personal self-interest as a force for family reinforcement and cultural reform. Most parents surely don't want to think about their children as financial investments, and most couples in love don't want to think about the consequences of divorce for themselves or for their children. In any event, many observers would argue that what is wrong with both the family and society is too much greed and selfishness and what is needed is a great moral awakening, not more pursuit of investments and personal gains.

Adam Smith was a philosophical optimist who believed that market incentives and moral goals were naturally compatible, not mutually exclusive; but it appears in retrospect that he was rather naive. As many analysts have noted, Smith's benign view of capitalism was grounded in a basic philosophical assumption about human nature that set natural limits on greed and on an individual's willingness to pursue worldly goods at the expense of basic morals and ethics. Smith's earlier book, *A Theory of Moral Sentiments*, postulated an innately moral and civilized individual based on every person's natural ability to empathize with others.

We now know that the manners, morals, and constraints of civilized human behavior aren't as innate as Smith assumed. Family dysfunction has demonstrated an alarming tendency to correlate with immoral and uncivilized behavior. Children abused or seriously neglected in childhood often exhibit as adults a sociopathic inability to empathize with other people. Moral sentiments, it seems, don't develop in a vacuum—they have to be created and nurtured early in the human development process. It could thus be said that moral sentiments come primarily from the same place that babies come from; that is, from families. From this perspective, strengthening the economic fibers of the family is a practical approach to restoring the moral fibers of our society.

It would certainly be wrong to create the impression that the only concerns of the family or of society are economic. It is equally wrong, however, to think it is possible to ignore the practical dimensions of life. In the words of Alan Wolfe, a social-science philosopher, the job of social science is to mediate between the sacred and the profane, profane meaning the scientific, biological, technological facts of life, the mindless part of life that has to be dealt with. Sacred means the things that give meaning to life for human beings, the reasons why we care.

Wolfe argues that part of human life is determined by the natural world, part by culture and tradition, and part by the individual mind, and what is unique about humans is that the human mind can reflect on both nature and culture and is capable of changing the rules by which we live. Nowhere, it seems, is there a greater need for reflection on the connections between the sacred and the profane and the rules by which we live than in the situation of the modern family at the end of this century.

THE CONTINUITY OF THE FAMILY

As much as this argument has been about modernism, postindustrialism, and the future of the family and as often as it has questioned the continued viability of some of our most hallowed traditions, the past still has much to say to us. In her commentary on Xenophon's *Oeconomicus*, for instance, Sarah Pomeroy notes a scene on a fifth-century (B.C.) Greek vase that has been interpreted by scholars as a pictorial predecessor of Xenophon's idea of marriage. The scene pictures the mistress of the house at a spinning wheel, the master of the house striding through the doorway, and Eros hovering overhead. Although cloth making has moved out of the household and both spouses are now going through the doorway, Xenophon's concept of marriage as an economic partnership bound by love is as applicable now as it was 24 centuries ago. The human family evolves; but in its essential aspects, it also endures.

APPENDIX
QUANTITATIVE DIMENSIONS OF A PARENTAL DIVIDEND

PURPOSE

The purpose of this appendix is to provide some quantitative perspective on how a parental dividend could actually work in practice. For parental dividends to be considered a practical possibility, it is necessary to have credible answers to technical questions such as:

How would a parental dividend compare with current Social Security benefits?

How, specifically, would it affect the rich versus the poor?

What impact would it have on the financial situation of families?

How would the parents of family caretakers be affected?

How strong would the pronatal effect be?

How could the transition be made from one system to another?

How would a parental dividend affect the economic balance between investment in human capital versus investment in tangible capital?

Teams of actuaries, statisticians, and economists would be required to work out all of the formulas involved in such questions; but a quantitative profile can be estimated by working through some numerical examples.

PROCEDURE

In order to see how converting Social Security to a parental dividend would work out mathematically, the low-, middle-, and high-income families represented in Table 5.3 of Chapter 5 can be used as examples. The following computations are based on both general assumptions about all families and specific assumptions about families at specific income levels.

GENERAL ASSUMPTIONS

1. Each family reproduces itself; that is, each family produces two children who have approximately the same lifetime earning capacity as their parents.
2. Parents become the recipients of the Social Security taxes paid by their own children. The employee payroll tax currently consists of a 15.3 percent tax, 12.4 percent of which goes for retirement, survivors', and disability payments and 2.9 percent of which goes for hospital insurance (Part A of Medicare). The 12.4 percent tax paid by each child is assumed to be put into a retirement trust fund for his or her parents. (The same thing could, of course, be done for health insurance; but the computations here are confined to retirement pensions.)
3. Parental trust funds are invested in the capital markets. Estimates of returns are computed on the basis of 3 percent and 6 percent real rates of return compounded annually. (The real rate of return, discounting for inflation, in the U.S. stock market has averaged about 7 percent over the past half century while the real rate of return on government bonds has averaged 2.3 percent.)
4. Retirement occurs at age 67 with an average remaining life expectancy of 16 years.

SPECIFIC ASSUMPTIONS

In order to compute lifetime taxes, trust-fund earnings, and retirement benefits, it is necessary to make specific assumptions as to the age at which parents have children, how long the children stay in school, and children's work profiles, all of which are likely to vary with income class. Spelling out the details of a family's life is a rather tedious process, but paying attention to the details of life is what any realistic proposal for achieving old-age security must do. As results depend on the assumptions, those chosen for these examples are deliberately modest.

The Low-Income Family
(Income < $35,500, av. = $22,100)

One parent averages $14,200 and the
more flexible parent averages $7,900

For purposes of estimation, the low-income family is assumed to have one child when the parents are 20 years old and another child when the parents are 23 (for simplicity, the parents are assumed to be the same age). Both children graduate from high school at age 18 and start working at $5.50/hour jobs such as manual laborer, convenience-store clerk, filling-station attendant, or fast-food service worker. Full-time work at $5.50 an hour generates an annual income of approximately $11,000.

The first child is assumed to start working when the parents are 38 years old. The 12.4 percent payroll tax ($1,364) that the child pays is deposited in a retirement trust fund for his or her parents. The second child begins work at a similar job when his or her parents are 41 years old, and those payroll retirement taxes are also deposited in the parental trust fund. Both children are assumed to get $200 annual raises so that they achieve their parents' average lifetime earning capacity of $14,200 per year by age 34.

If the parents retire at age 67, the first child will be 47 years old, earning $16,800, and paying a tax of $2,083 per year. The second child will be 44 years old, earning $16,200, and paying a tax of $2,009. If the trust fund accumulates at a 3 percent annual real rate of return, it will then have a value of $146,283.12. If the trust fund is then converted to a lifetime annuity at 6 percent nominal interest, the parents would receive a yearly income of $14,475.03 from the trust fund plus the $4,092 in taxes that their children will still be paying for an annual total of $18,567.03 in 1997 dollars. At a 6 percent real rate of return on trust-fund investment, the parental trust fund would be worth $230,179.13 at retirement, and the parents' annual pension would be $26,868.72.

The rate at which the trust fund is assumed to be annuitized at retirement is assumed to be at a nominal rate of 6 percent in both cases. At the present time, our annuity markets are not very robust because of technical problems, so it is difficult to know what the annuity options will be down the road. The problem with annuities from an insurer's standpoint is that people tend to self-select; i.e., people who expect to live a long time are the people most interested in buying annuities. If everyone were required to convert their parental trust funds to annuities at retirement, this problem could be alleviated. Availability of the inflation-indexed government bonds that the U.S. Treasury Department recently proposed to offer would be another significant contribution to the development of a reliable annuities market.

The Middle-Income Family
(Income = $35,500–$59,700, av. = $47,200)

One parent averages $30,900 and the
more flexible parent averages $16,300

The middle-income family is assumed to have one child at age 23 and a second child at age 26. Both children graduate from high school, spend two years in junior college or trade school, and enter the workforce when their parents are 43 and 46 years old, respectively. Each child starts out at an $9.00/hour job ($18,000 a year) such as mechanic, practical nurse, hairdresser, bookkeeper, and so on, and receives an annual raise of $700 that brings each of them up to their parents' earning capacity of $30,900 by age 39.

When the parents retire at age 67, the first child is earning $34,800 and paying $4,315 in retirement taxes. The second child is earning $32,700 and paying $4,055 in retirement taxes. At a 3 percent real rate of return on trust-fund investment, the parental trust fund would be worth $207,390.39 in 1997 dollars, which if converted to a lifetime annuity at 6 percent interest would pay $20,521.72 per year. Adding in the $8,370 per year that the children are still paying in taxes would give the parents an annual income of $28,891.72. At a 6 percent real rate of return on trust-fund investment, the trust fund would be worth $293,460.69 and the annual pension would be $37,408.56.

The High-Income Family
(Income > $59,700, av. = $89,300)

One parent averages $59,000 and the
more flexible parent averages $30,300

The high-income family is assumed to have a first child at age 25 and a second child at age 28. Both children attend college for five or six years, get a professional degree such as an MBA, and begin work at age 24. The parents are 49 years old when the first child enters the workforce and 52 years old when the second child begins working. Both children start at $36,000 a year and receive annual raises of $1,200. The children achieve their parents' lifetime average earning capacity of $59,000 at age 44.

When the parents retire at age 67, the first child is 42 years old, earning $57,600, and paying retirement taxes of $7,142. The second child would be 39 years old, earning $54,000, and paying taxes of $6,696. The parental trust fund would be worth $267,624.20. Converting the trust fund to a lifetime annuity at 6 percent interest would result in an annual payout of $26,481.99. Adding in the children's current tax payments of $13,838 would provide an annual payment of $40,319.99. At a 6 percent real rate of return on trust-fund investment, the trust fund would be worth $388,958.14 and the annual pension would be $52,326.24.

EFFECTS OF CARETAKING

Estimates of parental dividends computed in the preceding examples assume that each family produces two workers who stay in the labor force full time and are paid equally. That assumption is inconsistent with the argument of Chapter 5 which suggests that many families find it necessary for one parent to be more flexible and to sacrifice significant income opportunities for family caretaking. Whether both parents in a young family share the caretaking or one specializes in caretaking while the other specializes in market work, there are likely to be significant opportunity costs that reduce the caretakers' incomes and therefore reduce parental dividends for the parents of caretakers.

Realistically, parental-dividend estimates need to allow for the income losses of family caretakers. Again, some specific assumptions have to be made to estimate dollar amounts. For purposes of illustration, it is assumed in each case that the second child receives the same education as the first, enters the workforce at the same age, works full time for five years at the same salary, and receives the same raises as in the previous examples. It is then assumed that the second child drops out of the workforce to take care of two preschool children born three years apart. When the younger child enters kindergarten, the flexible parent is assumed to start working half time and to continue working half time for the next 10 years until the younger child is 15 years old, at which time the flexible parent returns to full-time work.

It is hard to guess what kind of part-time work a caretaking parent might get after being out of the workforce for eight years. For purposes of estimation, it is assumed that the caretakers would have to come back into the workforce at the salary rate at which they first began working adjusted for half time (half of $11,000 for the low-income worker) rather than the rate at which they left and that they receive comparable half-time raises ($100 a year for the low-income worker). The half-time low-income worker would be earning $6,400 at the end of 10 years, which would be converted to a full-time wage of $12,800 when full-time work is resumed with $200 annual raises.

By these assumptions, the second child of the low-income family would be earning $13,600 and paying $1,686.40 in taxes when the parents retire. At a 3 percent real rate of return on trust-fund investment, the parental trust fund would be valued at $110,163.77 and the parental dividend would be $14,670.34 (At a 6 percent real rate of return on trust-fund investment the trust fund would be worth $176,154.67 and the parental dividend would be $21,200.28). Similar computations at a 3 percent real rate of return on trust-fund investment would reduce the parental dividend to $20,483.83 for the middle-income family to $39,516.67 for the high-income family. At a 6 percent real rate of return, the comparable figures would be $27,216.40 for the middle-income family and $36,451.80 for the high-income family.

Table A.1 summarizes the computations in these examples and compares the estimated pension benefits to parents of two full-time workers and parents of one full-time worker and one part-time worker with an estimate of the benefits that the same families would receive under current Social Security formulas (as of 1997). Since these computations depend

Table A.1: *Comparison of Parental Dividends and Social Security*

	Income Status as Defined in Table 5.3		
	Low-Income Couple	Medium-Income Couple	High-Income Couple
Estimated			
1. 1997 Social Security Benefit	$13,405	$22,089	$28,966
2. Parental Dividend from 2 children who work continuously	$18,567* $26,869†	$28,892* $37,409†	$40,320* $52,326†
3. Parental Dividend from 1 continuous worker and 1 flexible caretaker	$14,671* $21,200†	$20,484* $30,185†	$29,517* $36,452†

*Computed at a 3 percent real rate of investment return on trust-fund investment compounded annually and converted to an annuity at 6 percent nominal interest in 1995 dollars.

†Computed at a 6 percent real rate of investment return on trust-fund investment compounded annually and converted to an annuity at 6 percent nominal interest in 1995 dollars.

very specifically on what people do and when they do it, there would be considerable variation among families; nevertheless these examples suggest that parents who invest in children and reproduce themselves in terms of earning capacity would be likely to receive parental dividends that equal or exceed current Social Security benefits while their children pay taxes at the same rate they are paying now. This is *not* an illusion because it is based on two forms of *real* investment:

- Investment in children who become productive workers
- Investment of children's taxes in trust funds that are invested in the capital market for a significant period of time prior to their parents' retirement and therefore create real investment capital.

Real wealth is therefore created in the form of productive labor and productive capital.

Comparing future benefits of a pension system funded by real investment with benefits in the current noninvestment system is undoubtedly a biased comparison that understates the benefits from converting to an investment system for several reasons:

1. Current Social Security benefit formulas (as of 1995) are likely to be revised downward as the baby boom retires precisely because the baby-boom generation hasn't invested enough in either labor or capital to support its retirement at current levels.
2. The comparisons made in Table A.1 also ignore the productivity gains that could reasonably be expected from increased investment in labor and capital.
3. Another element that must be accounted for in making comparisons is the fact that there would be an additional source of funding out of current tax levels from children who outlive their parents.

A POSTMORTEM FUND

In the present Social Security system, all workers pay taxes to support the retired generation, including workers whose parents are deceased. Since children generally outlive their parents, there is a significant portion of children's lifetime earnings paid into Social Security that a parental dividend would be unable to tap directly. If parents have a child at age 25 and the child begins working at age 23, the child will be 42 when the parents retire at age 67 and 52 when the parents die at the average age of 77. After their parents' deaths, children normally have about 15 more years to work before their own retirement, which is approximately a third of their working lives. The last third of a working life frequently contains the peak earning years, so a third of lifetime earnings is a conservative estimate of the share of children's earnings, which couldn't be assessed to pay a parental dividend directly. One-third of the Social Security tax collected in 1997 was approximately $135 billion.

In order not to create a substantial incentive for children to profit from their parents' demise, the tax that children pay for parents could continue to be collected after parents are deceased as Social Security taxes are now. Postmortem collections would provide a fund that could be used to augment parental dividends and to plug holes in the system outlined in the previous examples. The fund could be used to provide inflation adjustments to parental dividends, insurance for disability, and a safety net for indigent elderly who have invested in neither capital nor children or who have had bad investment luck in one form or another. Given that indigent elderly are already provided for by the S.S.I. program that is funded by general revenues, the postmortem fund could be used primarily for disability, dividend enhancements, and inflation insurance for parents, without requiring additional resources.

FAIRNESS FOR CARETAKERS: A JOINT RETURN FOR FAMILY BUSINESS

Table A.1 suggests that parents of one full-time worker and one flexible caretaker would tend to do better than they would under current Social Security formulas even with very modest returns on investment and without any enhancements from a postmortem fund. Parents of caretakers, however, would be penalized substantially relative to parents whose children stay in the labor force full time. If both children in these examples were to become flexible caretakers, their parents would be seriously hurt.

It could hardly be a profamily policy to institute a pension system that penalizes parents for producing children who become family caretakers. Such a system would be as unfair to many parents as the existing Social Security System that provides no rewards for being good parents. The logical remedy is that a husband and wife should share the support of their parents equally. In terms of their economic contributions to the next generation of families, parents of caretakers have earned as much claim to old-age support as the parents of wage earners. For purposes of parental support, it shouldn't matter which person in a marriage makes more money. Both are partners in the business of family.

Discussion of the marriage contract in Chapter 8 argued that the marriage contract that is in the interest of the state to sanction and to enforce is a commitment between two parties to take care of family business. The business of family is taking care of each other and taking care of family dependents. If parental dividends are calculated on the basis of a joint return of a couple's earnings and split equally between their parents' accounts, bias against parents of caretakers would be significantly reduced, especially if contributions to such accounts are required to be continued for a significant period after a divorce.

IMPLICATIONS FOR ECONOMIC PROGRESS:

INCENTIVES FOR PARENTAL INVESTMENT

It would be a static and unimaginative (not to mention undemocratic) interpretation of Table A.1 to assume that people are limited to reproducing children equal to themselves in terms of economic achievement. What is particularly significant about this table is that it opens the door for families to climb the economic ladder in their own lifetimes by investing in their children. The low-income family that currently receives an annual Social Security payment of $13,405 would receive, by the most conservative estimate, a parental dividend of $14,671 if they produce two children who achieve middle-income status through work and/or marriage. Sharing the rewards of parenting with parents would harness the forces of our economic system in support of the kinds of family investments that are crucial to economic productivity and economic progress.

INVESTMENT BALANCE

Parental trust funds would also provide substantial increases in capital investment, which would create the kinds of boosts to productivity and economic welfare that the more conventional proposals for privatization envision. It was argued previously that economic investment needs to be appropriately balanced between labor and capital because neither can produce very much without the other. Historically, about two-thirds of U.S. production has been attributed to labor and about one-third to capital. How would a dividend paid to parents partially through parental trust funds in the manner outlined above distribute resources between labor and capital? Table A.2 summarizes an approximation of the way workers' payroll taxes would be distributed according to the assumptions made in Table A.1.

Table A.2: *Distribution of Workers' Payroll Taxes*

Age of Worker	Status of Parents	Allocation of Taxes
Young	Still in Workforce	Investment Trust Fund for Parents
Early Middle Age	Retired	Dividend to Parents
Late Middle Age	Deceased	Postmortem Fund for Social Insurance

Most people have their children while in their 20s. Therefore, the majority of workers would be in their 40s when their parents retire and in their 50s when their parents die. Since young workers typically earn lower salaries, their greater numbers would be partially offset by their lower earnings. A rough estimate, therefore, of how workers' payroll taxes would be distributed in the previous examples would be approximately one-third invested in parental trust funds, one-third distributed directly in parental dividends, and one-third available in the postmortem fund to provide dividend enhancements and various forms of social insurance. Approximately one-third of children's taxes would therefore be invested in tangible capital through the trust funds, while two-thirds would go to the parents who produce the labor force. Given the historical productivity ratio between labor and capital in our economy, that ratio would seem to strike a prudent investment balance for achieving real economic and social security.

THE RISK FACTOR

How can parents be sure their sacrifices for childrearing will pay economic dividends in old age? Obviously, they can't. From an economic standpoint, childrearing can be as risky as most other forms of investment. The detailed assumptions required here for computing the examples summarized in Table A.1 make the estimated returns from investing in children very path-dependent; that is, dependent on what individual parents and children do and when they do it and on external forces beyond the control of individual families.

Given that the major payoff from children is still parental love, however (see Chapter 5), childrearing carries more insurance than most investments for people who want children for their own sake. Most parents would be well advised, however, to spread their retirement risks by putting money into pension funds as well if they can. Since many of the risks and worries of childrearing come from peer pressures, one could make a speculative argument that parental investment would be less risky for everyone if more parents stayed on the case and reduced the numbers of insufficiently supervised kids.

It is considerably harder for any one family to prevent destructive behavior when a lot of other kids are doing it. To the extent that a parental dividend would send a widely disseminated cultural message to all parents that investment in parental supervision and guidance is a valuable commodity, the degree of risk associated with childrearing might be reduced for all parents. Reducing the systemic risks associated with parenting would make the world a safer place for our economy's major investors.

At least the economic risks of receiving dividends from one's children are explicit and to some degree a function of parental effort. In collective systems like Social Security and Medicare, the risks are hidden and beyond the control of individuals. The public has naturally believed that by paying their Social Security taxes they were doing what they needed to do to be taken care of in old age as their parents and grandparents were. The system has never communicated the hard, cold fact to individuals that what is required for everyone to be taken care of in old age is parental investment in the next generation of children.

To the contrary, workers were specifically told in 1983 that if they paid extra taxes that generated surpluses the system would have sufficient funds when the baby boom reached retirement. Now, those same workers are nearing the end of their productive years and are being told for the first time that the system doesn't have enough workers with high enough productivity to continue supporting future retirees at the levels they expected. A parental dividend would at least tell people the truth about where the risks and requirements on the supply side of social security really are.

That Social Security and Medicare won't be there for people nearing retirement to the extent they were for earlier generations isn't something most individuals have had sufficient economic and demographic information to predict. Even if the public had the necessary information, there was nothing any one individual could have done about fixing the system. Collective schemes that have no real assets behind them contain the cruelest kinds of risks because such risks are bombs that can go off when people least expect them and hurt those people who have the least power to protect themselves. There will always be a need for a social safety net to take care of indigent elderly along the lines of the present S.S.I. program; but social insurance and pension investment are two different things that shouldn't be confused. The best way not to confuse them is to keep them separate.

LABOR-MARKET EFFICIENCY

One immediate benefit of privatizing Social Security is thought by economists to be increased incentives for people to choose work over leisure when they know their payroll taxes will go directly into their own pension funds rather than being transferred to someone else through the Social Security system. There are, in fact, large transfer elements in the current Social Security system such that the benefits people receive are only very loosely tied to the taxes they have paid. By linking pension benefits directly to contributions, privatization would, it is theorized, reduce the distortion of incentives for people to work and thereby reduce the "deadweight" efficiency losses of the current system. What this argument about the labor market ignores is that there won't be any laborforce to have its incentives distorted if parents don't make the necessary investments in the next generation of workers.

What would linking workers' contributions to benefits for their own parents do to labor-market incentives? It's hard to know. If it is viewed as insurance against having to support one's parents directly, workers could consider contributions to parental dividends as valuable as contributions to their own pension funds. Parental dividends would at least keep people's contributions within their families.

THE QUESTION OF FAIRNESS REVISITED

Considerable attention was paid in Chapter 6 to questions about how fair it would be to institute a parental dividend based on children's productivity. It is now possible to add some quantitative estimates to that discussion. Table A.1 indicates the numerical range that parental dividends would be likely to have. While middle- and upper-income parents would tend to gain more, the differences aren't nearly so large as might be imagined. Compared to the average financial net worth of such families, parental dividends would actually be more significant for the low-income family than for the middle- or high-income family (see Tables A.3 and A.4 in the following discussion).

Time is a major factor in reducing the discrepancies among income classes. High-income earners tend to stay in school longer and start their families later. If high-income parents produce children like themselves, their children will also tend to stay in school longer; so their parents would have significantly fewer years before retirement to collect and invest dividends from their children's earnings. The arithmetic of compound interest is such that delays in making contributions to trust funds tend to be quite costly. This is a major reason for the assertion in the discussion of fairness in Chapter 6 that the benefits of a parental dividend to high-income parents wouldn't be enormously larger than the benefits to low-income and middle-income families.

HOW PRONATAL WOULD A PARENTAL DIVIDEND BE?

Converting Social Security to a parental dividend would eliminate the free ride that nonparents and neglectful parents currently get, but it wouldn't require anyone in a modern economy to have children just for the sake of economic security in old age. There are many ways people can achieve long-term financial goals. Our capital markets are much better developed now than they were in 1935 when the Social Security Act was passed so that people have many investment options. There is now a whole menu of investment instruments available from which to choose: insured bank accounts, money-market funds, mutual funds, stocks, bonds, real estate, and so on. People have to invest in something, but not everyone has to invest in children.

It was argued in Chapter 6 that a parental dividend of any conceivable size wouldn't be likely to have a pronatal effect for people who don't really want children because childless individuals who invest the money they save would still come out ahead. Table A.3 provides some estimates of *how much* better a childless couple could expect to do by investing the time and money saved over a working lifetime. As Table A.3 indicates there would still be an enormous financial advantage for those who don't have children.

Computations for Table A.3 make the same assumptions with respect to when people work, how much they earn, and what return they get on their investments that were used for the computations of parental trust funds and dividends in Table A.1. If, for example, instead of having a child at age 20 the low-income couple saves the $7,127 that the USDA estimates such couples spend in the first year of a child's life and saves the extra $11,800 that the caretaking parent sacrifices to stay home with the baby and they invest their savings at a 3 percent real rate of return, their investments of the money saved in just one year of childlessness would be worth $69,490 in 1997 dollars (before taxes) by the time they are 67. Similarly, if they invest the money they could earn and save from the second year of a child's life by remaining childless, it would be worth $68,179 by age 67. Such numbers would accumulate to very large sums over the 18 years or more of children's dependency on their parents and over the lifetime of income sacrifices that the family caretaker makes.

Table A.3: *Value of the Investment Alternative for Childless Couples†*
(in 1997 pretax dollars)

Low-Income Couples	Middle-Income Couples	High-Income Couples
Net Worth at Age 67 of Savings from Being Childless		
$1,368,694*	$2,091,306*	$3,479,000*
$3,580,488**	$4,832,124**	$8,121,365**
Annual Payout if Converted to an Annuity *(at 6% interest for an average of 16 years)*		
$135,435*	$206,939*	$344,254*
$354,297**	$478,149**	$803,626**

†These numbers estimate what childless couples *could* earn, save, and accumulate with the time, energy, and independence that childlessness allows, which doesn't mean that such couples *would* invest all of the extra time and money available to them. Childless couples may use their extra time for leisure and their extra money for consumption rather than for investment.
*Assuming a 3% real rate of return on trust-fund investment
**Assuming a 6% real rate of return on trust-fund investment

Compared to low-income couples who have two children, a low-income childless couple that invests all of the money they can earn and save every year by not having children would have a total value of about $1.37 million when they are 67. (Assuming a 3 percent real rate of return on investment.) Similarly, such investments for a childless middle-income couple would result in a net worth of about $2.1 million and for the high-income couple about $3.48 million. At a 6% real rate of return on investment, the low-, middle-, and high-income nest eggs would be worth $3.58 million, $4.83 million, and $8.12 million respectively. These are conservative estimates of what it costs parents in time, money, and lifetime investment returns to have two children.

THE FINANCIAL SITUATION OF FAMILIES

The amounts of money that childless couples can earn, save, and accumulate by not having children make the parental dividend numbers in Table A.1 appear trivial by comparison. Compared to the financial advantages of remaining childless, a parental dividend of any imaginable size would be very small change. Compared to the financial situation of most families with children, however, the parental dividends estimated in Table A.1 are far from trivial. The wealth that would be returned to families by converting Social Security to a parental dividend is a very significant amount of money relative to the typical family's financial net worth.

According to the Federal Reserve's "Survey of Consumer Finances," the median net worth of a low-income family was $30,000 in 1995. By comparison, the present value of receiving an annual parental dividend of $14,671 for an average of 16 years discounted at a nominal interest rate of 6 percent is $228,272. Converting Social Security to a parental dividend would therefore create a retirement endowment for low-income families of more than 7 times their median net worth. Table A.4 compares retirement endowments of parental dividends to parents of one full-time earner and one flexible caretaker (as defined in Table A.1) with the median net worth of families at three income levels.

Table A.4: *Parental Endowments and Family Net Worth*

Income Status†	Low-Income Family	Middle-Income Family	High-Income Family
Median Family Net Worth in 1995:			
	$ 30,000	$ 54,900	$121,100
Financial Endowment Value of Parental Dividend at Age 67∞			
	$228,272*	$318,718*	$459,266*
	$329,859**	$469,660**	$567,171**
Ratio of Parental Endowment to Median Net Worth			
	7.6*	5.8*	3.8*
	11.0**	8.5**	4.7**

†The Federal Reserve's income categories don't match exactly those of the USDA on which Table A.1 is based. The categories used for this table are: Low = $10,000–$24,999, Middle = $25,000–$49,999, and High = $50,000–$99,999.
∞Financial Endowment Value is computed as the present value of the parental dividends estimated in Line 3 of Table A.1; that is, the amount that would have to be invested in the first year of retirement to generate the estimated parental dividend from one full-time worker and one flexible caretaker for an average of 16 years, in annual installments, using a nominal discount rate of 6 percent.
*Present value of 16-year annuity from trust-fund investment that averaged a 3 percent real rate of return
**Present value of 16-year annuity from trust-fund investment that averaged a 6 percent real rate of return

A problem with the comparisons made in Table A.4 is that there is a time discrepancy between net worth at retirement and median savings of all families in a particular income class, because savings tend to increase with age up to late middle age. According to the Federal Reserve study, median net worth for all families was $56,400 in 1995; but in the 50-64 age range, it was $110,800, a ratio of 1.96. If low-income families achieve the same ratio in the 50-64 age range, their savings would be ($30,000)(1.96) = $58,800. A parental endowment from their children of $228,272 would then increase their private net worth at retirement by 288 percent. For the middle-income family with a net worth of $110,800 in the 50-64 age range, a parental endowment of $318,718 would increase net worth by 187 percent. For the high-income family, a net worth at retirement of 1.96 times the median would be ($121,100)(1.96) = $237,356, and a parental endowment of $459,266 would increase net worth by 93 percent.

These comparisons indicate that while the parental dividends estimated in Table A.1 are trivial compared to the financial advantages of those who remain childless they would loom quite large in the financial situations of most families with children. They also indicate that relative to the financial net worth of low-, middle-, and high-income families, resulting family endowments would have greater weight for the families that are lowest on the income scale.

LOGISTICS OF TRANSITION: GETTING THERE FROM HERE

It is considerably easier to design a rational system for making the investments in labor and capital that are necessary for old-age support and for economic security in general than it is to figure out how to get out of the present noninvestment system. It would be easy if we could just wipe the slate clean and start over, but there isn't any way to terminate a chain-letter scheme without leaving someone holding the bag. It would be extremely inhumane to pull the plug on the existing system overnight while so many people are dependent on it at a time of life when they have few alternatives.

However irrational people's expectations of Social Security and Medicare may be, government (which is all of us) has played a major role in creating those expectations; and government (i.e., all of us) will have to take responsibility for the expectations created by making changes slowly. It has taken 60 years for the existing system to get into its current predicament, and it will take several decades to back out of it humanely. There is no quick fix for the baby-boom generation, which has invested relatively little in either children or capital. As a generation, baby boomers have relied on Social Security's illusion that someone else's children would take care of them in old age. Unfortunately, "someone else" didn't make the necessary investments in children either.

Table A.2 can be used as a rough guide to the financial implications for current and near-future retirees of converting Social Security to a parental dividend. Since no parental trust funds would exist initially, current retirees would lose the share of revenues paid into trust funds by younger workers whose parents are still in the workforce. Taxes paid by workers whose parents are retired would be distributed to parents at the expense of nonparents. The share of revenues paid by workers whose parents are deceased would be available to distribute as society sees fit—to enhance the dividends to parents and/or to provide a safety net for nonparents in addition to the S.S.I. system.

Diverting Social Security taxes paid by younger workers into trust funds for their parents would be a severe blow to a system that is already in trouble in terms of being able to meet the expectations of retirees. Withdrawing approximately a third ($132 billion in 1998) of current revenues from the system would squeeze current and near-future retirees rather drastically unless the difference was made up by allocations from general revenues. The sum needed to cover the gap would gradually decrease each year as proceeds from parental trust funds phase into the system. The system would be fully mature in an actuarial sense when parental trust funds of retirees contain contributions for the full working lives of their children. How long would that be?

If parents have a child at age 15 (to take an extreme case), the child enters the workforce at age 16, and parents retire at age 80 (to take another extreme), the child would pay into the parental trust fund for 49 years. For a more typical scenario of parents who have a child at age 24, the child enters the work force at age 22, and the parents retire at age 67, the period of trust-fund accumulation would be 21 years. If the system were converted immediately, it would take 25 to 30 years for most of the population to have fully matured parental trust funds when they retire. Since most parental investment is made before children enter the workforce, it would take another 15 or 20 years for the incentives for parental investment to have a full life-cycle effect on retirement pensions and perhaps several generations after that for the message about the economic value of family investment to become fully absorbed in the habits and perceptions of the culture. Although the full effects would take a long time to accumulate, productivity enhancements due to the trust-fund investments would start to take effect almost immediately.

All proposals for privatizing Social Security have the same problem; namely, how to finance real investment for future retirement out of current taxes and still maintain the benefits of current retirees. The short answer is that it can't be done without either raising taxes or cutting other forms of government spending, although numerous articles in *The Wall Street Journal* and elsewhere have suggested in glowing prose that it is a simple matter for countries to privatize their retirement systems the way Chile did in 1981. The following excerpt is typical:

The world is beating a path to Chile's door for good reasons. It privatized social security in 1981. And the new system has been an enormous boon, amassing $25 billion—or about 45 percent of gross domestic product—in accounts that resemble American IRAs. Officials are pleased. Workers are grateful. And labor leaders accept the idea. In short, Chile has set the standard for judging social security elsewhere.

What many would-be reformers have glossed over is the transition problems involved in going from one system to another. Our children's payroll taxes are already committed for the purpose of supporting current and future retirees for many years to come, which means that the system would have to be bought out or phased out in some manner. Chile bought out its Social Security system by giving its workers "recognition bonds" in exchange for their pension entitlements. The Chilean government *hopes* to pay off the bonds when they come due by selling state-owned industries, cutting defense and domestic expenditures to generate a budget surplus, and by getting increased tax revenues from a more productive economy due to workers' IRA investments. Bolivia is reportedly planning a similar kind of buyout financed by selling off state-owned electric utilities and state telephone, railway, and oil-and-gas monopolies. Chile and Bolivia aren't just privatizing their pension systems. They are also privatizing substantial portions of their socialized economies.

Governments in predominantly capitalistic economies don't own a lot of property that can be sold to fund their existing pension systems while they invest in new ones, nor are they in a fiscal position to generate budget surpluses without serious adjustments, although the U.S. Social Security System is currently collecting substantial surpluses (close to $100 billion in 1998). *If* the rest of government could be persuaded to cut spending or raise taxes sufficiently to stop consuming the Social Security surpluses, the surpluses that are projected to continue until about 2012 could be used to start an investment program.

Such a program would be similar to that suggested by Representative Porter in 1990 and by Senators Kerrey and Simpson in 1995, with the additional feature that endowing parents would tie the demand for old-age support directly to its major source of supply. Operating the kinds of personal investment programs proposed by Porter, Kerrey, and Simpson through parental trust funds would solve several problems simultaneously. It would generate tangible investment in our economy, tie support for old age to investments in real labor and real capital, and return dividends to our biggest and most important investors—our families.

NOTES

Preface

Page xi: See Vivianna A. Rotman Zelizer, *Morals &
            Markets: The Development of the Life Insur-
            ance Industry in the United States* (New Brun-
            swick: Transaction Books, 1983).

Chapter 1

Page 1:   Thomas J. Espenshade, *Investing in Children*
            (Washington, D.C.: The Urban Institute Press,
            1984).

Page 1:   "The implicit message to young Americans is
            frighteningly clear: Bearing and raising and nur-
            turing children may no longer be compatible
            with active pursuit of the American dream. No
            society can convey this message for long if it
            hopes to survive and prosper." Statement by
            Marian Wright Edelman, president of the Chil-
            dren's Defense Fund, commenting on the ana-
            lytical study *Vanishing Dreams: The Economic
            Plight of America's Young Families* (Washington,
            D.C.; Children's Defense Fund, 1992).

Page 1:   This is, of course, a very broad generalization.
            In fact, families have taken many forms and
            have been organized in various ways through-
            out history, a point that Stephanie Coontz
            makes clear in her book *The Way We Never
            Were* (New York: Basic Books, 1992). At least

211

since the writings of Plato and Aristotle, however, Western culture has idealized society as divided between public and private spheres and the family as correspondingly divided between men's work and women's work. See, for example, Jean Bethke Elshtain's *Public Man, Private Woman* (Princeton, N.J.: Princeton University Press, 1981).

Page 1:   Dominant economic models of the family, which are variations of the neoclassical equilibrium model, treat children as consumer goods and rationalize the status quo by portraying family choices as rational and efficient. While such models provide a very useful foundation for thinking about family problems, they don't capture what the public perceives as a situation of family disequilibrium and decline that is threatening our whole culture (see the following footnote), nor do the dominant models generally recognize the extent to which women's roles have been constrained within the family or the extent to which women have subsidized the market economy somewhat involuntarily with their reproductive and caretaking labor.

Page 2:   See, for example, William J. Bennett's *The Index of Leading Cultural Indicators* (New York: Simon & Schuster, 1994), which tabulates numerous social statistics such as divorce, single-parent families, illegitimacy, juvenile crime, and teenage suicide, all of which tell a depressingly familiar story of increasing family dysfunction. Examples of statistics indicating family decline include the facts that since 1960 the number of divorces has tripled, the number of unmarried pregnant teenagers has doubled, teen suicide has tripled, and violent crime has increased over 500 percent.

For what *Library Journal* calls "a powerful, extensively researched, and often shocking book that explores the plight of a vast number of our children today," see Sylvia Hewlett, *When the Bough Breaks: The Cost of Neglecting Our Children* (New York: HarperPerennial, 1992).

The same kind of picture is reported by the Carnegie Corporation. "Millions of infants and toddlers are so deprived of medical care, loving supervision and intellectual stimulation that their growth into healthy and responsible adults is threatened. The plight of the nation's youngest and most vulnerable children is a result of many parents' being overwhelmed by poverty, teenage pregnancy, divorce or work." "Study Confirms Worst Fears on U.S. Children," *The New York Times*, April 12, 1994, p. 1.

Page 4: The 15.3 percent payroll tax levied on wages and salaries to support the Social Security system is ostensibly split equally between employer and employee with the employee paying 7.65 percent and the employer paying 7.65 percent. There are basically three ways in which employers can pay their share of the tax: by reducing their profits, by raising the prices of the products they sell, or by reducing the employee's wage. Economists generally agree that the employer's share of the tax is viewed by the employer as a wage cost and that the employer pays lower wages because of it. The employee therefore pays for the employer's share with lower wages.

Page 5: Day-care regulations were reportedly proposed in Maryland that would require infants to be "held, played with, and talked to"; but the practical impossibility of monitoring such a requirement is obvious—an army of state inspectors couldn't enforce it. "Proposed Day-Care Rules in Maryland Require Holding and Talking to Infants," *Education Week*, Sept. 5, 1990, p. 18. Cited by Myron Lieberman, *Public Education: An Autopsy* (Cambridge, Ma.: Harvard University Press, 1993), p. 30.

Page 5: This question is raised very provocatively by Charles Murray in his book, *Losing Ground: American Social Policy, 1950-1980* (New York: Basic Books, 1984).

Page 6: Professor Frank Furstenberg, a sociologist at the University of Pennsylvania, says:

> "I think the conservative fear may be that all human beings are selfish at their core and that the pull of the market is so strong that women are going to become more like men, and invest less in their children." "Family Decay Global," *The New York Times*, May 30, 1995, p. A5.

Page 6: Richard T. Ely was the first president of the American Economic Association.

Page 6: Richard T. Ely, *Property and Contract in Their Relation to the Distribution of Wealth* (New York: The Macmillan Company, 1914).

Chapter 2

Page 9:   Adam Smith, *The Wealth of Nations*, Edwin Cannan, ed. (Chicago: University of Chicago Press, 1976), p. 477.

Page 10:   For an extensive discussion of the ways in which economic analysis has been affected and distorted by the omission of women's work from economic statistics, see Marilyn Waring's *If Women Counted* (San Francisco: HarperCollins, 1988). As Waring notes:

> Activities that lie outside the production boundary—that is, in every nation, the great bulk of labor performed by women in an unpaid capacity—are left out of the gross domestic product, as they are left out of the gross national product. It is not a large step from that point to leaving them out of policy considerations altogether.

Nuclear attack submarines are counted as part of a nation's output, but tending to one's family is not. "Family values" are nowhere to be found in our measures of economic welfare.

Page 10:   See, for example, Julie A. Nelson, *Feminism, Objectivity and Economics* (London: Routledge, 1996), especially Chapter 2, "Gender and Economics."

Page 10:   This extension of the "invisible hand" concept was suggested by Ulla Grapard in "Postmodern Theory and the Economic Discourse," a paper presented at the conference of The International Association for Feminist Economics, American University, Washington, D.C., July 25, 1992.

Page 11:   "Studying the Seasons of a Woman's Life," an article about Dr. Levinson's forthcoming book, *The New York Times*, September 14, 1987, p. A23.

Page 11:   James P. Rouark, *Masters Without Slaves: Southern Planters in the Civil War and Reconstruction* (New York: W.W. Norton & Company, 1977).

Page 12:   Shirley P. Burggraf, "Women, youth, and minorities and the Case of the Missing Productivity," AEA *Papers and Proceedings*, May 1984, 74(2), pp. 254-259.

An article by Diane J. Macunovich, "An Economist's Perspective," in *Social Security: What Role for the Future*, Peter A. Diamond,

David C. Lindeman, and Howard Young, eds. (Washington, D.C.: National Academy of Social Insurance, 1996), pp. 43-67 notes:

> It is a particular shortcoming of the economic literature that by focusing on the male-female wage gap, the productivity effects of women's "double burden" have been discussed solely in terms of the presumed lower productivity of women in the market due to their responsibilities in the home. For some reason the other side of this effect has not been considered seriously: that men with a stay-at-home wife will tend to be more productive than men with a working wife or no wife at all. (p. 59)

Page 12: *Social Security Accountability Report for Fiscal Year 1997, Office of Financial Policy and Operations, SSA Pub. No. 31-231, November, 1997, pp. 53-54.* "Present value" is a financial term. In this context, it means that $21-plus trillion would have to be invested now at current interest rates in order to pay the future claims of people already in the system (workers and retirees).

Page 12: "According to the Federal Reserve Flow of Funds accounts, the U.S. net wealth at the end of 1993 amounted to almost $17 trillion, excluding consumer durables." Henning Bohn, "Social Security Reform and Financial Markets," *Social Security Reform: Conference Proceedings*, Steven A. Sass and Robert K. Triest, eds., Federal Reserve Bank of Boston Conference Series No. 41, June 1997, p. 208.

Page 13: In the words of one editorial writer:

> As women's options in the workplace expanded, the number of likely candidates for this profession [teaching] diminished. A question put to more than 500 National Merit Scholars a few years ago revealed that only five—*five!* — aspired to teach.

"An Isolated Case," *The Tallahassee Democrat*, July 3, 1996, p. 12A.

Page 14: Katie Sherrod, "Churches Are in Conflict as Centuries of Patriarchy End," *Tallahassee Democrat*, July 21, 1991, p. B3. Reprinted from *Fort Worth Star-Telegram*.

Chapter 3

Page 15: Margaret Mead, *Male and Female: A Study of the Sexes Around the World.* (New York: Morrow, 1949), p. 59.

Page 15: Victor Fuchs, *Women's Quest for Equality* (Cambridge, MA.: Harvard University Press, 1988), p. 43.

Page 16: William Baumol, "On Method in U.S. Economics a Century Earlier," *The American Economic Review,* Dec. 1985, 75(6), pp. 1-12. Baumol stated that women's issues have continually been on the periphery of concern for the economics profession.

Page 16: Peter Drucker, "The Feminist Experiment," *The Wall Street Journal,* October 17, 1994, p. A14.

Page 16: As Drucker and others have noted, gender roles haven't always been based on physiology. Jobs that are considered "men's jobs" in some cultures are considered "women's jobs" in other cultures and the designation of "men's work" or "women's work" changes over time within the same culture. Drucker argues that the real dividing line between men's jobs and women's jobs has universally been one of power and social status and that the essence of the "feminist experiment" is letting women share high-status jobs.

Several sociobiologists argue the same thing and claim that the male's drive for status and dominance versus the female's need for gentleness and protection is biologically determined. See, for example, Yves Christen, *Sex Differences: Modern Biology and the Unisex Fallacy* (New Brunswick, N.J.: Transactions Publishers, 1991).

Many feminists argue that power and status are indeed the issue but there is no inherent basis in either biology or psychology that justifies most gender divisions of labor. They argue that even if gender divisions have some degree of biological basis, they have been appropriated and expanded as mechanisms of repression and exploitation. For an extensive survey of this approach, see Nancy Folbre, *Who Pays for the Kids?: Gender and the Structures of Constraint* (New York: Routledge, 1994).

Page 16: *Op. cit.,* p. 7.

Page 17: Barbara Bergman, *The Economic Emergence of Women* (New York: Basic Books, 1986, Chapter 1).

Page 17:   Sushila Gidwani, "Modern Economic Development Strategies and Female Economic Potential." Paper presented to CSWEP Panel at EEA meetings, Philadelphia, PA, April 1986.

Page 20:   Donald N. McCloskey, "Some Consequences of a Feminine Economics," Paper presented to CSWEP Panel at Southern Economic Association meetings, Orlando, FL, December 1989, p. 12.

Page 20:   "Feminism, they said, erodes the family values on which America was built." Summary of feminist backlash by *Business Week* reviewer of Susan Faludi's book, *Backlash: The Undeclared War against American Women*, Nov. 4, 1991, p. 12.

Page 20:   Kristin Luker, *Abortion and the Politics of Motherhood* (Berkeley: University of California Press, 1984), see especially Chapter 7.

Page 21:   "Women in the Law Say Path Is Limited by 'Mommy Track,'" *The New York Times*, August 8, 1988, p. A1.

Page 23:   George Gilder, *Sexual Suicide* (New York: Quadrangle/The New York Times Book Co., 1973), p. 4.

Page 23:   *Ibid.*, p. 6.

Page 23:   *Ibid.*, p. 7.

Page 24:   *Ibid.*, p. 13.

Page 24:   *Ibid.*, p. 15.

Page 24:   *Ibid.*, p. 25.

Page 27:   William Styron, *The Confessions of Nat Turner* (New York: Bantam Books, 1966), p. 131.

Page 27:   Barbara Bergman, "The Economic Risks of Being a Housewife," *AER Papers and Proceedings*, May 1981, 71(2), pp. 81-83. Bergman spells out a long list of reasons why an economically rational individual could find it very difficult to assume the role of housewife as it is currently structured.

Page 28:   Based on a survey by Executive Research Group, Wilton, CT, reported in "Managing," *The Wall Street Journal*, January 26, 1993, p. B7.

Page 28:   Patricia Aburdene and John Naisbitt, *Megatrends for Women* (New York: Villard Books, 1992), pp. 71-73.

Page 28:   According to an article by Susan B. Carter:

> If the nation had appropriately valued educational services and had used economic incentives rather than discrimination in other occupations to induce women to teach, the women who taught in the schools would have received a far larger share of society's resources.

"Occupational Segregation, Teachers' Wages, and American Economic Growth," *Journal of Economic History*, June 1986, 46(2), p. 383.

Page 31:   William Raspberry, "Our Economic System Downgrades Children's Importance," *Tallahassee Democrat*, July 30, 1991, p. 11A, reprinted from *The Washington Post*.

Page 31:   "··· the 'cruel institution of motherhood' is how the author Gena Corea once described the evolutionarily assigned role of the female in human reproduction." "Delayed Childbearing," *The Atlantic Monthly*, June 1995, p. 56.

Page 31:   As quoted by Alice Schwarzer in *After the Second Sex: Conversations with Simone de Beauvoir* (New York: Pantheon Books, 1984), p. 40.

Page 31:   Quoted by Guettel Charnie, *Marxism and Feminism* (Toronto: Canadian Women's Educational Press, 1974), p. 31.

Page 31:   Shulamith Firestone, *The Dialectic of Sex: The Case for Feminist Revolution* (New York: Bantam Books, 1971), as quoted by Guettel Charnie, *op. cit.*, p. 39.

Page 32:   Victor Fuchs, *op. cit.*, p. 4.

Page 32:   *Ibid.*, p. 61.

Page 32:   *Ibid.*, p. 115.

Page 32:   *Ibid.*, p. 141.

Page 32:   Barbara Bergman, *The Economic Emergence of Women, p. cit.*, p. 226.

Chapter 4

Page 37:   See "Social (in)Security: The Numbers Don't Add Up," cover story in *Time*, March 20, 1995, pp. 24-32 or "Is Nothing Sacred Anymore? Maybe Not," in *Business Week*, August 1, 1994, pp. 74-76.

Page 37: "Moynihan Battles View He Gave Up on Welfare Fight," *The New York Times*, June 18, 1995, p. 1.

Page 38: December 1994, p. 16.

Page 39: In the words of one of history's most determined social reformers:

> I doubt whether there is any subject in the world of equal importance that has received so little serious and articulate consideration as the economic status of the family—of its members in relation to the other units of which the community is made up. I say "articulate consideration" because what appears haphazard in our present arrangements for the family is probably the result of more deliberate purposing and choosing than appears on the surface, but it has been a sub-conscious and therefore inarticulate purpose and choice. . . . If the reader doubts it, let him consider any of the other units or classifications that have to be taken into account in framing the economic structure of society, that is in providing material means for its maintenance—capital and labour; rent, profits, and wages; production and distribution; collective and private enterprise, and so forth. Not one of them has been the subject, in general and in detail, of a never-ending stream of writing among economists, industrial experts, politicians and pressmen. The family too has, of course, been written about—as a problem of population by imperialists; of breeding by eugenists; in relation to endless problems of health, housing, and child welfare. But of the family as an economic unit—something which has its own claim, based on its own value to the nation, to its own share in the nation's wealth—there has been next to no consideration at all. The claim has been not so much disparaged or negatived as ignored.
>
> It [the family] is at once indispensable as a means to all the rest and, in a sense, an end in itself. Pluck from under the family all the props which religion and morality have given it, strip it of the glamour, true or false, cast round it by romance, it will still remain a prosaic, indisputable fact, that the whole business of begetting, bearing and rearing children, is the most essential of all the nation's businesses. If it were not done at all, the world would become a desert in less than a century. To the extent that it is done badly, a nation finds itself confronted in war time with the problem of making an A.1 army out of a C.3 population; in peace time with the competition of rivals that manage it better.

Eleanor Rathbone, *The Disinherited Family* (London: George Allen & Unwin Ltd., 1924), p. vii.

Rathbone's rhetoric concerning neglect and misunderstanding of the role of the family in our economic system is about as true today as it was when she wrote it in 1924. She would surely be somewhat gratified to observe the amount of public consternation currently being expressed over the subject of "family values" and could say with considerable justification: "I told you so."

Page 39:   Apparently, these types of questions are just beginning to creep into high-level discussions of public business. Secretary of Labor Robert Reich began an address at a Radcliffe Conference ("Work and Family: the New Economic Equation," Cambridge, Massachusetts, May 24, 1995) by saying that he had just come that morning from a meeting in Paris with finance ministers of major industrial countries and that even *finance ministers* (Reich's emphasis) were starting to say that family issues couldn't continue to be totally ignored in considering matters of national and international economic policy.

Page 39:   As Marilyn Waring (*op. cit.*, pp. 85-86) notes, the values of a wide variety of non-monetary activities such as forestry, hunting, and fishing are imputed in economic statistics in countries around the world.

Page 39:   There is, of course, a long history of social reformers who have understood very well where babies come from and have argued for family assistance programs of various kinds. While social activists have sometimes based their proposals for family assistance on arguments for recognizing the value of family work as well as on humanitarian concerns (Rathbone, *op. cit.*, for example), their arguments have never been integrated into the dominant political and economic models of how our culture works.

Page 39:   (Stanford, California: Stanford University Press, 1988.)

Page 40:   John Locke, *Two Treatises of Government*, 2nd ed., P. Laslett, ed. (Cambridge, MA.: Cambridge University Press, 1967), II, #183, II, #81-82, as quoted by Pateman, *op. cit.*, p. 53.

Page 40:   Jean Jacques Rousseau, *Emile or on Education*, tr. A. Bloom, (New York: Basic Books, 1979), p. 409, as quoted by Pateman, *op. cit.*, p. 109.

Page 40:   Immanuel Kant, *Anthropology from a Pragmatic Point of View*, tr. M.J. Gregor, (The Hague: Martin Nijhoff, 1974, p. 171), as quoted by Pateman, *op. cit.*, p. 101.

Page 41: Sir W. Blackstone, *Commentaries on the Laws of England*, 4th ed., J. DeWitt Andrews, ed. (Chicago: Callaghan and Co., 1899), Bk I, Ch. 15, #111, p. 442, as quoted by Pateman, *op. cit.*, p. 91.

Page 41: Cited in Pateman, *op. cit.*, p. 49.

Page 41: See especially Chapter 3.

Page 41: John Rawls, *A Theory of Justice* (Cambridge, MA.: The Belknap Press of Harvard University Press, 1971), as summarized by Pateman, *op. cit.*, pp. 42-43.

Page 41: According to Rawls:

> The principle of fair opportunity can be only imperfectly carried out, at least as long as the institution of the family exists. The extent to which natural capacities develop and reach fruition is affected by all kinds of social conditions and class attitudes. Even the willingness to make an effort to try, and so to be deserving in the ordinary sense is itself dependent upon happy family and social circumstances.

Rawls, *op. cit.*, p. 74.

Page 42: As summarized by Pateman, *op. cit.*, pp. 42-43.

Page 42: Stephanie Coontz, *The Way We Never Were* (New York: Basic Books, 1992), p. 59.

Page 42: Women's voices haven't gone entirely unheard. Harvard sociologist Theda Skocpol makes a very convincing case that even though American women were excluded from suffrage they were amazingly successful at making their voices heard in unconventional ways. Her analysis concludes that the extensive grassroots network of women's clubs across the country was a very effective and cohesive form of organization for promoting widows' pensions and limitations of women's working hours in the early decades of this century:

> In the welfare state literature, as in standard welfare historiography, "public life" is typically presumed to be an exclusively male sphere, with women regarded as "private" actors confined to homes and charitable associations. Debates have centered on the relative contributions of male-dominated unions, political parties, and bureaucracies to the shaping of labor regulations and social benefits designed to help male

breadwinners and their dependents. Established approaches often overlook social policies targeted on mothers and women workers. And they fail to notice the contributions of female-dominated modes of politics, some of which are not dependent on action through parties, elections, trade unions, or official bureaucracies.

Protecting Soldiers and Women: The Political Origins of Social Policy in the United States (Cambridge, MA.: The Belknap Press of Harvard University Press, 1992), p. 30.

Page 43:   "Pro-Life? or Pro-Death?" *The New York Times*, January 26, 1989.

Page 44:   The Center for the Future of Children reported 577,800 runaway and throwaway youths in 1988 of which at least 192,700 had no familiar and secure place to stay. The center also reported that at the end of FY 1992 442,000 children were in foster care, 659,000 children experienced foster care during the year, an additional unknown number of drug-exposed babies were waiting for foster care in hospitals, and 760,644 children between 10 and 18 years of age were admitted to custody in juvenile justice confinement facilities in 1988 with an additional 65,263 juveniles held in adult jails. A one-day census in 1989 indicated that 93,945 juveniles were incarcerated. See Richard E. Behrman and Linda Sandham Quinn, "Children and Divorce: Overview and Analysis," in *The Future of Children: Children and Divorce*, published by the Center for the Future of Children, The David and Lucille Packard Foundation, Volume 4, No. 1, Spring 1994, p. 14n.

Page 44:   C. Douglas North, Nobel lecture, "Economic Performance through Time," as printed in *American Economic Review*, Vol. 84, No. 3 (June, 1994), pp. 359-368.

Page 44:   "Growing Up in a Changing World: Challenges of Youth Today," conference sponsored by the Center for the Study of Human Development at Brown University, the Henry A. Murray Research Center of Radcliffe College, Brown University, the John D. and Catherine T. MacArthur Foundation, and the W. T. Grant Foundation, at Brown University, April 1994, as reported in *Murray Research Center News*, Fall 1994, p. 4.

Page 44:   Robert A. LeVine, "Human Parental Care: Universal Goals, Cultural Strategies, Individual Behavior," in Robert A. LeVine, Patrice M. Miller, Mary Maxwell West, eds., *Parental Behavior in Diverse Societies* (San Francisco: Jossey-Bass, Inc., 1988), p. 4.

Page 44: (New York: Simon and Schuster, 1994.)

Page 45: Erma Bombeck, syndicated columnist, "Having It All, Murphy Brown, May Be Too Much," *Tallahassee Democrat*, June 18, 1992, p. 16.

Page 45: Bill Cosby, *Fatherhood* (New York: Berkley Books, 1986), p. 61.

Page 45: One large actuarial study sponsored by Lutheran Brotherhood based on a survey of 270,000 teenagers in 600 communities identifies 16 external factors and conditions that correlate with positive child development: Family support, Parents as social resources, Parent communication, Other adult resources, Other adult communication, Parent involvement in school, Positive school climate, Parental standards, Parental discipline, Parental monitoring, Time at home, Positive peer influence, Music, Extracurricular activities, Community activities, Involvement with a faith community. See Peter L. Benson, Judy Galbraith, and Pamela Espeland, *What Kids Need to Succeed* (Minneapolis: Search Institute, Free Spirit Publishing, Inc. 1995), pp. 3-4.

The avowed purpose of the study was to identify specific things that parents, communities, schools, and churches could do to create a better environment for kids. The resulting list indicates that, yes, it takes a village to rear a child; but it also indicates the extent to which the burden falls primarily on parents.

Page 45: It isn't just women who have to think about giving up higher paying jobs because of exposure to possible causes of birth defects. Researchers are also concerned that exposure of men to certain toxins can cause sperm defects leading to heart abnormalities and mental retardation. See, "Research on Birth Defects Turns to Flaws in Sperm," *The New York Times*, January 1, 1991, p. A1.

Page 46: U.S. Department of Agriculture, Center for Nutrition Policy and Promotion, *Expenditures on Children by Families: 1997 Annual Report*, Miscellaneous Publication No. 1528-1997. The USDA computations were reported for the costs of children from birth to age 17. Their estimates are extended here to age 18 (the approximate age of high-school graduation) by adding an extra year at cost reported for the seventeenth year.

Page 46: "I was reared in a home without love," statement by Wesley Allen Dodd describing a childhood in which the major form of deprivation was emotional, quoted in "Child-Killer Awaiting

Noose May Have Slain Illusions Too," *The New York Times*, December, 1992, p. 1.

Page 46:   As Wade Horn, a clinical psychologist, notes:

> The consequences of lack of supervision can be far more drastic for teenagers than for younger children. When a six-year-old runs away, he gets to the end of the block. When a 16-year-old runs away, she may wind up on Hollywood Boulevard prostituting herself.

Quoted in "Working Parents' Torment: Teens After School," *The Wall Street Journal*, May 9, 1995, p. B1.

Dr. Ruby Takanishi of the Carnegie Council on Adolescent Development cites some grim statistics:

The number of teenagers who drink alcohol has climbed more than 30 percent since the 1950s; two out of three now say they have started drinking by the ninth grade.

Suicide, once extremely rare among teenagers, has become the third-ranking cause of death after accidents of all kinds and homicide; suicide rates nearly tripled from the mid-1960s to the mid-'80s among boys and girls 10 to 14 years old, and doubled among those 15 to 19.

Despite the availability of birth control, the rate of unwanted pregnancies among those 10 to 14 years old increased 23 percent from 1983 to 1987.

Rates for gonorrhea quadrupled among those 10 to 14 and tripled among those 15 to 19 from 1960 to 1988.

These statistics are quoted in "Teen-Agers Called Shrewd Judges of Risk: A reality far more grim than their parents' teenage years," *The New York Times*, March 2, 1993, p. B5.

Page 47:   According to an article, "Working Parents' Torment: Teens After School," *The Wall Street Journal, op. cit.*:

> Most child-care authorities agree that the risks adolescents face today are far more pernicious than even a decade ago. Working parents know all the perils: the accessibility of more addictive and hazardous drugs, for example, and the early age—14 or 15—that most kids now begin experimenting with alcohol. "There's a high level of what I call total, abject

fear about what's going to happen to their kids," says Rita Ghilani, an Ashland, Mass., consultant who conducts parenting workshops for corporate employees.

According to David Gelman, author of "A Much Riskier Passage," *Newsweek Special Issue*, Summer/Fall, 1990, pp. 10-16:

Today's teens are getting less attention from adults but they face greater dangers. . . .

These realizations are emerging just when the world has become a more dangerous place for the young. They have more access than ever to fast cars, fast drugs, easy sex—'a bewildering array of options, many with devastating outcomes,' observes Beatrix Hamburg, director of Child and Adolescent Psychiatry at New York's Mount Sinai School of Medicine.

Page 47: As Ellen Goodman, syndicated columnist, notes:

> Sooner or later most Americans become card-carrying members of the counterculture . . . All you need to join is a child . . . . At some point between Lamaze and PTA, it becomes clear that one of your main jobs as a parent is to counter the culture. What the media delivers to children by the masses, you are expected to rebut one at a time. . . . the call for parental responsibility is increasing in direct proportion to the irresponsibility of the marketplace. Parents are expected to protect their children from an increasingly hostile environment.

"Parents Struggle against Our Culture," *The Tallahassee Democrat*, August 16, 1991, reprinted from *The Boston Globe*.

Page 47: March, 1995, pp. 169-176.

Page 47: As the mother played by Shirley MacLaine in the movie *Turning Point*, asserted to her daughter in explaining the essential asset mothers have, " I know you."

Page 47: Penelope Leach, *Children First* (New York: Vintage Books, 1994), p. xv.

Page 48: According to an annual study by the Annie E. Casey Foundation reported in *Kids Count Data Book*:

> The neighborhood in which a child lives is a powerful influence . . . We can no longer be surprised by the terrible outcomes experienced by young people who grow up in

environments where drugs, violence, welfare and teen pregnancy are far more prevalent than safe schools, high-school diplomas, and good jobs.

Reported in *The Tallahassee Democrat*, April 25, 1994, p. 9A.

Page 48:   David Wood, author and pediatrician at Cedars-Sinai Medical Center in Los Angeles, is quoted in a *New York Times* article, "Education Transfers and Stops: Public Schools Struggling with High Student Turnover," March 16, 1995, p. B1:

> Children who move often are more likely to fail a grade and to have behavioral problems than those who do not, according to a 1993 study published in *The Journal of the American Medical Association.* Even a short move is often stressful.

The same conclusions were reached by a General Accounting Office study reported in, "How America's Mobility Hurts Poor Children," *Business Week*, June 6, 1994:

> While mobility can improve the efficiency of labor markets, it seems particularly high among the poor and disadvantaged. The effect on children can be particularly devastating . . . Among all income groups, frequent school-changers are more likely to perform poorly in reading and math, to repeat a grade, and to have health problems than children who have never changed schools.

Page 48:   A dramatized illustration of the very tangible risks involved in becoming a parent is Julia Roberts's character in *Steel Magnolias*. Shelby literally risks and eventually loses her life to have a child.

Page 49:   See, for example, Erich Fromm's *The Art of Loving*, especially II(2), "Love between Parent and Child" (New York: Harper & Row, 1956).

Page 49:   Examples of contemporary analysis of gender dimensions of parental roles include Hope Edelman's *Motherless Daughters: The Legacy of Loss* (New York: Addison-Wesley, 1994) and David Blankenhorn's *The Fatherless Society* (New York: Basic Books, 1994).

Artists and writers have expressed the need for parental role models in very compelling ways. See, for example, Camus's statement in the section entitled "Search for the Father" in his autobiographical novel, *Le Premier Homme* (*The First Man*) that Camus was writing at the time of his death in 1960, which has been published recently by his daughter. Camus's leading character, Jacques Cormery, whom critics claim to be indistinguishable from the author, says:

> I tried to discover as a child what was right and wrong since no one around could tell me. And now I recognize that everything abandoned me, that I need someone to show me the way, to blame and praise me . . . I need my father.

Quoted in a review by Paul Gray, "A Mesmerizing Encore from Camus," *Time*, May 16, 1994.

An equally compelling contemporary statement about fathers is made by director John Singleton in the movie *Boyz N' the Hood*. Laurence Fishburne's father character illustrates the enormous difference a mature and caring adult can make in the lives of sons like Trey.

Page 49: The "heroic compromises that marriage entails" are something that novelists, screenwriters, and actors are adept at portraying as indicated by, for instance, Richard Corliss's review of Jessica Lange's Oscar-winning performance in *Blue Sky*, "Jess Like a Woman," *Time*, April 10, 1995, p. 77.

Page 49: Effects of divorce on the lifetime welfare of children require longitudinal studies over extended periods. The difficulty of controlling for extraneous circumstances is formidable, but several studies have indicated that children of divorce have significantly reduced prospects in life. See, for example, the work of Judith Wallerstein, *Surviving the Breakup: How Children and Parents Cope with Divorce* (New York: Basic Books, 1980), Sara McLanahan and Gary Sandefur, *Growing Up With a Single Parent* (Cambridge, MA.: Harvard University Press, 1994). The issue here is not whether children are better off having divorced parents versus living in a severely dysfunctional family but simply the value to children of having the stable, caring attention of both parents on a daily basis.

Page 49: George McGovern, *Terry* (New York: Villard, 1996), p. 19.

Page 49: *Ibid.*, p. 75.

Page 50: "More Family, Less Saga for Mantle," *The New York Times*, June 12, 1995, p. C1.

Page 50: *Ibid.*

Chapter 5

Page 57: USDA, *op. cit.* The USDA estimates are presented explicitly for a second child to age 17. The estimates are projected for a first child to age 18 by adding an extra year at the rate computed as equal to the USDA computation for the seventeenth year and by adding a 24 percent differential for a first child relative to the second.

Page 59: Heather Joshi, "The Cost of Caring," in Carol Glendenning and Jane Millar, eds., *Women and Poverty in Britain: the 1990s* (New York: Harvester Wheatsheaf, 1992), p. 121.

Page 59: *Ibid.*, pp. 123-24.

Page 59: " . . .the negative effects of having two or more children appear to be large." Sanders Korenman and David Neumark, "Marriage, Motherhood, and Wages," *Journal of Human Resources*, Vol. XXVII, No. 2 (May 1992), p. 251.

Page 59: *Ibid.*

Page 60: Arthur Levine, President of Teachers College, Columbia University cites a national average per-pupil cost of roughly $6500 in "Why I'm Reluctantly Backing Vouchers," *The Wall Street Journal*, June 15, 1998, p. A28. Estimates of expenditures per pupil in public schools vary widely. In his book, *Public Education: An Autopsy* (Cambridge, MA: Harvard University Press, 1995), Myron Lieberman notes that official estimates exclude many things such as capital outlays, interest on school debt, and various other forms of expenditures not explicitly included in school budgets. Lieberman concludes:

> None of us knows the costs of public education, from our own pockets or the government's. These costs are extremely diffuse and intermingled with others beyond identification. Even with the help of a supercomputer, it is impossible to ascertain what any individual is paying for public education. (p. 139)

Page 61: See, for example, Richard Wright's "Our Cheating Hearts," an article adapted from *The Moral Animal: Evolutionary Psychology and Everyday Life*, in *Time*, August 5, 1994, pp. 44-52. Wright states:

> The genetic payoff of having two parents committed to a child's welfare seems to be the central reason men and women can fall into swoons over each other . . . One of the most obvious Darwinian predictions is that stepparents will tend to care less profoundly for children than natural parents. After all, parental investment is a precious resource. So natural selection should favor those parental psyches that do not squander it on nonrelatives who do not carry the parents' genes.

Wright cites the work of Martin Daly and Margo Wilson of McMaster University, who have found that American stepchildren are 100 times more likely to be fatally abused than children living with biological parents. In Canada the ratio is 70:1. Children under 10 are three to four times more likely to suffer nonfatal abuse when living with a stepparent and a biological parent instead of two biological parents.

Page 62: Julie B. Schor, *The Overworked American* (New York: Basic Books, 1992).

Page 62: As *New York Times* columnist Peter Passell notes:

> The formal limits that prevented women from combining financially rewarding work with childrearing are fading. But the practical constraints are proving very durable.

Passell's article cites a a study by Harvard economist Claudia Goldin based on data from the National Longitudinal Survey that tracks tens of thousands of Americans over their entire lives. Goldin found that by a very modest definition of career success (earnings equal to that of the lowest twenty-fifth percentile of college-age men) only about one in six college-educated women born between 1946 and 1956 has managed to combine children with a career. "Career and Family: College Women Look to the Past," NBER Working Paper #5188 (Cambridge, MA: National Bureau of Economic Research), 1995. Cited in "Economic Scene," *The New York Times*, September 7, 1995, p. C2.

Page 62: Theodore W. Schultz, "Fertility and Economic Values," in Theodore W. Schultz, ed., *Economics of the Family* (Chicago: University of Chicago Press, 1974), pp. 1-22. See also Gary S. Becker, *A Treatise on the Family*, Chapter 5, "The Demand for Children," (Cambridge, MA: Harvard University Press, 1981).

The theories of economists about fertility are now being put into practice by world-development agencies in Asia, Africa, and

Latin America. Emphasis on education and opportunities for women is replacing sterilization, implanting IUD's, handing out contraceptives, and imposing quotas on family size as the major focus of population planners. Higher education rates for women correlate dramatically with declines in infant mortality and fertility according to a report, "A New Approach to Population Control," *The New York Times*, April 13, 1994, p.1.

Page 63: According to Judith Bruce:

> Parents all over the world have an increasing awareness that their children will need literacy and numeracy. That means that instead of having their 6-year-old working with them in the fields, they have to pay for school fees, uniforms, transportation and supplies.

"Family Decay Global, Study Says," *The New York Times*, May 30, 1995, p. A5. Judith Bruce is the co-author of a report, "Families in Focus," issued by the Population Council.

Page 63: Wanda Minge-Klevana, "Does Labor Time Decrease with Industrialization? A Survey of Time-Allocation Studies," *Current Anthropology*, Vol. 21, No. 3, June 1980, p. 279.

Page 63: "Kids, Parents and the Economy," *The Washington Post National Weekly Edition*, July 3-9, 1995.

Page 63: Minge-Klevana notes that one characteristic that stands out in comparisons of time-allocation studies across cultures and stages of economic development is the extraordinary amount of time that mothers in the U.S. spend chauffeuring children. The more educated the mother, the more time she allocates to travel for her children, presumably for the purpose of providing them with "developmentally appropriate experiences," *op. cit.*, p. 284.

Page 64: Lawrence Katz, former chief economist at the Department of Labor, said: "It is remarkable how constant labor's [two-thirds] share has been over the last 150 years," quoted in "Productivity Is All, But It Doesn't Pay Well," *The New York Times*, June 25, 1995, p. E4.

Page 64: "In an attempt to identify any changes in total labor time between food-producer families of less industrial societies and wage-labor families of postindustrial societies, I have surveyed a number of the most comprehensive time-allocation studies to date. The survey brings into question certain theoretical assumptions about the evolution of family labor, in particular that transition from food-producing household economies to industrialized wage labor brings about the demise of the family as a labor group." Minge-Klevana, *op. cit.*, p. 285.

Page 65: Richard Dawkins, *The Selfish Gene* (Oxford: Oxford University Press, 1989).

Page 65: Marilyn Waring, *If Women Counted*, *op. cit.*, p. 29.

Page 65: Bronislaw Malinowski, A *Scientific Theory of Culture* (Chapel Hill: The University of North Carolina Press, 1944), p. 36.

Chapter 6

Page 68: This is the premise of Nobelist Gary Becker's A *Treatise on the Family*, *op. cit.*

Page 68: Becker's formulation of the basic equation for investing in human capital is given in his book, *Human Capital* (Chicago: University of Chicago Press, 3rd ed., 1993), p. 32, as follows:

$$\sum_{t=0}^{n-1} \frac{R_t}{(1 + i)^{t+1}} = \sum_{t=0}^{n-1} \frac{E_t}{(1 + i)^{t+1}}$$

when E_t and R_t are the present values of receipts and expenditures, i is the market discount rate, t is the time period, and n is the number of time periods.

Page 70: See Arthur B. Kennickell, Martha Starr-McCluer, and Annika E. Sunden, "Family Finances in the U.S.: Recent Evidence from the Survey of Consumer Finances," *Federal Reserve Bulletin*, Vol. 83, No. 1 (January, 1997), p.6.

Page 70: "Many Baby Boomers Save Little, May Run Into Trouble Later On," *The Wall Street Journal*, June 6, 1995, p. 1. (Source: Merrill Lynch & Co. study based on U.S. Census Bureau data.)

Page 72: "Holding Parents Responsible as Children's Misdeeds Rise," *The New York Times*, April 10, 1996, p. A1.

Page 73: Becker's family-optimization model shows the number of children and the quality of children to be interactive variables. Increasing the number of children magnifies the cost of increasing the quality of children and vice-versa. A *Treatise on the Family, op. cit.,* Chapter 5 (The Demand for Children).

Page 73:   A prominent financial advisor tells parents they should save for retirement rather than paying for their children's college education. See, "Letters from the Money Front," by Jane Bryant Quinn, *Newsweek,* March 14, 1994, p. 49.

Page 75:   On the subject of capitalism and morality, James Q. Wilson states:

> Critics of capitalism argue that wealth confers power, and indeed it does, up to a point. But this is not a decisive criticism unless one supposes, fancifully, that there is some way to arrange human affairs so that the desire for wealth vanishes. The real choice is between becoming wealthy by first acquiring political or military power or by getting money directly without bothering with conquest or domination. Max Weber put it this way: All economic systems rest on greed, but capitalism, because it depends on profit, is the one that disciplines greed. (p. 59)

James Q. Wilson, "Capitalism and Morality," *The Public Interest,* Number 121, Fall 1995, pp. 42-60.

Page 76:   A consensual contract between newborn babies and their parents was argued by both Hobbes and Pufendorf as a way of including everyone in the social contract. Locke and Rousseau, on the other hand, rejected such an idea and argued that parental power was temporary. ". . . at the age of maturity, sons become as free as their fathers and, like them, must agree to be governed." Carole Pateman, *The Sexual Contract, op. cit.,* pp. 83-84.

Page 76:   I am indebted to Kate Elgin, Bunting Fellow in Philosophy, 1994-95, for making this point.

Page 77:   Nina Darnton, "Mommy vs. Mommy," *Newsweek,* June 4, 1990, pp. 64-67.

Page 77:   "Women, Give Sisters a Break," *The Tallahassee Democrat,* October 10, 1990, p. 5D.

Page 77:   Amartya Sen, *Inequality Reexamined* (Cambridge: Harvard University Press, 1992), p. x. John Rawls, *A Theory of Justice, op. cit.,* p. 62.

Page 78:   Rawls, *op. cit.,* p, 62.

Page 78:   A paper written by Hilde Bojer of the University of Oslo provocatively asks what difference it would make if the rational agents negotiating a social contract behind Rawls's hypothetical "veil of ignorance" considered the fact that everyone begins life as a helpless infant and every rational agent has a 50% chance of being born female. In discussion of the paper, Julie Nelson, surely speaking for many women, offered to supply the veil for such an experiment.

Hilde Bojer, "Children and Distributional Justice," paper presented to the International Association of Feminist Economists, American University, July 24, 1996.

Page 78:   Ted Schultz, *op. cit.*, Chapter 4, "The Economics of the Value of Human Time," pp. 59 – 84:

> During the 1900-1909 period, using the official concept of national income, employee compensation accounted for about 55 percent, compared to 75 percent in 1970. Between 1909 and 1970, the changes in the shares of income other than employee compensation were as follows: proprietors' income declined from about 24 to 8 percent, rental income from 9 to 3 percent, and net interest from 5.5 to 4.1 percent, whereas corporate profits rose from 7 to 9 percent. The latter two income components fluctuated widely over this period, as would be expected in view of the uneven performance of the economy. (p. 79)

Page 78:   A particularly graphic example of what an unparented and unsocialized child can be like is provided by the story of Randi Anderson, a foster child in New York who was beaten to death by the 20-year-old son of her foster mother because she got on his nerves. "Fatal Beating Points Up A System in Crisis," *The New York Times*, September 19, 1992, p. 1. According to the article:

> Randi Anderson, 5 years old and 3 feet 7 inches tall, scrawled on the walls of her foster home with lipstick. She stole money from her foster mother's purse. She broke all her toys. She hoarded food. She defecated on the floor.

Page 78:   Bill Cosby, *op. cit.*, see especially p. 61.

Page 79:   As evidence of the economic value of parental attention, Ted Schultz cites a study by Arleen Leibowitz, "Home Investment in Children," in *Economics of the Family: Marriage, Children, and*

Human Capital, ed. Theodore W. Schultz (Chicago: University of Chicago Press, 1974).

Page 79:   One philosopher who has considered the conflicts between freedom and equality at the family level is James Fishkin in his book, *Justice, Equal Opportunity, and the Family* (New Haven: Yale University Press, 1983). As Fishkin notes:

> The conflict with liberty cannot be avoided. It appears in a particularly excruciating form directed at the family. Once the role of the family is taken into account, the apparently moderate aspiration of equal opportunity produces conflicts with the private sphere of liberty—with autonomous family relations—that are nothing short of intractable. (p. 4)

Page 79:   Theodore W. Schultz, "Fertility and Economic Values," in *Economics of the Family*, Theodore W. Schultz, ed. (Chicago: The University of Chicago Press, 1974):

> From the point of view of the sacrifices that are made in bearing and rearing them [children], parents in rich countries acquire mainly future personal satisfactions from them, while in poor countries children also contribute substantially to the future real income of their parents by the work that children do in the household and on the farm and by the food and shelter they provide for their parents when they no longer are able to provide these for themselves. Children are in a very important sense the *poor man's capital*. (p. 7)

Page 80:   As the psychiatrist Alvin F. Pouissant notes in his introduction to Bill Cosby's *Fatherhood (op. cit.)*:

> Recent evidence suggests that the fathering role, or the ability of fathers to support their children's healthy growth, is equivalent to mothers if men develop the attitudes and skills to be good parents. This often requires that they give up old-fashioned ideas about so-called manliness, "who wears the pants in the family," and what constitutes "women's work" as opposed to "men's work." (p. 9)

Page 81:   Syndicated columnist, "Nurturing: Diversity Needed in Programs Aimed at Young Blacks," *The Tallahassee Democrat*, March 8, 1994, p. 9A.

Page 82:   Amartya Sen, *op. cit.*, p. 1.

Page 82:   See, for example, Edward O. Wilson, *Sociobiology: The New Synthesis* (Cambridge: Harvard University Press, 1975), especially Chapter 27, "Man: From Sociobiology to Sociology."

Page 82:   See, for example, Sara Blaffer Hrdy, *The Woman Who Never Evolved* (Cambridge: Harvard University Press, 1981).

Page 82:   Gary S. Becker, A *Treatise on the Family, op. cit.*

In his presidential address to the American Economic Association, entitled "Family Economics and Macro Behavior," Becker stated:

> . . .parents' investments in children are a far more important source of an economy's capital stock than are bequests or the life-cycle accumulation of physical capital.

Printed in *The American Econmic Review*, Vol. 78, No. 1 (March, 1988), pp. 1-13.

Page 82:   Theodore W. Schultz, *The Economics of the Family, op. cit.* and Richard T. Ely, *op. cit.*

Page 83:   In economic language, parental investment of time and resources needs to be integrated into endogenous growth theory. While there has been increasing emphasis on human capital and culture as determinants of economic progress at both theoretical (Douglas North's Nobel Lecture, *op, cit.*) and empirical (World Bank, "Where Is the Wealth of Nations?," in *Monitoring Environmental Progress* (Washington, D.C.: The International Bank for Reconstruction and Development, 1995), pp.57-61.) levels, there is no formal recognition of the role of family investment in economic-growth models.

Investment in human capital is still counted only when it occurs in the market place, and the process of cultural development is considered impenetrable by economic analysis. Since culture formation has a large intergeneration-transmission component that depends substantially on what parents pass on to children, understanding where human capital and culture come from requires paying attention to where children come from, economically speaking.

A major cultural factor in economic growth is thought to be the ability of a particular population to absorb technology (see

North). In contrast to the theorists who profess to be mystified about where such ability comes from, any parent who has ever had the job of helping with homework or convincing a nine-year-old child that learning fractions is more fun than yacking with friends knows where the ability of a culture to absorb technology comes from.

Page 83: Folbre articulated this model in a lecture at the Public Policy Institute of Radcliffe College, June 6, 1995. Folbre's concept of the family is presented in "Children as Public Goods," *AEA Papers and Proceedings*, May 1994, pp. 86-90, and in her book, *Who Pays for the Kids?* (London: Routledge, 1994) in which she outlines her suggestions for public policy with respect to the family. See especially pp. 248-59.

Page 84: Folbre acknowledges that even the most generous of the European family-support systems pay only a fraction of the costs of childrearing. *Who Pays for the Kids?*, *op. cit.*, p. 250.

Page 84: This is another point that Kate Elgin, *op. cit.*, helped to clarify.

Page 84: Amartya Sen, "Gender and Cooperative Conflicts," in Irene Tinker, Ed., *Persistent Inequalities: Women and World Development*, (New York: Oxford University Press, 1990), pp. 123-149.

Page 84: Edward O. Wilson, *On Human Nature* (Cambridge, MA: Harvard University Press, 1978), p. 82.

Page 85: A conversation with Professor Wilson, May 3, 1995. See his book, *Sociobiology*, *op. cit.*, especially Chapter 20, "The Social Insects," Chapter 16, "The Nonhuman Primates," and Chapter 27, "Man: From Sociobiology to Sociology."

Ants have a uniquely collective method of reproduction centered around a fertile queen and a large number of sterile workers, a system that results in a high proportion of shared genes. In "diploid" reproduction, some of the queen's eggs are fertilized by a male and some aren't. Fertilized eggs hatch as females while unfertilized eggs hatch as males. The result is that sisters have three-fourths of their genes in common with each other whereas mothers and daughters only share half of their genes. Sisters therefore have more genetic reason to cooperate with each other than they do to produce their own offspring.

Page 85: The following excerpts are from a *USA Today* article on the results of several studies of stepfamilies:

> Many kids living in stepfamilies do no better on numerous measures of well-being—and sometimes worse—than kids in single-parent homes, some of the new studies show.
>
> "That is just an astonishing finding but it is verified in numerous important studies," says David Blankenhorn, author of *Fatherless in America.*
>
> The research doesn't bode well for what many say is the family form of the future.

Similar conclusions were reported by psychologist Nicholas Zill, sociologist Sarah McLanahan of Princeton, an NIH study, an extensive study of 17,000 children in Great Britain, and Rutgers University sociologist David Popenoe, author of *Life without Father* in "Some Worse Off When Parent Marries Again," *USA Today,* January 4, 1996, p. D1.

Chapter 7

Page 87: Professor Kotlikoff, an economist at Boston University, in a presentation to the American Economic Association, "Privatization of Social Security at Home and Abroad," San Francisco, January 7, 1996.

Page 87: "Liberté, Egalité, and Utter Gridlock," *The New York Times,* December 10, 1995, p. E5.

Page 87: For a review of social-security systems around the world, see *Averting the Old Age Crisis: A World Bank Policy Research Report* (Oxford: Oxford University Press, 1994).

Page 88: "Ending the Great Terror of Life," *AARP BULLETIN Special Report,* June 1995, p. 1.

Page 89: Alicia Munnell, assistant secretary of the Treasury for Economic Policy, listed "a sense of community" as one of the major virtues of the Social Security system. Chancellor's Distinguished Lecture Series, University of Massachusetts at Boston, April 19, 1995. A feeling of community sharing is an illusion, however, when what is really happening is that everyone is getting more out of a system than they put into it by operating an intergeneration pyramid scheme.

Page 90: A few brave politicians did try to tell the truth about the 1983 "cure" that raised Social Security taxes for the express purpose of generating a surplus that would make the system solvent when the baby boom reached retirement. Senator Moynihan pointed out that since the surpluses were being put into government bonds that financed the federal deficit, the Social Security surpluses were in effect being spent and wouldn't be there for future retirees.

Moynihan advocated rescinding the tax increase since it burdened wage earners disproportionately. See "Of Budgets and Truth," *The New York Times*, January 3, 1990, p. A13; Daniel Patrick Moynihan, "To My Social Security Critics," *The New York Times*, February 9, 1990.

At about the same time, Representative John Porter advocated investing the surpluses in individual IRA accounts, which would actually be there for retirement. See "What's Wrong—and Right—With the Porter Plan," *The Wall Street Journal*, February 8, 1990.

Page 91:   The first beneficiary of the program was Ida Mae Fuller of Ludlow, Vermont. On January 31, 1940, she received a Social Security check for $22.54. The retired law clerk continued to receive benefits for the next 35 years until her death shortly before her 100th birthday. In all, she had "contributed" $22 to the system; she collected a total of $20,000. This account is given by Dorcas R. Hardy, former Commisioner of Social Security, and C. Colburn Hardy in their book, *Social Insecurity* (New York: Villard Books, 1991), p. 10.

Page 92:   Through the end of the 1980s, retirees in this country received between two and four times as much from Social Security as they could have obtained if they had placed their tax contributions in a high-yielding private pension, according to Sylvia Hewlett, *When the Bough Breaks, op. cit.*, p. 177.

Page 92:   *AARP Bulletin*, July 1995, p. 12.

Page 93:   Even the most radical reformers who want to junk the whole pay-as-you-go system and convert Social Security to an investment program fail to recognize any contribution that family investment needs to make to old-age security.

Page 94:   As Deborah Steelman, a former associate director of the Office of Management and Budget, explained:

When lawmakers "fixed" Social Security five years ago, they said they would collect enough money to put the Social Security Trust Fund on solid footing for the next 75 years; they would "prefund" it, saving enough money over the next 10 to 20 years to pay for benefits to the huge generation that will retire 20 to 40 years from now. This sounded fine, so they passed a law requiring a series of payroll tax increases to accumulate the necessary funds and to make Social Security "safe" for all future generations.

Only one slight hitch: The Social Security Trust Fund doesn't save money; it lends it to the U.S. government. The U.S. government, in turn, spends not only every dollar it collects through income taxes but also every dollar it borrows from the trust fund, on today's basic programs: education, highways, law enforcement, and the like.

The biggest borrower on this continent—the U.S. government—borrows money to pay for these programs from the largest, and the fastest-growing source of financing on this continent, the Social Security Trust Fund. And if you think the government is saving for the day it has to pay this money back, think again. "Who's Going To Pay Back All the Money Borrowed from Social Security?" *Washington Post National Weekly Edition*, March 28-April 3, 1988, p. 29.

Page 94: It has been calculated by Laurence Kotlikoff that if current fiscal policies persist the lifetime net tax burdens of future generations are likely to be 21 percent greater than those of young Americans today. *Generational Accounting* (New York: Free Press, 1992), p. 29.

Page 95: It is not uncommon for two parents to have to work at three or more jobs to keep their heads above water financially. See, for example, "Working Harder, Getting Nowhere," *Time*, July 3, 1995, pp. 17-20; or "Here Comes the Four-Income Family," *Money*, February, 1995, pp. 149-155.

Page 95: The Social Security benefit is estimated according to the basic Social Security formulas for 1997. A wage base is constructed from the employee's earnings record, and the benefit is computed as 90 percent of the first $5,460 of annual earnings, 32 percent of the next $32,892, and 15 percent of any remainder. The Medicare figure is computed from the total expenditures reported divided by the number of enrollees. See "1998 Annual Report of the Board of Trustees of the Federal Supplemantary Medican Insurance Trust Fund" and "1998 Annual Report of the Board of Trustees of the Federal Hospital Insurance Trust Fund." U.S. Government Printing Office, Washington: 1998.

Page 96:   "Social Security Fact Sheet," *op. cit.*

Page 99:   A loose interpretation would be "too much of one thing and not enough of other things." Barring continuous technological innovation verging on the miraculous, the concentration of investment solely on machines would encounter the law of diminishing returns. As one analyst notes, "You cannot build enough steel mills to solve the Social Security Problem." C. Eugene Steuerle, "Plans for a Comprehensive Reform Package, " in Steven A. Sass and Robert K. Triest, *op. cit.*, p. 306.

Page 99:   See Martin Feldstein, "Social Security, Induced Retirement, and Aggregate Capital Formation," *Journal of Political Economy,* 1974, Vol. 83, 905-926; Martin Feldstein, "Perceived Wealth in Bonds and Social Security: A Comment," *Journal of Political Economy,* 1976, Vol. 84, 331-335; S.C. Hu, "Social Security, the Supply of Labor, and Capital Accumulation," *American Economic Review,* June 1979, 69, 274-283; Dean R. Leimer and Selig Lesnoy, "Social Security and Private Saving: New Time-Series Evidence," *Journal of Political Economy,* June 1982, 90, 606-642.

Page 99:   Two very different theories have been proposed for the apparent absence of a "wealth-illusion" effect of Social Security:

■   There isn't any illusion. People know there isn't any real wealth to back up the system, so rational consumers increase their personal saving by an equivalent amount to compensate for the missing wealth. The major proponent of this hypothesis has been Robert J. Barro. See, "Are Government Bonds New Wealth?" *Journal of Political Economy,* November/December 1974, 82, 1095-1117. Since Social Security is essentially an unfunded liability of the federal government, it has the same financial implications as the rest of the government's unfunded debt.

■   A wealth-illusion effect of Social Security may well exist, but it can't be identified statistically because of technical problems in the data and limitations of our analytical tools. See James Tobin, *Asset Accumulation and Economic Activity* (Chicago: The University of Chicago Press, 1980).

Page 99: Henry J. Aaron, *Economic Effects of Social Security* (Washington, D.C.: The Brookings Institution, 1982).

Page 99: The same demographics that are pushing up the stock market in the high-saving years of the baby-boom generation are expected to drive it down when the people who are investing now for retirement try to cash in their investments because the next generation is too small to absorb what the baby-boom generation will be trying to sell.

> That imbalance could send share prices tumbling by one-third over 15 or 20 years, in the view of experts who have begun examining the potentially lethal combination of demographics and finance.

Scott Thurm, "Retiring Baby Boomers Could Deflate Stock Market," *San Jose Mercury News*, reprinted in *The Tallahassee Democrat*, April 28, 1996, p. 5C.

Page 100: David C. Lindeman, "Introduction," *Social Security: What Role for the Future* (*op. cit.*), pp. 19-20.

An even more implicit reference to this problem is contained in the proposals of the 1995 Social Security Advisory Council, when they specify that projections of investment returns from putting some portion of Social Security collections into the stock market depend on the market's ability to maintain its historical level of performance. See, for example, Edward M. Gramlich, "Different Approaches for Dealing with Social Security," Economic Perspectives, Vol. 10, No. 3 (Summer, 1996), p. 59.

The market for capital won't be maintained if there isn't a productive workforce to complement it or if, what is saying the same thing, there isn't a younger generation that is affluent enough to buy stocks at their historical prices.

Page 100: Robert Eisner, a former president of the American Economic Association, emphasizes the point that even private pension funds can be deceptive:

To a considerable extent—to a greater extent in recent decades, with the development of private pension programs, than in earlier times—the elderly *feel* [emphasis mine] that they are providing for themselves. From the standpoint of the elderly as a group or the economy as a whole, there is a certain self-deception here. Aside from some real property that they may have, particularly houses, the elderly provide themselves only with pieces of paper—stocks, bonds, pension and insurance checks, bank deposits, and cash under the mattress. Society must produce the goods and services that these pieces of paper can be used to buy. Otherwise they amount to just that—pieces of paper.

The Misunderstood Economy (Boston: Harvard Business School Press, 1995), p. 124.

Page 102: See, for example, "Europeans Redefine What Makes a Citizen," *The New York Times*, January 7, 1996, p. E6:

The anti-immigrant mood is widespread in Europe these days, and it's one of the reasons why the 15-nation union has not yet made good on a promise made five years ago to do away with internal border controls and create a true common market that could eventually stimulate the economic growth needed to bring down chronic high unemployment.

Page 102: The World Bank estimates that 86 percent of the increase in world population over 60 by 2030 will occur in transitional socialist economies and developing countries while only 14 percent will occur in the developed economies. *Averting the Old Age Crisis: A World Bank Policy Research Report* (New York: Oxford University Press, 1994), p. 2.

Page 102: See, for example, *Work and Family: Policies for a Changing Workforce*, National Research Council, Marianne A. Ferber and Brigid O'Farrell, eds., with La Rue Allen (Washington, D.C.: National Academy Press, 1991).

Page 102: Child allowances, free medical care, free education through university, subsidized household assistance, home care for the elderly, household appliances, and rent subsidies for poor families are all part of the French family-assistance package. See "To French, Solidarity Outweighs Balanced Budget," *The New York Times*, December 20, 1995, p. 1.

Page 105: The World Bank estimates that in Australia, for instance, public health spending per person over age 65 is six times that per person under age 15 and that "the proportion of the population that is old explains 92 percent of the variance in public health plus pension spending in a large sample of industrial and developing countries. The Bank Report also notes the interaction between pension expenditures and health caused by the fact that better health care enables people to live longer and thus need more retirement support. *Averting the Old Age Crisis, op. cit.*, pp. 43-47.

Page 105: This statistic is cited by Robert J. Samuelson in "Dole's Risky Opportunity," *Newsweek*, May 20, 1996, p. 47, as reported by the Watson Wyatt consulting firm.

Page 105: Quoted in, "The Wealth of Nations: A 'Greener' Approach Turns List Upside Down," *The New York Times*, September 19, 1995, p. B5, referring to the monograph, *Monitoring Environmental Progress* (Washington, D.C.: The World Bank, 1995).

Page 105: "Where Is the Wealth of Nations?" in *Monitoring Environmental Progress, Ibid.*, p. 63.

Page 106: According to Dr. Gerard Miller, a psychoanalyst and political commentator, "'The message was that 'market rules are not our problem, and don't expect us to be reasonable anymore,'" quoted in "To French, Solidarity Outweighs Balanced Budget," *op. cit.*

Page 106: Pateman concludes after an extensive analysis that "fraternity" as employed by the Enlightenment philosophers was never intended to mean "community" except in a superficial and misleading way. In the context of social-contract theory, "fraternity" specifically meant the bonds among brothers. See Chapter 4, "Genesis, Fathers, and the Political Liberty of Sons," *The Sexual Contract, op. cit.*, pp. 77-115:

> Liberty, equality *and* fraternity form the revolutionary trilogy because liberty and equality are the attributes of the fraternity who exercise the law of male sex-right. What better notion to conjure with than 'fraternity,' and what better conjuring trick than to insist that "fraternity" is universal and nothing more than a metaphor for community. (p. 114)

Chapter 8

Page 109: Quoted from *Newsweek* by Wendy Kaminer in "It's All the Rage: Crime and Culture," *Radcliffe*, Fall/Winter, 1995, p. 30.

Page 109: Interview on CBS Evening News in segment focusing on Jane Austen's surprising popularity in Hollywood, December 15, 1995. Three movies produced in 1995 were based on Austen's books: *Clueless*, *Sense and Sensibility*, and *Persuasion*.

Page 109: Quoted from "Once Just a Princess, Suddenly a Feminist," *The Daily Telegraph*, by America Online, December 3, 1995.

Page 109: Statement by a character in *Rich in Love* by Josephine Humphreys (New York: Penguin Books, 1987), pp. 56-57.

Page 110: Virginia Satir, quoted by Maggie Scarf in her book, *Intimate Worlds* (New York: Random House, 1995), p. xxx.

Page 110: See, for instance, "Daughters of Murphy Brown," *Newsweek*, August 2, 1993, p. 58-59.

Page 110: "The Fatherhood Deficit," *The World & I*, November 1995, p. 63.

Page 110: According to Rebecca Blank, professor of economics at Northwestern University:

> The data indicate that rising nonmarital birth rates are primarily caused by a decline in fertility among married women, combined with a growing share of unmarried women in the population.

"Teen Pregnancy: Government Programs Are Not the Cause," *Feminist Economics*, Vol. One, No. Two, Summer 1995, p. 47.

According to David Popenoe, Associate Dean for Social and Behavioral Sciences of Rutgers University and Co-chairman of the Council of Families in America, white family structure has achieved a statistical profile in the 1990s similar to what the Moynihan Report described in the black family with considerable alarm in the 1960s:

> For example, in 1965, 51 percent of black teen-age mothers were single; in 1990, among white teen-age mothers, 55 percent were single. In 1965, 26 percent of black babies were born out of wedlock; in 1990, 19 percent of white babies were born to unwed mothers.

See "The Controversial Truth: Two-Parent Families Are Better," *The New York Times*, December 26, 1992, p. A19.

Page 110: According to Frank F. Furstenberg, Jr.:

> Until the latter part of the nineteenth century, divorce was largely proscribed by law and shunned in practice. . . . Roughly 5% of marriages ended in divorce just after the Civil War compared with an estimated 36% in 1964. . . . There was a sharp increase in the incidence of divorce from the mid-1960s to the late 1970s. During a span of a decade and a half, divorce rates for married women more than doubled (from 10.6 per 1,000 in 1965 to 22.8 in 1979), pushing the risk of divorce much higher for all marriage cohorts, especially those wed after the mid-1960s. Some researchers speculated that a majority of all marriages contracted in the 1970s and later would end, especially when both informal separations and formal divorces were counted.

"History and Current Status of Divorce in the United States," in *The Future of Children*, Volume 4, Number 1, Spring 1994, p. 29. Furstenberg notes that although there are some indications that the U.S. divorce rate is now declining, "the United States has led the industrialized world in the incidence of divorce and the proportion of children affected by divorce."

Page 110: "No-Fault Divorce Law Is Assailed in Michigan, and Debate Heats Up," *The Wall Street Journal*, January 5, 1996, p. 1.

Page 111: A concern articulated by anthropologist David W. Murray in the Spring, 1994, issue of *Policy Review* as cited by William Raspberry, *Washington Post* columnist, in "The Bonds and the Benefits of Being Married," reprinted in *The Tallahassee Democrat*, April 13, 1994, p. F1.

Page 112: According to Robert Haveman and Barbara Wolfe, *Succeeding Generations: On the Effects of Investment in Children* (New York: Russell Sage Foundation, 1995):

> A number of studies have investigated the correlates of marital and cohabitational patterns among young adults, with most of the analyses focusing on the intergenerational transmission of these patterns . . . . Numerous theoretical linkages suggest an intergenerational pattern of marital experiences. These include linkages through:

(1) economic resources or status attainment (single-parent families tend to have fewer economic resources than do intact families)

(2) educational attainment (children growing up in single-parent homes tend to have lower levels of schooling, with schooling being an alternative for marriage or cohabitation)

(3) parental social control (single parents tend to have less time to monitor and socialize children)

(4) earlier maturation (children growing up in single-parent households tend to be asigned responsibilities, rights, and authority earlier than those in intact families)

(5) attitudes regarding nonmarital sex, cohabitation, early-marriage, and marital dissolution (children growing up in a disrupted family—or in a family that married early, or that married postpregnancy, or that remarried after divorce—are likely to have distinct attitudes toward marriage, cohabitation, and marital dissolution). (pp. 74-75)

Haveman and Wolfe cite studies by Arland Thornton, "Influence of the Marital History of Parents on the Marital and Cohabitational Experiences of Children," *American Journal of Sociology,* 96: 868-894, 1991; and by P. Lindsay Chase-Lansdale and E.M. Hetherington, "The Impact of Divorce on Life-Span Development: Short and Long Term Effects," in Paul Baltes, David Featherman, and Richard Lerner (eds.), *Life-Span Development and Behavior* (Hillsdale, NJ: Lawrence Erlbaum Associates, 1991).

Page 113: Edward Rothstein, "Connections: Miss Manners has been keeping an eye on cyberspace and she is not amused," *The New York Times,* December 25, 1995, p. 25.

Page 113: *On Human Nature, op. cit.,* p. 163.

Page 115: Amartya Sen, "Gender and Cooperative Conflicts," in *Persistent Inequalities: Women and World Development.* Irene Tinker, ed. (New York: Oxford University Press, 1990), p. 124.

Page 115: See, for example, the comments of Simone de Beauvoir, Juliet Mitchell, and Shulamith Firestone quoted in Chapter 3.

Page 115: According to Rathbone:

> If the present system tells hardly on the wives and children of the wage-earner even when the latter is ordinarily industrious and affectionate, how do they fare when he is a shirker or a bully? Few people who have not been in contact with the facts realize how completely such a man has his family at his mercy, and how little the law does to protect them against anything but his worst excesses. . . . hardly any form of suffering can be worse than that which goes on day by day in a working-class home, where either husband or wife is really bad.

Rathbone, *op. cit.*, pp. 87-88.

Page 115: In Bergman's words:

> The disadvantages to playing the role of full-time homemaker are so great that it is unlikely that significant numbers of men would want to serve in it. If the occupation continues to exist, it will continue to be part of the female domain and hence inherently disadvantaged. Since this is the case, equality of the sexes and women's welfare would be better served if younger women were to avoid entering the role even temporarily and if the socially sanctioned 'option' to assume the role were to disappear.

Barbara Bergman, *op. cit.*, p. 226.

Page 115: Economist Victor Fuchs states:

> A comparison of age earning profiles for men and women demonstrates that, while women's earnings lag only slightly behind men's during women's early years in the labor force, women miss out on the rapid increase in earnings men experience in their late twenties and thirties, the peak childbearing years for women. Taking these factors together, Fuchs, concludes that 'I do' has a very different price for women than for men.

June R. Carbone, "A Feminist Perspective on Divorce," *op. cit.*, p. 184, quoting Victor Fuchs in *Women's Quest for Equality* (*op. cit.*).

Page 115: "The Bargain Breaks," *The Economist*, December 26th, 1992– January 8th, 1993, p. 37.

Page 115: Sen notes that the ratios of missing females are lower in the southern provinces of India (Karnataka, Andhra Pradesh, Tamil Nadu, and Kerala) where women have more opportunities for work outside the home than in the northern provinces (Punjab and Haryana) where there are fewer such opportunities. "Gender and Cooperative Conflicts," *op. cit.*, p. 139.

Page 115: "Thirty percent of all female murder victims in 1986 were killed by their husbands or boyfriends, compared with 6 percent of male victims killed by wives or girlfriends," Susan Moller Okin, *Justice, Gender, and the Family* (New York: Basic Books, 1989), p. 128. Moller cites several sources including *Report to the Nation on Crime and Justice*, 2nd ed. (Washington, D.C.: Government Printing Office, March 1988), p. 33.

Page 116: The link between fairness in distribution and the cooperation needed for efficient production was considered a major argument against imperialism and slavery by leading classical economists. According to Thomas Sowell:

> Both imperialism and slavery were regarded as *losing* ventures, for they inhibited the creation of wealth while concentrating on its appropriation. Classical economists saw the gains from imperialism going to a small class of wealthy businessmen and colonial officials to be greatly outweighed by the costs paid by the taxpayers to maintain an empire.

Classical Economics Reconsidered (Princeton, NJ: Princeton University Press, 1974), p. 11.

Sowell cites extensive quotes from Adam Smith's *An Inquiry into the Nature and Causes of the Wealth of Nations* (New York: Modern Library, 1937), p. 415; David Ricardo's *The Works and Correspondence of David Ricardo* (Cambridge University Press, 1957), Vol. I, pp. 133-134; and John Stuart Mill's *Principles of Political Economy*, ed. W. J. Ashley (London: Longmans, Green and Co., 1909), pp. 580-581, to demonstrate the classical economists' understanding of unfair distribution and expropriation as both moral and economic problems.

Page 116: If, to cite one of many possibilities, one spouse is required by an employer to move to a place where the other spouse is unable to find an equal job.

Page 116: "Gender and Cooperative Conflicts," *op. cit.*, p. 132.

Page 116: Albert O. Hirschman is cited by Okin as an economic theorist who developed the connection between relative exit positions and power within relationships:

The idea that the mutuality or asymmetry of a relationship can be measured by the relative capacities of the parties to withdraw from it has been developed extensively by Albert O. Hirschman, in two books written many years apart. In his 1970 book entitled *Exit, Voice and Loyalty,* Hirschman makes a convincing connection between the influence of voice by members within groups or institutions and the feasibility of their exit from them.

According to Okin, Hirschman made a similar argument twenty-five years earlier about the crucial influence of the *relative* potential of exit options in a two-party relationship on the power structure of the relationship in *National Power and the Structure of Foreign Trade* (Berkeley: University of California Press, 1945; expanded ed. 1980). See Susan Moller Okin, *Justice, Gender and the Family (op. cit.),* p. 137.

Page 117: *Justice, Gender, and the Family, op. cit.*

Page 118: Scarf, *op. cit.,* pp. 102-103.

Page 118: *Ibid.,* p. 125.

Page 119: *Ibid.,* p. 36.

Page 119: *Ibid.,* p. 74.

Page 119: *Ibid.*

Page 120: June R. Carbone, "A Feminist Perspective on Divorce," in *The Future of Children: Children and Divorce,* Volume 4, Number 1, Spring 1994, p. 187.

Page 120: *Ibid.,* p. 188.

Page 120: Mary Ann Mason, *The Equality Trap* (New York: Simon & Schuster, Inc., 1988), p. 50.

Page 120: *Ibid.,* p. 53.

Page 121: *Ibid.,* p. 64.

Page 121: "No-Fault Divorce Law Is Assailed in Michigan, and Debate Heats Up," *The Wall Street Journal,* December 5, 1996, p. 1. Mary Ann Mason (see preceding reference) cites studies that show an average 72 percent decline in children's standard of living one year after divorce (p. 64).

Page 121: As Carbone notes:

> [in some states] courts consider the "best interests of the child"[in awarding custody] prospectively only. In such determinations, the father's greater financial resources, even if they are the product of his lack of involvement with the children during the marriage, might outweigh the mother's greater contact and emotional commitment.

June R. Carbone,"A Feminist Perspective on Divorce," *op. cit.*, p. 188.

Page 121: Judge Joseph Q. Tarbuck made such a decision in a Pensacola, Florida, court in August of 1995 in the case of John and Mary Ward and their 11-year-old daughter. John Ward's parental qualifications included having spent eight years in prison for the second-degree murder of his first wife, being accused of molesting a teenage girl, and being $1400 behind in paying child support. "Judge Places Girl With Killer Rather than Lesbian Mom," *The Tallahassee Democrat*, February 1, 1996, p. 1.

Page 121: "An Unwed Mother for Quayle," *The New York Times*, September 24, 1992.

Page 122: "When the Bough Breaks," *The Economist, op. cit.* The article cites the work of Sara McLanahan on surveys of groups of children in the U.S. over time and similar results from studies based on surveys of British children born in a single week in 1946 and 1958.

Page 122: Cited by David Popenoe in "The Controversial Truth: Two-Parent Families Are Better," *The New York Times, op. cit.*

Page 122: "'New' Marines Illustrate Growing Gap between Military and Society," *The Wall Street Journal*, July 27, 1995, p. 1.

Page 122: Quoted in "No-Fault Divorce Law Is Assailed in Michigan, and Debate Heats Up," *The Wall Street Journal*, January 5, 1996, p. 1.

Page 122: "Modifying the No-Fault Divorce Law Is Bad Idea," *The Tallahassee Democrat*, April 7, 1996, p. 1C.

Page 123: Sanford N. Katz, "Historical Perspective and Current Trends in the Legal Process of Divorce," in *The Future of Children: Children and Divorce, op. cit.*, p. 44.

Page 123: A measure was introduced in the Michigan legislature in February 1996 that would revoke the no-fault provision of divorce law in contested divorce cases, and similar legislation was also being drafted in Iowa and talked about in Idaho, Georgia, and Pennsylvania. As reported by *The New York Times*:

> In those instances [contested cases], a divorce would not be granted unless the plaintiff could demonstrate that a marriage partner had been physically or mentally abusive, had a problem with alcohol or drugs, had committed adultery, had deserted the home or had been sentenced to prison. Governor John Engler, a Republican, has promised to sign the bill if it passes.

"No-Fault Divorce Is Under Attack," *The New York Times*, February 12, 1996, p. A8.

Page 124: *Ibid.*

Page 124: *Ibid.*

Page 125: Maggie Gallagher, "Why Make Divorce Easy?" *The New York Times*, February 20, 1996, p. A15.

Page 125: Quoted by Thomas Tetzinger Jr. in "The Front Lines: Case Affirms Depth of Duty Expected of Business Partners," *The Wall Street Journal*, March 29, 1996, p. B1.

Page 126: J. Seltzer and I. Garfinkel, "Inequality of Divorce Settlements: An Investigation of Property Settlements and Child Support Awards," *Social Science Research* (1991) 19:82-111, cited by Jay D. Teachman and Kathleen M. Paasch in "Financial Impact of Divorce on Children and Their Families," *The Future of Children*, *op. cit.*, p. 77.

Page 127: Working at home is an option that is becoming increasingly feasible technologically. According to a recent *New York Times* article:

> As many as 40 million people work at least part time at home, with about 8,000 home-based businesses starting daily, according to IDC/Link of New York, an electronics information research group.

The same article highlights the need to rethink zoning restrictions against residential businesses in order to allow today's families the kind of flexibility they need. A Miami Beach resident, Sharon Kersten, says: ". . .I feel it is a family-values issue—parents can work at home and be with their children." See "Your

Work at Home: Does the Town Board Care?," *The New York Times,* July 14, 1996, p. F1.

Flexible housing designs that have the potential of helping families organize work in ways that better serve their needs is another possible technical solution. Subsidizing experiments in cooperative housing is among Bergman's many creative suggestions for things that government could do to be of service to families in the way that agricultural research has helped farmers. Barbara Bergman, "High-Service Housing—The Family Care Mall," *The Economic Emergence of Women (op. cit.),* pp. 295-298.

We have already monetized such household functions as food production and preservation and clothing manufacture. It is possible to imagine ways of communalizing or monetizing additional areas of "women's work" in ways that would still leave parents in charge of rearing their children. Some families have organized co-ops to share various domestic functions. The Winslow Co-Housing Group of Winslow, Washington, built a $3.9 million "village" of 30 units housing 70 people with the goal of providing day care, elderly care, recycling, and optional communal dinner. According to Columbia University Professor of Architecture, Gwendolyn Wright:

> Co-housing has a future not as a solution to all our housing problems or social ills, but as a viable option within a market system that needs far more diversity.

Reported in "A Communal Type of Life with Dinner for All and Day Care, Too," *The New York Times*, September 27, 1990, p. B1.

Page 127: According to a *Time* article:

> There is some evidence that many people, women in particular, have 'downshifted' in an effort to cope [with work and family]. Juliet Schor, author of *The Overworked American,* found in a national survey of 1,000 people last year that 28% of the respondents had made a voluntary life-style change that involved a significant reduction in earnings: moved to a less stressful job, turned down a promotion or refused relocation. More and more mothers work part-time, though they routinely make less an hour than full-time workers doing the same job. Since 1990 the nation's mostly female temp force has mushroomed more than 85 percent."

"The Stalled Revolution," *Time,* May 6, 1996, p. 63.

Page 127: See "Women Are Becoming Equal Providers," *The New York Times*, May 11, 1995, p. A27.

Page 127: This is a major argument in Okin's book, *Justice, Gender, and the Family, op. cit.*

Page 128: Katha Pollitt, "Bothered and Bewildered," a comment on the Murphy Brown controversy, in *The New York Times*, July 22, 1993, p. A19.

Page 129: May, 1990. See, for example, Elizabeth Drew, "Barbara Bush at Wellesley: A Lesson . . . ," *The Washington Post National Weekly Edition*, May 14-May 20, 1990.

Page 129: According to a 1994 poll by the Labor Department's Women's Bureau:

> 15 percent of working women would want to work full time regardless of money
> 33 percent would prefer to work part time
> 31 percent would prefer to care for their families full time
> 20 percent would prefer to do volunteer work

Quoted in "The New Providers," *Newsweek*, May 22, 1995.

Page 129: "Women Are Becoming Equal Providers," *op. cit.*

Page 130: The theory of assortative mating (i.e., the tendency of people to choose mates similar to themselves on scales of social and economic attractiveness) has been developed extensively by Gary Becker. He cites statistical evidence that:

> The simple correlations between intelligence, education, age, race, nonhuman wealth, religion, ethnic origin, height, place of origin, and many other traits of spouses are positive and strong.

Gary S. Becker, *A Treatise on the Family* (Cambridge, MA.: Harvard University Press, 1981), p. 75.

One indicator of how similar marriage partners tend to be is Becker's computation from a 1967 U.S. Bureau of the Census tape that college-educated men are 15 times as likely to marry college-educated women as are men who never completed high school. See also Shoshana Grossbard-Schechtman's discussion of homogamy and positive sorting in *On the Economics of Marriage* (Boulder, Co.: Westview Press, 1993), pp. 2-3, 76, 105, 116, 131, 144-156, 295-296.

Page 130: Haveman and Wolfe (*op. cit.*), p. 99.

Page 130: Professor Laurence Kotlikoff included a "joint return" for Social Security in his recommendations presented to the American Economic Association, "Privatization of Social Security at Home and Abroad," *op. cit.*

Page 131: See, for example: L.J. Weitzman, *The Divorce Revolution: The Unexpected Consequences for Women in America* (New York: Free Press, 1985), p. 388; M. Fineman, "Implementing Equality: Ideology, Contradiction, and Social Change," *Wisconsin Law Review* (1983):789-886; H.H. Kay, "An Appraisal of California's No-Fault Divorce Law," *California Law Review* (1987) 75:291-319; J. Singer, "Divorce Reform and Gender Justice," *North Carolina Law Review* (1989) 76:1103-21, cited in June R. Carbone, "A Feminist Perspective on Divorce," *op. cit.*, p. 193.

Page 133: "One issue consistently overlooked in the child support literature is the effect of high marginal tax rates on absent fathers when child support payments get added to federal, state, and social security taxes." Steven Pressman, Review of *Small Change: The Economics of Child Support* by Andrea H. Beller and John W. Graham (New Haven: Yale University Press, 1993), in *Journal of Economic Issues*, 28 (September 1994), p. 945.

Page 134: "Paying the Price for Being Married," *The Washington Post National Weekly Edition*, July 18-24, 1994, p. 21.

Page 134: Alicia H. Munnell, *The Future of Social Security* (Washington, D.C.: The Brookings Institution, 1977), p. 86. Munnell lists the tax rate explicitly paid by the employee as 1 percent but goes on to cite economic analysts who have concluded that the matching contribution ostensibly paid by the employer is effectively deducted from the wages that employers actually pay to their employees. Like most economists, Munnell concludes that employees actually pay both the employee's and the employer's contributions to the payroll tax.

Page 135: (New York: Harper & Row, 1956), pp. 112 and 24, respectively.

Page 136: Irving Kristol, "Sex Trumps Gender," *The Wall Street Journal*, March 6, 1996, p. A20. In the process of arguing that the women's movement has been seriously misguided in seeking sexual equality, Kristol writes:

> . . ."no fault" is an ingenious way for married men to gain their sexual freedom while leaving their ex-wives in poverty and loneliness. I have, in conversation with friends, suggested that only wives should have the right to a no-fault divorce. They are amused but regard such a breach of "sexual equality" as just too unthinkable.

Page 136: *The Wall Street Journal*, March 19, p. A19.

Page 136: A study by Lynne Casper, a Census Bureau demographer, indicates that 16 percent of children were cared for primarily by fathers in 1993. See, for example, "Mr. Mom Is Back at the Office," *The Washington Post National Weekly Edition*, May 13-19, 1996, p. 34.

Page 137: As the head of the Florida Governor's Task Force on Domestic Violence notes concerning a the case of a murdered spouse:

> She did everything right. She did all the things she was supposed to do and she's dead. What makes the failure even more jarring is that Florida's domestic-violence laws are considered some of the best in the country.

Robin Hassler, quoted in a newspaper article about Penny Knowles who was shot by her husband in a Tallahassee parking lot even though she had taken all available legal steps to protect herself and her daughter. "Laws Couldn't Keep Knowles Alive," *The Tallahassee Democrat*, February 22, 1996, p. A1.

The same article quotes Kelly Otte, executive director of the local Refuge House for battered women:

> It scares them so badly that some women are either more desperate than ever to get out, or they're postponing their plans to leave. They're asking, why bother to get away if he's going to kill them? You can bet they're thinking of staying.

Page 137: While jobs are becoming increasingly mobile, elderly parents who live into their 80s and 90s are causing families to be less mobile. The "graying of America" is going to be a restriction on the economic choices of many families. Excerpts from a recent report describe the problem:

Just over a year ago, after much soul-searching, Robert W. Crispin turned down a plum job as one of the top three executives of a prestigious company on the West Coast. He decided instead to stay in Hartford, within easy visiting distance of his ailing 90-year-old father-in-law in northwest Pennsylvania.

"We tried to figure out ways to deal with this," Mr. Crispin said. "We talked about opportunities to travel back to the East. But traveling transcontinental every couple of weeks is not easy, and I was very concerned about how my wife would agonize, and how much she would have to be away from me and my 14-year-old daughter."

Just when corporations were getting used to the "trailing spouse"—the wife or husband whose career puts obstacles in the way of business moves—a new problem is cropping up. The graying of America is starting to create "trailing parents," who pose even bigger relocation hurdles.

"For More and More Job Seekers, An Aging Parent Is a Big Factor," *The New York Times*, January 1, 1996, p. 1.

Page 140: Katherine Davis, "I'm Not Sick, I'm Just in Love," *Newsweek*, July 24, 1995, p. 12.

Page 140: A study published in 1986 by David Bloom, Neil Bennett, and Patricia Craig reported that at age 30 college-educated white women have a 20 percent probability of marriage, at age 40 a 5 percent probability, and at age 50 a 1 percent probability. In 1989, a revision of the study was published that omitted some of the more controversial findings. Concerning the whole topic, Andrew Cherlin, Johns Hopkins University sociologist, commented:

The point that Bloom and Bennett made was valid even if the number is low. It is difficult to develop a successful marriage and a successful career at the same time. The greater point here is not which number is right but why did so many people care? We're still unsure about how women combine work and marriage today and a lot of people are still concerned about it.

Quoted in "Study on Marriage Patterns Revised Omitting Impact on Women's Careers," *The New York Times*, November 11, 1989, p. 9.

Page 141: Quoted in opening line by Jean Bethke Elshtain, *Democracy on Trial* (New York: Basic Books, 1995), p. xi.

Page 141: See, for example, "Do You, Tom, Take Harry," *Newsweek*, December 11, 1995, pp. 82-84 or "Let Them Wed," cover story in *The Economist*, January 6-12, 1996, pp. 68-71.

Page 142: Laurence H. Tribe, *The Clash of Absolutes* (New York: W.W. Norton & Company, 1990).

Page 143: "In Single Motherhood, Japan Trails the World," *The New York Times*, March 13, 1996, p. A1.

Page 143: *Ibid.*

Page 143: Jean Bethke Elshtain, *op. cit.*, p. 60.

Page 144: *Ibid*, p. 62.

Page 144: The case for using the market place to reduce stress on the political system was made very eloquently by Milton Friedman in his book, *Capitalism and Freedom*. In Friedman's words:

> The use of political channels, while inevitable, tends to strain the social cohesion essential for a stable society . . . Fundamental differences in basic values can seldom if ever be resolved at the ballot box; ultimately they can be decided, though not resolved, by conflict. The religious and civil wars are a bloody testament to this judgment. . . . The widespread use of the market reduces the strain on the social fabric by rendering conformity unnecessary with respect to any activities it ecompasses.

> Milton Friedman, *Capitalism and Freedom* (Chicago: University of Chicago Press, 1962), pp. 23-24.

Chapter 9

Page 147: This is the essence of the analysis by John E. Chubb and Terry L. Moe, *Politics, Markets, and America's Schools* (Washington, D.C.: The Brookings Institution, 1990). In the words of Chubb and Moe, "existing institutions cannot solve the problem, because they *are* the problem . . . ," p. 3.

Most serious critics of education are careful to distinguish between the institution and the individuals who work within it. Myron Lieberman, for example, makes the following statement:

> The decline of public education does not negate the fact that many individuals asociated with it perform invaluable services that deserve our respect and gratitude. My analysis

concerns the strengths and deficiencies of educational systems, not of the persons associated with them.

Myron Lieberman, *Public Education: An Autopsy* (Cambridge, Ma.: Harvard University Press, 1993), p. viii.

Page 148: "Putting Teachers on the Defensive," *The Washington Post National Weekly Edition*, March 25-31, 1996, p. 39 reports a survey of teacher attitudes concerning schools and parents. The survey reported that teachers gave low marks to many parents.

> Parents matter—a lot, these teachers said. Asked to name the single most important thing public schools need to help students learn, 31 percent of the teachers interviewed said "involved parents."

> "The single most important factor in a child's success in education is the parents," said one teacher in Grand Rapids, Mich. "After that, it's the teacher—but only after the parents."

The most startling and unexpected statement of this proposition was presented by James S. Coleman in his famous report, "Equality of Educational Opportunity," undertaken under Section 402 of the Civil Rights Act of 1964 to establish a basis for equalizing educational opportunities. Coleman expected simply to establish what everyone (at least every liberal) thought they knew—that segregation and funding disparities were crippling the ability of black children to learn. What Coleman found, instead, was that socioeconomic characteristics of parents such as education and income had much more correlation with children's academic achievements than any school characteristics such as funding, curricula, degree of integration, facilities, and so on.

Coleman's findings were substantially confirmed by the influential work of Christopher Jencks and his colleagues in the 1970s, which concluded that "family background, intellectual inheritance (e.g., IQ), and luck accounted for the bulk of variation of educational attainment (e.g., test scores) while other aspects of socioeconomic success that seemed far more amenable to change— such as parental economic position, school resources, and educational segregation—were found to play a relatively minor role." Summarized in Robert Haveman and Barbara Wolfe, *Succeeding Generations: On the Effects of Investments in Children* (New York: Russell Sage Foundation, 1995), p. 62.

A 1992 report by the National Assessment of Educational Progress, conducted by the U.S. Department of Education's National Center for Educational Statistics, also reports achievement gains by black students that are difficult to correlate with the school variables that Coleman and Jencks tested, and therefore seem attributable to the students' families according to David J. Armor, "Families Spur Black Students' Gains," *The Wall Street Journal*, June 30, 1992. Article adapted from an essay in the Summer 1992 issue of *The Public Interest*.

Page 148: Susan B. Carter reports in "Occupational Segregation, Teachers' Wages, and American Economic Growth," *Journal of Economic History*, June 1986, 46(2):

> If the nation had appropriately valued educational services and had used economic incentives rather than discrimination in other occupations to induce women to teach, the women who taught in the schools would have received a far larger share of society's resources. (p. 383)

Page 148: "Of the students who score in the bottom 20 percent on standardized college entrance exams, 40 percent become education majors," reported in "The Failure of Teacher Ed," *Newsweek*, October 1, 1990, p. 1.

Page 149: Haveman and Wolfe report that while only about 60 percent of those aged 25-29 in 1960 had graduated from high school by 1989 85.5 percent of the same age group were high-school graduates. (*op. cit.*), p. 145.

Page 149: As Leo Sandon, professor of religion and newspaper columnist, notes in connection with a bill passed by the Florida legislature to permit "voluntary" prayers at public-school commencement exercises, at sporting events or at a "secondary-school-related noncompulsory student assembly":

> Until the end of the nineteenth century, the United States was virtually a Protestant nation. Not officially, but *de facto*. As late as 1925, historian Andre Siegfried could speak of Protestantism as America's "only national religion." In many ways that generalization was still true in 1925, but less true than in 1900. It is untrue in 1996.

"The Prayer Bill: Longing for a Protestant Past," *The Tallahassee Democrat*, May 11, 1996, p. D1.

Myron Lieberman (*op. cit.*) elaborates on this point:

> By virtually any criterion—income, religion, language, eth-
> nicity, value orientation, family type—the United States is
> becoming a more heterogeneous society. This trend, espe-
> cially in social, cultural, and lifestyle matters, is generating
> more conflict than public education can constructively
> absorb. Its resources are increasingly devoted to conflict
> management instead of to education, and its ability to pro-
> vide high-quality education is correspondingly weakened.
> (p. 36)

As an example of the degree of divisiveness in public-school
issues, Lieberman notes that the official list of speakers at a public hearing on the "Chancellor's Plan for Expanded HIV/AIDS
Education Including Condom Availability" in the New York City
schools (1990) included 28 religious organizations, 27 community
organizations, 22 elected officials, 21 health organizations, 17
AIDS-related organizations, 14 teachers, 14 parents, 8 gay/lesbian
organizations, 5 higher educations institutions or organizations,
and 1 research organization as well as 77 speakers with no speci-
fied affiliation.

Page 150: Glenda and Jim Conley petitioned the Leon County (Florida)
School System to let their third-grade daughter attend the
school closest to where her parents work rather than the school
district assigned on the basis of their residence. "This is where
we are when school is in session," the parents said. The parents'
request was flatly refused even though the assigned school was at
capacity and the school of the parents' choice was under capacity. Parental convenience was denied as a valid consideration in
school assignment. The Conleys appealed the decision and
eventually won their case and even succeeded in getting the
School policy changed subject to approval by principals at both
schools. Their battle is typical of the kind of effort parents have
to make to get even the smallest consideration from a school
bureaucracy. Reported by Community Columnist Mary Ann
Lindley, *The Tallahassee Democrat*, March 7, 1996, p. 10A.

Page 150: "Plainfield High is part of a radical redesign going on in some
schools around the country: moving an extensive array of social
services, like the program here for teen-age mothers, into the
schools. The idea uses schools to reach troubled families whose

problems are crippling their children's abilities to learn, and to connect them with social services they need," "Schools to Help With Life as Well as Learning: Social Work Goes to School," *The New York Times*, April 15, 1991, p. 1.

Page 150: Pressure to fit into the grooves of an increasingly regimented school system together with less parental attention at home are blamed by critics for the fact that the number of school children taking Ritalin (the "fidgety pill") has increased 2 1/2 times since 1990. "'It takes time for parents and teachers to sit down and talk to kids,' says Dr. Sharon Collins, a pediatrician in Cedar Rapids, Iowa. . .," quoted in "Ritalin: Are We Overmedicating Our Kids?," *Newsweek*, March 18, 1996, p. 52.

Another symptom of school rigidity according to some experts is the extent to which middle-class parents are holding children back from starting kindergarten in order to give them an extra year to get ready for what is perceived as increasing demands on kindergartners to master academic skills:

> Some who study child development suggest that delayed school entry is inevitable in an educational system that has become too rigid and structured in the early grades and ignores the intellectual growth rates of individual children.

Reported in "Deciding if It's Time for Kindergarten or Time to Wait a Year," *The New York Times*, July 20, 1995, p. C4.

Page 151: "A Post-Trial Question: Should Adulterer Teach?" *The New York Times*, August 17, 1991, p. 6.

Page 152: Fred M. Hechinger, "About Education," *The New York Times*, November 8, 1989, p. 24.

Page 152: Joanne Jacobs, Knight-Ridder Wire Service Report, "Perestroika in U.S. Schools?" *The Tallahassee Democrat*, October 28, 1989, p. A13.

Page 153: Arthur T. Costigan, a teacher in a public high school, "Even Socrates Couldn't Teach in N.Y.C. Schools," *The New York Times*, July 1, 1989, p. 15.

Page 154: *Newsweek*, May 1, 1989, p. 64.

Page 155: "Race for Public School Slots is Acute," *The New York Times*, May 29, 1989, p. 20.

Page 155: By August of 1996, 25 states had authorized charter schools in some form. "Optimism Guides Charter School," The Tallahassee Democrat, August 18, 1996, p. B1.

Page 156: "Bronx Elementary School May Be Too Good for Its Own Good," *The New York Times*, August 10, 1991, p. 12.

Page 157: Owen Ullmann, Knight Ridder Washington Bureau, reported in "Report: Soviet Economy Is in Severe Trouble," *The Tallahassee Democrat*, December 22, 1990, p. 1.

Page 157: According to an article in *The Tallahassee Democrat* a couple of years ago, Leon High School with approximately 1,800 students, considered by many to be the preeminent public high school in Florida's state capital, had *seven* football coaches—one head coach and six assistants. The same high school also has facilities for basketball, soccer, tennis, and various practice fields, but sometimes puts 50 students in honors classes.

While the main purpose of a voucher system would be to break the government monopoly on the management of education, basic standards of curriculum, safety, and performance in use of taxpayers' money could still be implemented.

Page 158: Excerpts from "Array of Opponents Battle over 'Parental Rights' Bills," *The New York Times*, May 1, 1996, p. 1:

> Congress and state legislatures around the country are becoming battlegrounds over politically charged "parental rights" bills, pitting conservative and religious-right groups seeking broader protections for parents against education, public health, and liberal organizations who say such laws are major threats to children and schools.
>
> The model language for the bills, adapted from a 1925 Supreme Court ruling and proposed by a "pro-family" group called Of the People, which is promoting such laws, states, "The right of parents to direct the upbringing and education of their children shall not be infringed."
>
> "What we're trying to insure through this legislation is very simple: that schools reinforce rather than undermine the values parents teach to our children in our homes, churches and synagogues," said Ralph Reed, head of the Christian Coalition. . . .

> A coalition of more than 40 education, health, women's child advocacy and civil liberties groups are organizing to rally against the proposals. . . .
>
> "As an attorney, I can tell you this is another lawyers' relief act or full employment act," said August W. Steinhilber, general counsel for the National School Boards Association. "And it would raise total havoc with the curriculum. The irony is that everyone is saying the curriculum should be enriched and broadened, but this would give parents veto power over almost anything they didn't like."

Page 161: *Time*, March 26, 1990, p. 72.

Page 161: "A New Jersey Town Is Troubled by Racial Imbalance between Classrooms," *The New York Times*, August 11, 1994, p. A12.

Page 162: *Ibid.*

Page 162: John Miller, "Why School Choice Lost," *The Wall Street Journal*, November 4, 1993, p. A14.

Page 162: Of 25,500 ninth-grade black and Hispanic students who were originally enrolled in segregated, nonselective high schools in Chicago in 1980, only 9,000 graduated four years later, of which 4,000 read at or below the junior level, and only 2,000 read at or above the national average. Statistics cited by William Julius Wilson in *The Truly Disadvantaged* (Chicago: The University of Chicago Press, 1987), p. 58.

Page 163: A newspaper columnist describes some of the forms guerilla parenting can take:

> School is starting and all's not right with the educational world. Here in North Florida, school leaders may be getting more of that coveted parental involvement than they ever dreamed of—or really want.

Guerilla parenting is the name of the game.

> In Jefferson County, where more than two-thirds of the students are black—but two-thirds of the teachers are white—protesting black parents have been keeping their kids out of the classroom in droves . . .
>
> Leon County has its problems, too, but it's geographic discrimination rather than racial that troubles the parents of

Fort Braden Elementary. They're steamed over perceived neglect of the little 1930s-style school located amid the mobile-home parks and bait shops ofState Road 20 West.

The last straw was when, instead of new bricks and mortar to alleviate school overcrowding, two more mobile units were recently added to a campus that already has 11 portables. Parents say Fort Braden's getting short shrift compared with the staff and equipment riches of, say, Killearn Lakes [a relatively rich residential area] in the north, where a new $11.4 million school is opening. . .

Outspoken guerrilla parenting can be practiced solo, too. Karen Williams, a state employee, is fighting to get her eldest daughter, Jennifer, enrolled in Florida State University without the requisite immunizations . . . She's trying to get Florida to join 22 other states that allow philosophical exemptions from immunization shots. She's persuaded state Senator Sherry Walker to introduce such a bill in the Legislature. And she's thinking of hiring a lawyer.

Mary Ann Lindley, "Or They May Learn About Heads and Stone Walls," *The Tallahassee Democrat*, August 26, 1990, p. 12A.

Page 163: "End of School Year Has Parents Frantic," *The Tallahassee Democrat*, May 23, 1995, p. 1B.

Page 164: "Parents Clean, Shovel, Even Teach, to Aid Schools," *The Wall Street Journal*, June 12, 1995, p. B1.

Page 164: Mary Ann Lindley, "Hiring a School Volunteer Is One Mom's Solution," *The Tallahassee Democrat*, November 29, 1994. p. D1.

Page 164: "Private Gifts to Public Schools Bring Questions of Fairness," *The New York Times*, December 27, 1988, p. 1.

Page 164: March 9, 1992.

Page 164: A statistic quoted by Stephanie Coontz, *The Way We Never Were, op. cit.,* p. 2.

Page 165: "Shock Value: Bill That Would Allow Teachers to Carry Stun Guns into School Is Given Approval by Committee," *The Tallahassee Democrat*, February 20, 1991, p. C1.

Page 165: "As Armed Forces Cut Back, Some Lose a Way Up in Life," *The New York Times*, May 7, 1990, p. 1.

Page 167: Milton Friedman, *Capitalism and Freedom op. cit.*, p. 102.

Page 167: David Tyack and Larry Cuban, *Tinkering Toward Utopia* (Cambridge, MA: Harvard University Press, 1995), quoted by Peter Applebome, "Can the Schools Stand and Deliver?," *The New York Times*, March 24, 1996, p. 4E.

Page 168: "Many of the city's public schools are 'patronage troughs' for political leaders and aspiring politicians," according to James F. Gill, chairman of the Joint Commission on Integrity in the Public Schools, reported in "School Boards in New York Accused of Payroll-Padding," *The New York Times*, March 14, 1990, p. A16. Typical stories include those of District 27 in Ozone Park, Queens, in which dozens of unnecessary jobs were said to have been awarded to friends and supporters of school-board members at an annual cost of almost $1 million and that of Districts 19 and 32 whose superintendents reported that their school boards had hired 150 unnecessary workers at a cost of almost $2 million a year.

Page 168: Mancur Olson, *The Rise and Decline of Nations* (New Haven: Yale University Press, 1982).

Page 169: William Raspberry, *Washington Post* columnist, "Forget the Figure about More Blacks in Jail than School," printed in *The Tallahassee Democrat*, April 7, 1996, p. 1F.

Page 170: *Ibid.*

Chapter 10

Page 173: One notable exception to the general trend toward depriveleging working-class families is the earned-income tax credit (EITC) that began in 1975 but was only recently expanded to its present level in 1993 (an estimated $21 billion in 1995). See Robert J. Barro, "Workfare Still Beats Welfare," *The Wall Street Journal*, May 21, 1996, p. A22. The EITC was no sooner expanded to a significant level, however, before it was targeted for demise by influential politicians; so it may or may not survive.

Page 175: William Julius Wilson, *The Truly Disadvantaged, op. cit.*

Page 176: As Glenn Loury, a prominent black economist, notes:

> The dilemmas of the underclass pose in stark terms the
> most pressing, unresolved problem of the social and moral

societies: how to reconcile individual and social responsibility. The problem goes back to Kant. The moral and social paradox of society is this: On the one hand, we are determined and constrained by social, cultural, not to mention biological forces. Yet on the other hand, if society is to work we must believe that and behave as if we do indeed determine our actions. Neither of the pat political formulas for dealing with this paradox is adequate by itself. The mother of a homeless family is not simply a victim of forces acting on her; she is in part responsible for her plight and that of her children. But she is also being acted on by forces—social, economic, cultural, political—larger than herself. She is not an island; she is impacted by an environment; she does not have complete freedom to determine her future. It is callous nonsense to insist that she does, just as it is mindlessness to insist that she can do nothing for herself and her children until "society" reforms.

Glenn C. Loury, *One By One* (New York: The Free Press, 1995), p. 29.

Page 176: As Loury (*op. cit.*), p. 103 states:

Networks of social affiliation among families and individuals, while most often not the consequence of calculated economic decisions, nevertheless exert a profound influence upon resource allocation, especially those resources important to the development of the productive capacities of human beings. . . .

Parenting services, for example, are not available for purchase on the market by a developing person but accrue as the consequence of the social relations between mother and father. So the allocation of parenting service among the prospective workers in any generation is the consequence of the social activities of members of the preceding generation.

Page 176: Charles Murray, *Losing Ground, op. cit.*

Murray is hardly alone in believing that welfare programs have perverse long-run effects that outweigh short-term benefits on very poor populations. In the words of a black minister: "'Whosoever wrote the welfare bill knew exactly how to mess up a race of folk,' said the Reverend Fairro J. Brown, pastor of the Selmont Community Baptist Church in Selma," quoted in, "In Selma Everything and Nothing Changed," *The New York Times*, August 2, 1994, p.1.

Page 177: Richard J. Herrnstein and Charles Murray, *The Bell Curve: Intelligence and Class Structure in American Life* (New York: Free Press, 1994).

Page 177: The apparent contradiction between Murray's two hypotheses was noted in a panel discussion entitled "Economic Outcomes, Family Background, and Ability: The Bell Curve through the Economist's Lens," chaired by Harvard economist Claudia Goldin at the annual meeting of the American Economic Association in San Francisco, January 6, 1996.

Page 177: Thomas Sowell, *Ethnic America* (New York: Basic Books, Inc., 1981).

> Substantial reshuffling of the rankings of nations and races at different stages of history undermine genetic explanations in general. . . .
>
> Polish Americans had average IQs around 85 during the 1920s (compared to a national norm of 100), but in the 1970's their IQ level was 109. This 24-point rise in IQs was not only remarkable in itself but was also larger than the current black-white IQ difference (15 points). Italian Americans likewise rose over the years from IQs averaging in the low to mid-80s to IQs around the national average. Perhaps the most dramatic changes have been among Jewish Americans. Jewish soldiers in World War I averaged some of the lowest scores on mental tests of any of the numerous ethnic groups tested. Within a decade, this economically rising and rapidly acculturating group had achieved an average IQ level above that of Americans in general. (pp. 281-82)

Chapter 11

Page 181: Tom Fiedler and Nick Mason, Voices of Florida, reported in "Campaign 96: Candidates Back Elusive Family Values," *The Tallahassee Democrat*, February 25, 1996, p. 4C.

Page 182: James Carville, *We're Right, They're Wrong* (New York: Random House, 1996).

Page 182: Even though women got the right to vote in 1920, few other laws changed before the 1960s and 1970s. It wasn't until 1975 that the U.S. Supreme Court guaranteed women the right to sit on juries; and about the same time women were guaranteed the right to have credit in their own names. Before that, women who divorced had no credit history: car insurance was automatically canceled; already installed telephones required new deposits. It was only in the 1980s and 1990s that most state laws pertaining to domestic violence, sexual assault and sexual harassment began to change. See, for example, Sherry Stripling, "It's Not Ancient Herstory: Women Won Rights Only Recently," *Seattle Times*, reprinted in *The Tallahassee Democrat*, August 27, 1995, p. 2E.

Page 182: Jean Bethke Elshtain, *Private Man, Public Woman* (*op. cit.*).

Page 184: Adrienne Rich, *Of Woman Born* (New York: W.W. Norton & Company, 1986), p. ix.

Page 184: Sarah B. Pomeroy, *Xenophon Oeconomicus: A Social And Historical Commentary* (Oxford: Clarendon Press, 1994), p. 31.

Page 185: The economic unit with which Xenophon was concerned was the *oikos*, a term that Pomeroy indicates can be translated as "household," "family," or "estate," with the property dimensions of the term predominating. The *oikos* included family members, slaves, animals, buildings, and lands, and all of the goods produced, consumed, and disbursed by the household.

Page 185: The Peloponnesian War, fought between Athens and Sparta over which city would dominate Greece, lasted from 431 to 404 B.C. A major impetus for Sparta's willingness to fight such a long and expensive war was apparently its fear that a powerful enemy might encourage its helots to revolt. See, for example, *World History* (London: Ivy Leaf, 1989), pp. 696-97. Given the crucial role of slaves in the *oikos*, such a revolt would have undermined the substructure of the Greek family economy.

Page 186: See, for example, Peter G. Peterson, "Will America Grow Up before It Grows Old?" *The Atlantic Monthly*, May, 1996, pp. 55-86. Peterson is a co-founder of the Concord Coalition along with former senators Warren Rudman and Paul Tsongas.

Lester Thurow, MIT economist, makes a similar argument about intergenerational conflict: "No public interest is served by making parents rich at the cost of making children poor." In "The Birth of a Revolutionary Class," *The New York Times Magazine*, May 19, 1996, pp. 10-11.

Page 189: Apparently, there was no Eve in Adam Smith's life, as he was by all accounts the most confirmed of bachelors. See, for example, E. Ray Canterberry, *The Literate Economist* (New York: Harper-Collins, 1995), p. 41.

Page 189: In the words of MIT economist Lester Thurow, "No one doubts it. . . . Capitalism's nineteenth- and twentieth-century competitors—fascism, socialism, and communism—are all gone." *The Future of Capitalism* (New York: William Morrow and Company, Inc., 1996), p. 1.

Page 190: Government-enforced parental dividends would represent explicit, partial commodification of children as opposed to the kind of implicit commodification of children that has existed in traditional families by social custom and the kind that is currently embodied in our Social Security system by law.

In her book, *Contested Commodities* (Cambridge, MA.: Harvard University Press, 1996), Stanford Law Professor Margaret Jane Radin explores the issue of what should and should not be commodified consistent with the humanistic values of our culture. Radin argues for a concept of "partial commodification" in many cases but worries that the explicit market-commodification language of economic analysis is morally threatening in and of itself when it is applied to human beings.

Given that most people would wish to avoid injecting market language into family affairs any more than necessary, having the state write an intergenerational contract and a prenuptial contract that provide basic economic infrastructure for family functions would seem to be a more humane alternative than putting the burden of negotiations on individual family members, especially since parents, children, and caretakers are not in a position to negotiate sufficiently to protect their legitimate interests.

Page 190: See, for example, Charles Krauthammer, "A Social Conservative Credo," *The Public Interest*, No. 121, Fall 1995, pp. 15-22.

Page 190: According to Professor Coase:

Adam Smith makes sympathy the basis for our concern for others. We form our idea of how others feel by considering how we would feel in like circumstances. The realization that something makes our fellows miserable makes us miserable, and when something makes them happy, we are happy.

Coase quotes Smith as follows:

How selfish soever man may be supposed, there are evidently some principles in his nature, which interest him in the fortune of others, and render their happiness necessary to him though he derives nothing from it, except the pleasure of seeing it. . . . The greatest ruffian, the most hardened violator of the laws of society, is not altogether without it.

R.H. Coase, Essays on Economics and Economists (Chicago: The University of Chicago Press, 1994), pp. 95-96.

Page 190: The statistical coincidence between absent fathers and immoral behavior is quite dramatic: Almost two-thirds of rapists, three-quarters of adolescent murderers, and the same percentage of long-term prison inmates are reported to be young males who grew up without fathers in the house. See, for example, Chapter 7 in "Life without Father," in Irving Kristol, *Neo-Conservatism* (New York: Free Press, 1996), pp. 67-71.

Page 191: Alan Wolfe, *The Human Difference: Animals, Computers, and the Necessity of Social Science* (Berkeley: University of California Press, 1993). The following passage is an example of the kind of mediation between nature and culture by social science that Wolfe has in mind:

Contemporary conservatives yearn for a world that no longer exists, lamenting in the process the fact that real-world people have not only made their compromises with modernity but sometimes find it appealing. Women are unlikely to leave the workplace, even if families could afford it, stop having abortions, and devote full-time to their families, no matter how vigorously conservatives urge them to do so. To be a realist is to accept the fact that gender relations have changed precisely because people have minds as well as bodies and that, once changed, they are never again likely to be the same. Conservatives who demand legislation requiring parental approval for abortions, in appealing to an imagined family structure, are much the same as postmodernists calling for androgynous social arrangements; the one demand is as unreal as the other. If liberals often have a hard time believing that people can be racist or inegalitarian, conservatives refuse to believe that homosexuals will not go away, secularism is here to stay, most people have minds of their own, and modernity survives because most people find it beneficial. (pp. 153-54)

Page 191: Pomeroy, *op. cit.*, p. 133.

Appendix

Page 194: Quoted in "Can Retirees' Safety Net Be Saved?" *The New York Times*, February 18, 1996, p. F1.

Page 198: See note for page 95 concerning method of computing Social Security benefits.

Page 204: "Parents exist who do not know where their kids are, what they're doing and who their friends might be. This stuns me because love means setting limits; it annoys me because it makes my job as a parent so much harder," statement by Andrea Brunais, editorial writer for *The Tallahassee Democrat* in "Adolescence: Is there no safe place for teenagers?" November 12, 1995, p. F1.

Page 204: In a paper entitled "Privatizing Social Security at Home and Abroad" which was presented to the American Economic Association in San Francisco on January 7, 1966, Professor Laurence Koflikoff estimated that reducing the distortion of incentives to work by putting Social Security taxes into private pension funds would be equivalent to a 4 percent increase in the annual consumption and leisure levels of future generations.

Page 204: For example, while people retiring in 1997 whose average earnings were less than $5,460 per year got pensions equal to 90 percent of their preretirement income, people whose average earnings exceeded $38,352 got only 15 percent of their preretirement income over that amount, even though they may have paid taxes on income up to the income cap of $65,400. Some authors have expressed the hope that by keeping Social Security more or less as it is it can continue to serve a major redistributive function. See, for example: Joseph F. Quinn and Olivia S. Mitchell, "Social Security On the Table," *The American Prospect*, May-June, 1996, pp. 76-81.

Whatever course Social Security takes in the future, however, much of the hidden redistribution that currently occurs within Social Security will be exposed. The distribution issue has been politically dormant until now because all contributors have been getting more from the system than they put in, so no one has been disposed to complain. Redistribution will become a very different matter, however, when it becomes an issue of one group making sacrifices to subsidize another especially since the relatively well off are excused from most of the redistribution in the current system. The redistribution falls most heavily on individuals with lifetime average incomes high enough to be in the minimum-benefit range (>$38,352) but under the cutoff point for paying Social Security taxes ($68,400 in 1998). Wage and salaries above $65,400 escape the redistribution altogether as do other forms of income such as profits, rents, interest, dividends and capital gains.

Page 207: This was a major point of Martin Feldstein's Richard T. Ely address to the American Economic Association about Social Security reform, "The Missing Piece in Public Policy Analysis," January 5, 1996, reprinted in *American Economic Association Proceedings*, May 1996.

Page 207: Arthur B. Kennickell and Martha Starr-McCluer, "Changes in Family Finances from 1989 to 1992: Evidence from the Survey of Consumer Finances," *The Federal Reserve Bulletin*, October, 1994, pp. 861-882.

Page 208: *Ibid.*, p. 865.

Page 210: Use of such terms as trust fund, insurance, and earnings base in Social Security literature give the strong impression that Social Security is a fully funded insurance system.

Page 210: James M. Smalhout, "Can Chile's Social Security Reform Be Duplicated?" *The Wall Street Journal*, August 18, 1995, p. A11.

Page 210: Some authors have acknowledged that converting to a privatized retirement system wouldn't be painless. See, for example, Paul Craig Roberts' article, "The GOP Contract Is Too Timid," *The New York Times*, December 3, 1994, p. 23. Roberts warns that privatization will be "financially challenging" and that large amounts of general revenue would have to be used to support those in retirement and near-retirement while younger workers are moved into IRAs and similar plans.

The Advisory Council on Social Security has proposed several alternatives for financing a restructuring of Social Security. The Schieber Plan suggests a combination of a new 1 percent sales tax and deficit financing that could grow to $1.2 trillion in 40 years while The Gramlich Plan would add an additional 1.6 percent to the current payroll tax, "Where Candidates Fear to Tread," *Time*, April 1, 1996, p. 38.

Whatever form investment of Social Security funds takes, it won't make any difference in our economy's productivity unless there is a net increase in saving in the total economy. If the federal government simply increases its borrowing to cover the reallocation of Social Security funds into private investment, it will just shuffle funds around but will have little if any effect on total investment.

Page 210: "Bolivia Is Selling Off State Firms to Fund Its Citizens' Future," *The Wall Street Journal*, August 15, 1995, p. 1.

Page 210: Bob Kerrey and Alan K. Simpson, "How to Save Social Security," *The New York Times*, August 15, 1995, p. A17.

INDEX